# Chemistry

Robert Taggart

WALCH EDUCATION®

POWER BASICS

**Senior Author** ........ Robert Taggart
**Editorial Director** ........ Susan Blair
**Project Editor** ........ Holly Moirs
**Director of Marketing** ........ Jeff Taplin
**Senior Production Editor** ........ Maggie Jones
**Interior Design** ........ Mark Sayer
**Cover Design** ........ Roman Laszok
**Typesetting** ........ Sheila Russell
Mark Sayer
Ian Weidner
**Editorial Staff** ........ Elizabeth Lynch
Richard Lynch
Kate O'Halloran
Mary Rich
Erica Varney

1 2 3 4 5 6 7 8 9 10
ISBN 978-0-8251-5625-0



J. Weston Walch, Publisher
40 Walch Drive • Portland, ME 04103
www.walch.com

Printed in the United States of America

# Table of Contents

# To the Student

Welcome to *Power Basics® Chemistry,* a course designed to help you understand the basic concepts of chemistry. This knowledge is vital for your work at school, in testing situations, on the job, and in other parts of your life.

**Unit 1, Matter and Measurement,** will review basic information about matter and how it is measured. The concepts in this unit lay the foundation for understanding and applying concepts in the three units that follow.

**In Unit 2, Properties of Matter,** you will learn basic information about atoms and molecules. You will explore the structure of matter, the periodic table, and periodic trends.

**Unit 3, Transformations of Matter,** will help you learn about chemical reactions, stoichiometry, and bonding. This section builds on the concepts in the first two units and lays the foundation for applications in Unit 4.

**Unit 4, Topics in Chemistry,** will teach you about intermolecular forces, solutions, and acids and bases.

There are many special features in these pages that make learning easier. "Tips" give you hints for mastering the ideas and facts more quickly. "In Real Life" sections show you how the skills you are learning are applied in the world around you. "Think About It" questions ask you to think about chemistry in new ways.

We hope you will use *Power Basics Chemistry* to master skills that will help you understand and appreciate the world around you. And, we hope you enjoy yourself as you learn!

# UNIT 1

## Matter and Measurement

# LESSON 1: Chemistry and the Scientific Method

GOAL: To define chemistry and matter; to understand the scientific method of inquiry

## WORDS TO KNOW

| | | |
|---|---|---|
| **atoms** | **hypothesis** | **scientific method** |
| **chemistry** | **matter** | **theory** |
| **experiment** | **problem** | |

## What Is Chemistry?

Most people are more aware of the role of physics in their lives than they are of the role of chemistry. For example, anyone who has driven a car knows something about velocity and acceleration. Fewer people are aware, however, of the chemical reactions that are taking place in the car's engine to convert gasoline to carbon dioxide, water, and the energy needed to power the car. Anyone who has turned on an electric light knows something about electricity. But fewer people are aware of the composition of the filament in the lightbulb or the chemical reactions that produce the light. Finally, anyone who has run or walked up a hill knows something about gravity, but fewer people are aware of the structure of the hemoglobin in their blood that makes it possible to bring oxygen to and remove carbon dioxide from their muscles.

**Chemistry** is the study of the composition, structure, and properties of matter and the changes that matter undergoes. **Matter** is anything that occupies space and has mass. For example, automobiles, animals, and air are matter, but ideas, actions, and feelings are not. If you are eating a sandwich for lunch, then you, the sandwich, and the paper it is wrapped in are matter. But the act of lifting the sandwich to your mouth and the feeling of fullness you have after you have finished the sandwich are not matter.

The study of the properties of matter is based on the properties of atoms. **Atoms** are the smallest possible particles of a substance that are recognizable as that substance. When chemists study the composition of matter, they are studying the kinds of atoms that matter contains. When chemists study the structure of matter, they are studying the way in which atoms are organized in matter.

**IN REAL LIFE**

Many people who have never studied chemistry use it every day. For example, a farmer who applies fertilizer to a field is doing a chemistry experiment. So is a postal worker who puts on sunscreen before delivering the mail, a chef who bakes a cake, and a firefighter who puts out a fire. Chemistry is everywhere!

## PRACTICE 1: What Is Chemistry?

Decide whether the following is matter (**M**) or not matter (**NM**). Write the correct letter or letters on each line.

M **1.** a dog

NM **2.** studying for an exam

NM **3.** worrying about an upcoming exam

M **4.** the pencil used for taking an exam

NM **5.** a joke that makes you laugh

M **6.** Earth, the Sun, and the Moon

NM **7.** an idea for reducing the federal budget deficit

M **8.** the Statue of Liberty

## The Scientific Method

What we know about chemistry (or any science) has come about from the systematic (step-by-step) research of thousands of women and men over many years. These scientists have proposed ideas about matter and designed experiments to test their ideas. The process of proposing and testing is called the **scientific method.**

The scientific method consists of the following five steps:

1. Define the **problem.** Before any experiment can be conducted or any problem can be solved, a specific question or problem must be defined. In the nineteenth century, for example, the French wine-making industry was unable to consistently make sweet wine. Some barrels produced sour wine instead. A scientist named Louis Pasteur was asked to find out how wine spoils.

2. Gather information. In order to solve a problem, you must know as much about it as possible. Information may be gathered by observing nature, by reading about related research in the library or on the Internet, or by communicating with experts in the field. Louis Pasteur gathered information by observing nature. He examined samples of the sweet and sour wines under a microscope and discovered germs in the sour wine that were absent in the sweet wine.

3. Propose a **hypothesis.** A hypothesis is a possible explanation for the gathered information. Louis Pasteur's hypothesis was that germs in the sour wine were the cause of the sourness.

4. Conduct an experiment. An **experiment** tests the validity of a hypothesis. Scientific experiments are controlled so that only one factor is changed at a time. The results of changing the one factor can then be compared with the unchanged event. Louis Pasteur's controlled experiment was to divide a barrel of sweet wine into two separate casks. He then introduced the newly discovered germs into one cask and left the other cask undisturbed. The undisturbed cask remained sweet while the wine with the added germs turned sour.

5. Develop a theory. A **theory** is an idea that is based on experimental results. A theory attempts to explain experimental results already obtained and to predict experimental results not yet obtained. Louis Pasteur concluded from his experiments that his hypothesis about the germs was correct. Furthermore, he predicted that germs may cause diseases.

IN REAL LIFE

Most milk sold today is pasteurized. This means it has been heated to a temperature that kills harmful germs but does not greatly change its chemical makeup. Pasteurization was originally developed by Louis Pasteur and was a direct result of his controlled experiments with sweet and sour wine. Now, every time you buy a carton of milk at the store, you are directly benefiting from Pasteur's careful use of the scientific method.

It is important to understand that experiments can disprove a theory, but they cannot prove one. A theory is not a fact. A theory is just the scientist's best guess or conclusion, based on current observations and experiments, of what is going on. Experiments may support a theory for a time, but new experiments may disprove the theory. In the case of Louis Pasteur, the experiments of other scientists helped validate his germ theory of disease. These experiments did not prove that Pasteur's theory was correct, however. In fact, other scientists eventually found evidence that contradicted Pasteur's theory in some ways.

When this happens, a theory must be discarded or changed to match the new experimental results. The new theory is then subjected to the same kind of testing as the old one. Pasteur's theory was revised in light of later experiments, and may be revised further as new experiments are conducted.

Experimental results must never be changed to match a theory. It doesn't matter how clever or interesting the theory is. It is common for scientists to repeat experiments several times in order to make sure that their results are consistent and reproducible. If you get one result one time and a different result a second time, then you must keep repeating the experiment until you get a consistent result. Only then can you believe the result. A good experiment is one that can be repeated by someone else and still give the same result.

## PRACTICE 2: The Scientific Method

Decide if each statement on the following page is true (**T**) or false (**F**). Write the correct letter on each line.

T **1.** A theory is a best guess that can be disproved but not proved.

T **2.** A controlled experiment changes more than one factor at a time.

T **3.** A hypothesis is a tentative explanation for the gathered information.

F **4.** The scientific method consists of a process of proposing ideas and conducting experiments to test the ideas.

F **5.** The *second* step in the scientific method is to define the problem.

T **6.** A theory attempts to explain experimental results already obtained and to predict experimental results not yet obtained.

T **7.** The *first* step in the scientific method is to define the problem.

F **8.** Louis Pasteur concluded from his experiments that his hypothesis about the germs was not correct.

**TIP**

Sometimes you can simplify a complicated idea by organizing it into a flowchart. A flowchart is a diagram that leads you step-by-step through a process. Some flowcharts are organized from left to right. Others are organized from top to bottom. If a flowchart is organized from left to right, it begins with the box that is farthest left and follows the arrows to the right. If a flowchart is organized from top to bottom, it begins with the top box and follows the arrows down. Using a flowchart carefully will help you avoid errors and give you a handy visual reminder of what an idea means.

1. Define the problem.
↓
2. Gather information.
↓
3. Propose a hypothesis.
↓
4. Conduct an experiment.
↓
5. Develop a theory.

# LESSON 2: Classification of Matter

GOAL: To understand the difference between many kinds of substances and mixtures

## WORDS TO KNOW

| | | |
|---|---|---|
| **chemical formula** | **heterogeneous mixture** | **molecule** |
| **compound** | **homogeneous mixture** | **subscript** |
| **element** | **mixture** | **substance** |

## Substances and Mixtures

Matter can be categorized as either substances or mixtures. A **substance** has a constant (unchanging) composition and distinct properties. Gold, oxygen, and pure water are substances. The properties of gold are distinct from the properties of oxygen and pure water. For example, gold is a shiny yellow metal at room temperature; oxygen is a colorless gas; and pure water is a colorless liquid.

A **mixture** contains two or more substances that keep their individual identities when they are combined. Milk, air, brass, and tap water are mixtures. Milk is a mixture of water, fats, and proteins. Air is a mixture of nitrogen, oxygen, ozone, carbon dioxide, other gases, and bits of dust. Brass is a mixture of copper and zinc. Tap water is a combination of water and various minerals.

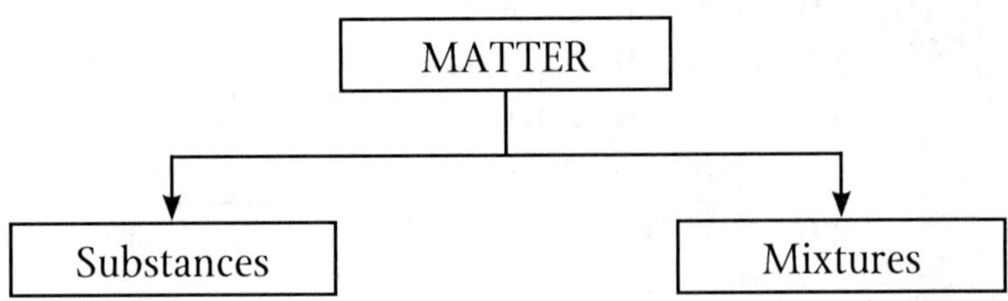


There are two more important things to remember about mixtures. First, the substances in all mixtures are physically mixed but not chemically combined. This means that it is possible to separate a mixture into the substances that make it up without a chemical reaction.

For example, it is possible to separate milk into water, its various fats, and its various proteins, because milk is a mixture.

Second, the composition of a mixture changes depending on where the mixture is obtained and/or how it is prepared. For example, a sample of air obtained in Los Angeles, California, will probably be different from a sample of air obtained in Denver, Colorado, because of differences in humidity, altitude, and levels of pollution.

## PRACTICE 3: Substances and Mixtures

Decide if each statement that follows is true (**T**) or false (**F**). Write the correct letter on each line.

__T__ **1.** Milk can be classified as a mixture.

__F__ **2.** Gold can be classified as a mixture.

__F__ **3.** A sample of water obtained from a faucet in New Jersey will be exactly the same as a sample collected in Warsaw, Poland.

__T__ **4.** A substance has an unchanging composition and distinct properties.

__T__ **5.** A mixture contains two or more substances that retain their individual identities when combined.

__F__ **6.** The properties of gold are exactly the same as the properties of oxygen.

__T__ **7.** It is possible to physically separate a mixture into the substances that make it up.

## Homogeneous and Heterogeneous Mixtures

Mixtures can be further categorized as either homogeneous or heterogeneous, depending on how they appear. A **homogeneous mixture** has no visible boundaries between the substances that make it up. As a result, a homogeneous mixture has a uniform (changeless) composition throughout and is often called a solution.

Perfume, milk, and rubbing alcohol are homogeneous mixtures. Perfume is a mixture of fragrances, water, and alcohol, but the amounts of each are the same throughout the bottle. Milk is a mixture of water, fats, and proteins. Whether you drink from the top, the middle, or the bottom of the bottle, you are getting the same mixture of water, fats, and proteins. Rubbing alcohol is a mixture of 70% isopropyl alcohol and 30% water throughout the bottle. There are no parts that are only isopropyl alcohol or only water.

A **heterogeneous mixture** has visible boundaries between the substances that make it up. As a result, the composition of a heterogeneous mixture varies. Oil-and-vinegar salad dressing, granite, and beefsteak are heterogeneous mixtures. Salad dressing may appear to be homogeneous after mixing, but the oil and vinegar will eventually separate into two distinct layers if left to stand.

If you look closely at granite, you will see specks of different colored rocks. Some specks are quartz, while others are mica and other rocks. You can see the boundaries between the different rocks that make up granite. The same is true of beefsteak. Beefsteak is a mixture of bone, fat, blood, and muscle. You can see where the bone leaves off and the muscle begins. Even if you grind the steak into hamburger, it is still a heterogeneous mixture because you can see regions of fat that are separate from regions of muscle.

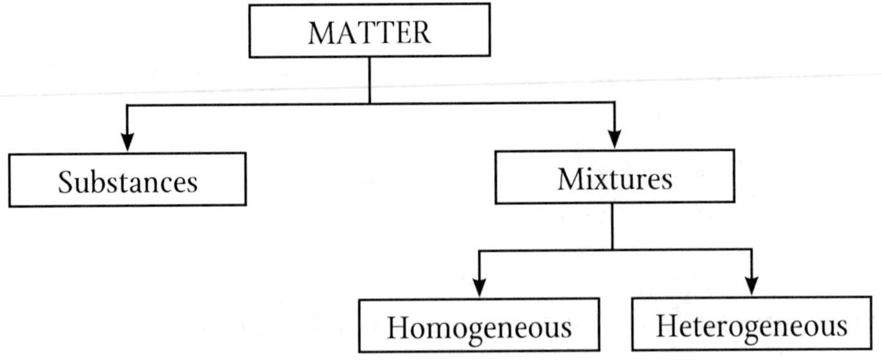


## PRACTICE 4: Homogeneous and Heterogeneous Mixtures

Decide if each statement on the following page is true (**T**) or false (**F**). Write the correct letter on each line.

T 1. Mixtures can be categorized as either homogeneous or heterogeneous.

T 2. Tap water is a homogeneous mixture.

F 3. A heterogeneous mixture can also be called a solution.

F 4. A heterogeneous mixture has no visible boundaries between the substances that make it up.

T 5. A homogeneous mixture has a uniform composition throughout.

F 6. Beefsteak is a homogeneous mixture.

T 7. Rubbing alcohol is a homogeneous mixture.

T 8. Granite is a heterogeneous mixture.

## Elements and Compounds

Substances can be further categorized as elements or compounds. An **element** is a substance that cannot be broken down into simpler substances by chemical means. An element consists of only one kind of atom. Hydrogen, oxygen, iron, and uranium are elements. So are helium, nitrogen, copper, and lead. In fact, scientists have so far identified 115 different chemical elements (and they are always looking for more). Each element has unique properties.

A **compound** is a substance made up of two or more elements that are chemically joined in a fixed (uniform) composition. Carbon dioxide, ammonia, hydrogen peroxide, and sodium chloride (table salt) are compounds.

Water is a chemical compound made up of the elements hydrogen and oxygen in a two-to-one ratio. All samples of pure water contain two hydrogen atoms and one oxygen atom chemically joined together into a unique substance. If water were simply a mixture of the elements hydrogen and oxygen, then there would be a physical way to separate it into the two elements, and the properties of water would be the combined properties of the hydrogen and the oxygen. Instead, the properties of water are distinct from the properties of either hydrogen or oxygen. For example, at room temperature, water is a colorless liquid, hydrogen is a colorless and very flammable gas, and oxygen is a colorless gas.

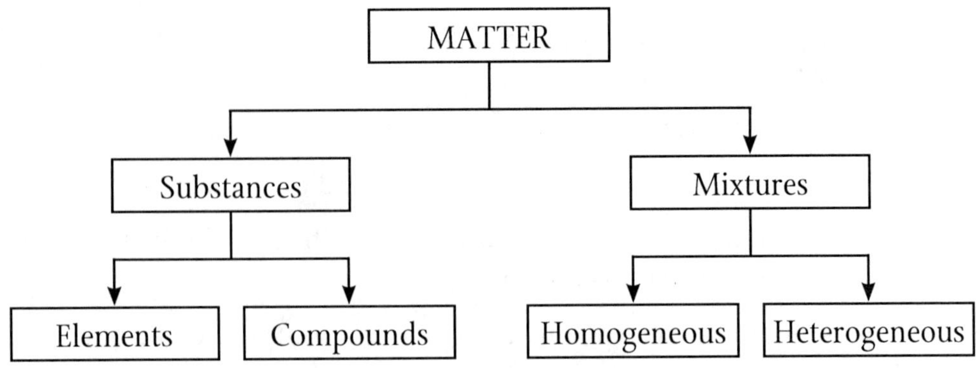


## PRACTICE 5: Elements and Compounds

Decide if each statement that follows is true (**T**) or false (**F**). Write the correct letter on each line.

_____ **1.** An element cannot be broken down into simpler substances by chemical means.

_____ **2.** A compound is a mixture of two or more separate elements.

_____ **3.** A compound contains two or more elements chemically joined in a fixed composition.

_____ **4.** If compounds are made up of elements, then elements must be made up of compounds.

_____ **5.** The properties of carbon monoxide, a chemical compound that contains one carbon atom and one oxygen atom chemically joined together, are distinct from the properties of the elements carbon and oxygen.

_____ **6.** An element consists of only one kind of atom.

_____ **7.** So far, scientists have identified 211 different chemical elements.

## Elements and Their Symbols

Of the 115 chemical elements discovered so far, 91 occur in nature and 24 have been made in laboratories. Each has a unique name. Traditionally, the person or persons who discover an element have the honor of naming it. As a result, the names of elements have many different origins.

Chlorine is a pale green gas. It is named for the Greek word *chloros,* which means "light green." Argon is a gas that does not react with other elements. It is named for the Greek word *argos,* which means "inactive." Helium is named for the Greek word *helios,* which means "sun." It was discovered by scientists who were studying the Sun at the time.

Some elements are named for countries. Polonium is named for Poland and germanium is named for Germany. Others are named for continents, such as americium for the Americas and europium for Europe. Still others are named for famous scientists, such as curium for Marie and Pierre Curie and fermium for Enrico Fermi.

Each chemical element has a unique symbol, too. The symbol of an element is a one- or two-letter abbreviation for its name. The first letter of the symbol is always capitalized, and the second letter is always lowercase. Each symbol is unique so that the different elements can be easily distinguished. For example, it would only cause confusion if the letter "C" were used to symbolize carbon, cobalt, and chromium. Instead, "C" is used for carbon, "Co" is used for cobalt, and "Cr" is used for chromium.

The symbol of an element is often the first letter or the first two letters of the English name of the element. Examples include "H" for hydrogen, "O" for oxygen, "N" for nitrogen, "P" for phosphorous, "Ba" for barium, "Ca" for calcium, "Li" for lithium, and "Mo" for molybdenum.

The symbols of other elements correspond to the first letter of the English name plus another letter from that name. Examples include "Mg" for magnesium, "Mn" for manganese, "Rb" for rubidium, and "Pt" for platinum.

Still other elements have symbols that bear no relationship to the English name of the element. Examples include "Au" for gold, "Hg" for mercury, "Pb" for lead, and "W" for tungsten. The origin of the "Au" for gold is the word *aurum,* which is Latin for "shining dawn." The origin of the "Hg" for mercury is *hydrargyrum,* which is Latin for "liquid silver." The origin of the "Pb" for lead is *plumbum,* which is Latin for "lead" (meaning heavy). Finally, the origin of the "W" for tungsten is wolframite, a mineral that contains tungsten.

The only way to remember the different elements and their symbols is to memorize them. In order to help you learn their names and symbols, some of the more common elements are listed in the following table.

| Name | Symbol | Name | Symbol | Name | Symbol |
|---|---|---|---|---|---|
| Aluminum | Al | Hydrogen | H | Potassium | K |
| Barium | Ba | Iodine | I | Silicon | Si |
| Bromine | Br | Iron | Fe | Silver | Ag |
| Calcium | Ca | Lead | Pb | Sodium | Na |
| Carbon | C | Magnesium | Mg | Sulfur | S |
| Chlorine | Cl | Mercury | Hg | Tin | Sn |
| Chromium | Cr | Nickel | Ni | Titanium | Ti |
| Copper | Cu | Nitrogen | N | Tungsten | W |
| Fluorine | F | Oxygen | O | Uranium | U |
| Gold | Au | Phosphorous | P | Zinc | Zn |

## PRACTICE 6: Elements and Their Symbols

Decide if each statement that follows is true (**T**) or false (**F**). Write the correct letter on each line.

T **1.** Each chemical element has a unique name.

T **2.** The symbol for carbon is C.

F **3.** The symbol for tin is Tn.

F **4.** The symbol for both cobalt and chromium is C.

T **5.** Each chemical element has a unique one- or two-letter symbol.

T **6.** Helium is named for the Greek word *helios,* which means "sun."

T **7.** Hg is the symbol for mercury.

F **8.** The symbol for oxygen is Oxy.

## THINK ABOUT IT

If some elements are named for places or famous scientists, what are the elements californium and einsteinium named for? If you discovered a new element, what would you name it? What symbol would you use for it? Write your answers on a separate sheet of paper.

## Molecules

A **molecule** is a combination of two or more atoms that are chemically bound together in a specific shape. These atoms may be atoms of the same element or atoms of different elements. Therefore, molecules are not necessarily the same as chemical compounds. Remember, chemical compounds are made up of two or more elements that are chemically joined in a fixed composition.

Water is a compound and a molecule. It consists of two hydrogen atoms and one oxygen atom chemically bound together. It is a compound because it contains two different elements (hydrogen and oxygen). It is a molecule because it contains two or more atoms.

Other molecules that are also compounds include carbon dioxide, carbon monoxide, ammonia, and sucrose (cane sugar). A molecule of carbon dioxide consists of one carbon atom and two oxygen atoms. A molecule of carbon monoxide consists of one carbon atom and one oxygen atom. A molecule of ammonia consists of one nitrogen atom and three hydrogen atoms. A molecule of sucrose consists of 12 carbon atoms, 22 hydrogen atoms, and 11 oxygen atoms.

Hydrogen gas is a molecule that is not a compound. It consists of two hydrogen atoms chemically bound together. It is a molecule because it contains two or more atoms. It is not a compound because the two atoms are the same element.

Other molecules that are also not compounds include oxygen gas, nitrogen gas, chlorine gas, and ozone. Oxygen gas consists of two oxygen atoms, nitrogen gas consists of two nitrogen atoms, chlorine gas consists of two chlorine atoms, and ozone consists of three oxygen atoms.

## PRACTICE 7: Molecules

Decide if each statement that follows is true (**T**) or false (**F**). Write the correct letter on each line.

__F__ **1.** Molecules and chemical compounds are the same thing.

__T__ **2.** Water is a compound and a molecule.

__T__ **3.** Hydrogen gas is a molecule that is NOT a compound.

__T__ **4.** A molecule is a combination of two or more atoms that are chemically bound together in a specific shape.

__F__ **5.** A molecule of ozone consists of three helium atoms.

__T__ **6.** A molecule of ammonia consists of one nitrogen atom and three hydrogen atoms.

__F__ **7.** Carbon dioxide and carbon monoxide are molecules that are NOT compounds.

__T__ **8.** A molecule of sucrose consists of 12 carbon atoms, 22 hydrogen atoms, and 11 oxygen atoms.

## Chemical Formulas

A molecule of water consists of two hydrogen atoms and one oxygen atom chemically bound together. Chemists often express the same information in a shorthand called a chemical formula. A **chemical formula** uses numbers and the symbols for the elements to indicate which elements are present in a substance and how many atoms of each element are present in the substance.

The chemical formula for water is $H_2O$. “H” is the symbol for hydrogen, and “O” is the symbol for oxygen. The **subscript** “2” after the “H” for hydrogen tells you that each water molecule has two hydrogen atoms. There is no subscript “1” after the “O” for oxygen, because no number is used when only one atom of an element is present in the substance.

Other chemical formulas include $CO_2$ for carbon dioxide, CO for carbon monoxide, $NH_3$ for ammonia, $C_{12}H_{22}O_{11}$ for sucrose (cane sugar), $O_2$ for oxygen gas, $N_2$ for nitrogen gas, $Cl_2$ for chlorine gas, and $O_3$ for ozone.

## PRACTICE 8: Chemical Formulas

Decide if each statement that follows is true (**T**) or false (**F**). Write the correct letter on each line.

T **1.** The chemical formula for water is $H_2O$.

T **2.** A chemical formula indicates which elements are present in a substance and how many atoms of each element are present in the substance.

F **3.** In a chemical formula, a subscript "1" is used to indicate that only one atom of an element is present in the substance.

F **4.** The chemical formula for carbon dioxide is the same as the chemical formula for carbon monoxide.

T **5.** The chemical formula for carbon dioxide is $CO_2$, and the chemical formula for ammonia is $NH_3$.

T **6.** If the chemical formula for aspirin is $C_9H_8O_4$, then each molecule of aspirin contains nine carbon atoms, eight hydrogen atoms, and four oxygen atoms.

F **7.** The chemical formula for oxygen gas is $O_2$, and the chemical formula for ozone is $O_3$.

F **8.** The chemical formula for carbon monoxide is $C_1O_1$.

### THINK ABOUT IT

Chemistry formulas can appear to be difficult. The way the numbers are shown, and the use of symbols rather than words, can make them look more complicated than they are. But chemical formulas are basically recipes. They are not much different from a recipe you would use to make chocolate chip cookies. Instead of cups or teaspoons of an ingredient, a chemical recipe calls for atoms.

# LESSON 3: States and Changes of Matter

**GOAL: To learn the different states of matter; to understand the changes matter undergoes**

## WORDS TO KNOW

| | | |
|---|---|---|
| **boiling** | **evaporation** | **melting point** |
| **boiling point** | **freezing** | **physical change** |
| **chemical change** | **freezing point** | **physical properties** |
| **chemical properties** | **gas** | **solid** |
| **condensation** | **liquid** | **sublimation** |
| **deposition** | **melting** | |

## Solids, Liquids, and Gases

Matter can exist in three different physical forms, or states. These are called solids, liquids, and gases. Ice, for example, is the solid form of water. When ice melts, it forms liquid water. When liquid water boils, it forms water vapor (gaseous water). Ice, liquid water, and water vapor are all the same chemical compound (water), but their physical properties (such as shape and volume) are very different.

A **solid** has its own fixed shape and volume. If you drop a dime into a cup, the dime maintains its shape and volume. It does not conform to the shape of the cup. If you keep adding dimes, you will eventually fill the cup. There will be spaces between the dimes, however, because the dimes will not conform to the shape of the other dimes, either. You may even be able to overfill the cup with dimes.

A **liquid** has a fixed volume but not a fixed shape. If you pour 8 ounces of orange juice into a 10-ounce glass, the orange juice maintains its original volume (8 ounces), but it conforms to the shape of the glass because it is fluid. If you try to pour 12 ounces of orange juice into the 10-ounce glass, then you will end up with 10 ounces of orange juice in the glass and 2 ounces in your lap. You cannot overfill a container with a liquid.

A **gas** has neither a fixed shape nor a fixed volume. If you add a gas such as helium to a container, the helium conforms to the shape of the container because gases are fluid, too. Note that the helium fills the entire container because gases do not have fixed volumes. If you take the helium from the original container and put it into a larger container, the helium will expand to fill the larger container. Similarly, if you take the helium from the original container and put it into a smaller container, the helium will contract to fill the smaller container. Gases expand and contract to entirely fill their containers because gases do not have fixed shapes or volumes.

| State of Matter | Fixed Shape | Fixed Volume | Examples |
|---|---|---|---|
| solid | yes | yes | ice, dry ice, gold, table salt, a dime |
| liquid | no | yes | liquid water, coffee, maple syrup, rubbing alcohol |
| gas | no | no | water vapor, carbon monoxide, carbon dioxide, hydrogen, helium |

Except for ice, dry ice, and water vapor, the examples listed in the table are assumed to be at normal room temperature (25°C). This is an important assumption because solids can be turned into liquids or gases if the temperature is raised high enough. For example, gold can be turned into a liquid at the very hot temperature of 1064°C. Gold can be turned into a gas at 3080°C. Similarly, gases can be turned into liquids or solids, and liquids can be turned into solids if the temperature is lowered enough. For example, hydrogen becomes a liquid at –253°C and a solid at –259°C. These are extremely cold temperatures.

## PRACTICE 9: Solids, Liquids, and Gases

Decide if each statement that follows is true (**T**) or false (**F**). Write the correct letter on each line.

____ **1.** The three states of matter are solids, liquids, and gases.

____ **2.** Dry ice (solid carbon dioxide) is a solid because it has its own fixed shape and volume.

_____ **3.** Coffee is a liquid because it has neither a fixed shape nor a fixed volume.

_____ **4.** Carbon monoxide is a gas because it has neither a fixed shape nor a fixed volume.

_____ **5.** Liquid water and water vapor are both fluid, but liquid water has a fixed volume.

_____ **6.** Ice, liquid water, and water vapor are different chemical compounds because their physical properties are very different.

_____ **7.** Ice, liquid water, and water vapor are the same chemical compound in different physical forms.

_____ **8.** A liquid has its own fixed shape and volume.

## Physical Changes Versus Chemical Changes

You learned in Lesson 1 that chemistry is the study of the composition, structure, and properties of matter and the changes that matter undergoes. The changes that chemists study are those that change the properties of a substance. Examples of changes that occur in everyday life include dissolving sugar in hot coffee, burning wood in a fireplace, and digesting food.

There are two kinds of changes: physical changes and chemical changes. In a **physical change,** the physical properties of matter change, but the chemical properties do not. **Physical properties** can be determined without the formation of new materials. **Chemical properties** can be determined only by the formation of new materials. Breaking a window, melting ice, and opening a can of corn are all physical changes, because only the physical properties of the matter are changed. The window's glass is still glass, it is just in smaller pieces. The water that makes up the ice is still water, it is just a liquid instead of a solid. The metal in the can of corn is still the same metal whether or not the top is intact.

In a **chemical change,** the chemical properties of matter change. New substances are formed. Burning propane in a camp stove is a chemical change because propane is turned into carbon dioxide and water in the process. Carbon dioxide and water are chemical substances that are different from propane. Sodium metal reacts violently with chlorine gas to produce sodium chloride (table salt). This is a chemical change, because table salt is a different chemical substance from either sodium metal or chlorine gas.

The rusting of iron is a chemical change because the iron reacts with oxygen and water to produce an iron oxide. The iron oxide is a different chemical substance from iron metal, oxygen, or water. Dynamite explodes when TNT decomposes to various gases and releases a lot of energy. This is a chemical change because the gases are different chemical substances from TNT.

## PRACTICE 10: Physical Changes Versus Chemical Changes

Decide if the following changes are physical (**P**) or chemical (**C**). Write the correct letter on each line.

__P__ **1.** carving a turkey

__C__ **2.** burning butane in a lighter

__P__ **3.** melting snow

__P__ **4.** mowing the lawn

__C__ **5.** digesting food

__C__ **6.** tarnishing silver

__P__ **7.** sharpening a pencil

__C__ **8.** exploding firecrackers

### THINK ABOUT IT

Most of us use physical and chemical changes to our advantage every day. If you make pea soup on a gas stove, then you are burning methane. The methane becomes carbon dioxide and water. So, burning methane is an example of a chemical change. If you make more soup than you can eat at one meal, you can freeze the rest for later. Frozen (solid) pea soup is the same, chemically, as liquid pea soup. So, freezing the soup is an example of a physical change. What other physical and chemical changes can you think of in your daily life?

## Changes of State

The molecules of a solid are held tightly to one another by attractive forces and are closely packed together. The individual molecules move slightly, but not nearly as much as the molecules of a liquid or a gas. As a solid is heated, the molecules move more and more. At a certain temperature, the movements strain the attractive forces to their limit. Heating the solid any more breaks the attractive forces between the molecules. When this happens, the solid changes to a liquid. The process of a solid changing to a liquid is called **melting.** The temperature at which a solid melts to a liquid is called the **melting point.** The melting point of water is 0°C.

If the temperature of the liquid is lowered again, the molecules of the liquid will slow down again. At a certain temperature, the movements will be so slow that the attractive forces will bind the molecules again. When this happens, the liquid changes into a solid. The process of a liquid changing into a solid is called **freezing.** The temperature at which a liquid freezes into a solid is called the **freezing point.** The freezing point of water is 0°C, which is the same as the melting point of water. In fact, the melting point and freezing point of a substance are always the same temperature.

The molecules of a liquid are also held together by attractive forces, but these forces are different from the strong attractive forces that hold solids together. The attractive forces in a liquid are weaker, so the molecules in a liquid are not nearly as closely packed together as the molecules of a solid. The individual molecules of a liquid can slip past one another, so they move more than the molecules of a solid.

As a liquid is heated, the particles in the liquid move faster. At a certain temperature, the particles in the liquid move fast enough to break free of their attractive forces. When this happens, the liquid changes into a gas. This process is called **boiling,** and it can happen at any location throughout the liquid. A liquid can also become a gas through **evaporation.** Evaporation happens only at the surface of a liquid. It happens when the occasional particle gains enough kinetic energy to escape the attractive forces of the liquid. Evaporation can happen at many different temperatures for a liquid, whereas boiling can only happen at one temperature for a given set of conditions. This temperature is called the **boiling point.** The boiling point of water, for example, is 100°C.

If the temperature of a gas is lowered again, the molecules of the gas will slow down. At a certain temperature, the movements will be slow enough that the attractive forces can bind the molecules again. When this happens, the gas changes to a liquid. The process of a gas changing to a liquid is called **condensation**. The temperature at which a gas condenses to a liquid is the same as the boiling point, because condensation is the opposite of evaporation.

Under the correct conditions, the molecules of a solid can move fast enough to completely break away from one another and change to a gas without becoming a liquid first. The process of a solid directly becoming a gas is called **sublimation**. Dry ice (solid carbon dioxide) sublimes. It becomes gaseous carbon dioxide without first becoming liquid carbon dioxide.

Naphthalene sublimes, too. Naphthalene is the chemical compound in mothballs. You can tell naphthalene sublimes because you can smell the mothballs and because the mothballs get smaller over time. You would not smell the mothballs unless some of the naphthalene molecules were in the gas phase.

The opposite of sublimation is deposition. **Deposition** occurs when a gas becomes a solid without first becoming a liquid. An example of deposition is the formation of ice crystals on a cold window during the winter. Water vapor changes to solid water (ice) without first becoming liquid water.

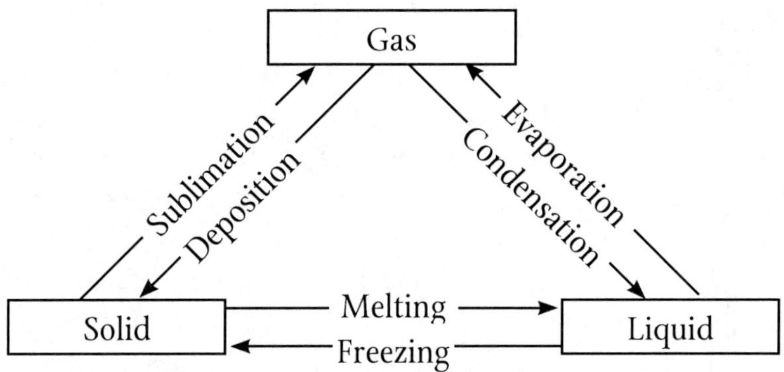

## PRACTICE 11: Changes of State

Decide if each statement that follows is true (**T**) or false (**F**). Write the correct letter on each line.

__T__ **1.** Melting is the opposite of freezing.

__F__ **2.** Sublimation is the process of a liquid changing into a gas.

__T__ **3.** Sublimation is the process of a solid changing directly into a gas.

__T__ **4.** Condensation is the opposite of evaporation.

__F__ **5.** Sublimation is the opposite of evaporation.

__T__ **6.** Sublimation is the opposite of deposition.

__F__ **7.** Deposition is the opposite of condensation.

__T__ **8.** If liquid water evaporates to water vapor at 100°C, then water vapor condenses to liquid water at 100°C, too.

__F__ **9.** Attractive forces are stronger in liquids than they are in solids.

__T__ **10.** Attractive forces are weaker in gases than they are in liquids.

### THINK ABOUT IT

Imagine it is winter, and a lot of snow has fallen where you live. You get a break from the snowstorms for about a week, but the temperature does not rise above 0°C during that time. The huge snowdrift in front of your house does not get plowed or shoveled, but it is getting noticeably smaller. Since the temperature does not rise above the freezing point of water, the snow is not changing to liquid form. How can the snowdrift get smaller? (Think about what is happening to the water molecules in the snow.) Write your answer on a separate sheet of paper.

# LESSON 4: Measuring Matter

GOAL: To learn how scientists measure things

## WORDS TO KNOW

| | | |
|---|---|---|
| **absolute zero** | **Fahrenheit scale** | **scientific notation** |
| **Celsius scale** | **heat** | **temperature** |
| **conversion factor** | **Kelvin scale** | **volume** |
| **density** | **mass** | **weight** |

## Units of Measure

When scientists conduct experiments (step 4 of the scientific method on page 5), they measure things. They may measure how fast a reaction occurs or how much material they get from a reaction. Whatever they measure, scientists always report a number and a unit, such as 5.73 seconds or 3.1 grams. The unit tells you what was measured (seconds or grams, for example), and the number tells you how much of that thing was measured (5.73 and 3.1, for example).

IN REAL LIFE

You probably rely on numbers and their units more than you realize. Imagine giving yourself cough syrup if the instructions said to take "two every four hours." Would you take two teaspoonsful, two tablespoonsful, or two bottles? The choice could mean the difference between life and death. Imagine asking your boss for a raise. She agrees to give you "five more." If she means five dollars more per hour, then that is probably a pretty good raise. If she means five dollars more per week, then it is not such a good raise. If she means five cheese sandwiches a year, then you may want to look for another job.

The units of measure most familiar to you are probably the English units used in the United States. In the English system, feet measure length or distance, gallons measure volume, and pounds measure weight. Unfortunately, it can get pretty confusing trying to use these different units because there is no logical connection between them. For example, there are 12 inches in a foot, but there are 5280 feet in a mile. There are 32 ounces in a quart, but there are also 16 ounces in a pound. The 32 ounces in a quart are different from the 16 ounces in a pound because one measures volume and the other measures weight.

Most scientists use the metric system of measurement instead of the English system. Meters measure length or distance, liters measure volume, and grams measure mass (not weight). In the metric system, all units are in multiples of ten, so it is easy to use different units. The following table shows the prefixes scientists use to divide meters, liters, and grams into smaller quantities or to group them into larger ones. The examples in the table use only meters, but they apply equally well to liters or grams. Meters are abbreviated with the symbol m, liters with the symbol L, and grams with the symbol g.

| Prefix | Symbol | Number Value | Example |
|---|---|---|---|
| giga | G | 1,000,000,000 | A gigameter (Gm) is one billion meters. |
| mega | M | 1,000,000 | A megameter (Mm) is one million meters. |
| kilo | k | 1000 | A kilometer (km) is one thousand meters. |
| | | 1 | One meter is one meter. |
| centi | c | 0.01 | There are one hundred centimeters (cm) in a meter. |
| milli | m | 0.001 | There are one thousand millimeters (mm) in a meter. |
| micro | μ | 0.000001 | There are one million micrometers (μm) in a meter. |
| nano | n | 0.000000001 | There are one billion nanometers (nm) in a meter. |

## PRACTICE 12: Units of Measure

Decide if each statement that follows is true (**T**) or false (**F**). Write the correct letter on each line.

__T__ **1.** In the metric system, meters measure length, liters measure volume, and grams measure mass.

__T__ **2.** The abbreviation for meters is m, liters is L, and grams is g.

__F__ **3.** A micrometer (μm) is larger than a gigameter (Gm).

__T__ **4.** There are 1000 grams (g) in a kilogram (kg).

__T__ **5.** There are 1000 milliliters (mL) in a liter (L).

__T__ **6.** If the abbreviation for a centimeter is cm, then the abbreviation for a centigram must be cg.

__F__ **7.** A milligram (mg) is larger than a kilogram (kg).

__T__ **8.** If there are one billion nanometers (nm) in a meter, then there are one billion nanograms (ng) in a gram.

### Converting Between Different Units

Sometimes it is necessary or desirable to convert measurements from one kind of unit to another. In order to do this, you need a **conversion factor**, which is a number that tells you how many of one unit equals the same amount in another unit. For example, the conversion factor between feet and inches is 1 foot equals 12 inches. Both "1 foot" and "12 inches" are equivalent (equal) quantities, but they are expressed in different units.

$$1 \text{ ft} = 12 \text{ inches}$$

If you divide both sides by 12 inches, you get the conversion factor for going from a quantity in inches to an equivalent quantity in feet.

$$\frac{1 \text{ ft}}{12 \text{ inches}} = \frac{12 \text{ inches}}{12 \text{ inches}} = 1$$

The conversion factor, $\frac{1 \text{ ft}}{12 \text{ inches}}$, equals 1 because the numerator (1 ft) and the denominator (12 inches) are equal. Therefore, multiplying a quantity by a conversion factor changes the units of the quantity, but it does not change the value of the quantity.

For example, suppose you are given 24 inches of rope and are asked to figure out how many feet long it is. First, multiply 24 inches by the conversion factor for going from inches to feet (1 ft/12 inches).

$$(24 \text{ inches}) \times \left(\frac{1 \text{ ft}}{12 \text{ inches}}\right) = ?$$

Next, notice that the units "inches" are in both the numerator and the denominator. When that occurs, they cancel each other out. What you are left with, then, is the following:

$$(24) \times \left(\frac{1 \text{ ft}}{12}\right) = \left(\frac{24 \text{ ft}}{12}\right) = 2 \text{ ft}$$

You now have the answer you were looking for. Two things tell you it is the answer you were looking for. First, the number went down. You know that a foot is a larger unit than an inch, so you should expect the number of feet to be less than the equivalent number of inches. Second, unwanted units (inches) canceled to leave you with the desired units (ft). When you choose the correct conversion factor, unwanted units will cancel and leave you with the desired units.

Suppose you had multiplied 24 inches by the conversion factor "12 inches/1 ft," instead:

$$(24 \text{ inches}) \times \left(\frac{12 \text{ inches}}{1 \text{ ft}}\right) = ?$$

The conversion factor "$\frac{12 \text{ inches}}{1 \text{ ft}}$" is a legitimate conversion factor because 12 inches and 1 ft are equivalent quantities. Unfortunately, using this conversion factor does not lead to the cancellation of unwanted units in this problem. Also, the number will go up ($24 \times 12 = 288$), and then common sense should tell you that you should never get more feet from an equivalent quantity of inches.

The conversion factor "$\frac{12 \text{ inches}}{1 \text{ ft}}$" can be used to go from a quantity in feet to the equivalent quantity in inches. For example, suppose you are given a board that is 1.5 feet long and are asked how many inches long it is.

$$(1.5 \text{ ft}) \times \left(\frac{12 \text{ inches}}{1 \text{ ft}}\right) = ?$$

Once again, notice that the units "ft" are in both the numerator and the denominator. When that occurs, they cancel each other out. What you are left with is the following:

$$(1.5) \times \left(\frac{12\text{ inches}}{1}\right) = (1.5) \times (12\text{ inches}) = 18\text{ inches}$$

This is the answer you were looking for because the unwanted units (ft) canceled and left you with "inches" as the units. Also, the number went up. The number should go up because an inch is a smaller unit than a foot.

The conversion between English units and metric units is done the same way as converting between inches and feet or feet and inches. All you need is the correct conversion factors. The following table provides the conversion factors you need to convert from English units to metric units and from metric units to English units.

| | **English to Metric** | **Metric to English** |
|---|---|---|
| Length | 1 inch = 2.54 cm<br>1 foot = 0.3048 m<br>1 mile = 1.609 km | 1 cm = 0.3937 inches<br>1 m = 3.281 feet<br>1 km = 0.6214 miles |
| Mass | 1 ounce = 28.35 g<br>1 pound = 0.4536 kg | 1 g = 0.0353 ounces<br>1 kg = 2.205 pounds |
| Volume | 1 gallon = 3.785 L<br>1 quart = 0.9464 L | 1 L = 0.2642 gallons<br>1 L = 1.057 quarts |

In order to find out how many centimeters long a 24-inch rope is, find the appropriate conversion factor in the table.

$$1\text{ inch} = 2.54\text{ cm}$$

Divide both sides by 1 inch to get the conversion factor for going from a quantity in inches to an equivalent quantity in centimeters.

$$\left(\frac{1\text{ inch}}{1\text{ inch}}\right) = \left(\frac{2.54\text{ cm}}{1\text{ inch}}\right) = 1$$

Next, multiply the 24-inch rope by the conversion factor for going from inches to centimeters.

$$(24\text{ inches}) \times \left(\frac{2.54\text{ cm}}{1\text{ inch}}\right) = ?$$

Notice that the units "inches" are in both the numerator and the denominator. When that occurs, they cancel each other out. What you are left with is the following:

$$(24) \times \left(\frac{2.54 \text{ cm}}{1 \text{ inch}}\right) = (24) \times (2.54 \text{ cm}) = 60.96 \text{ cm}$$

Once again, two things tell you that this is probably the correct answer. First, unwanted units canceled and left you with the desired units. Second, the number went up. A centimeter is a smaller unit than an inch, so you should expect the number of centimeters to be greater than the equivalent number of inches.

Suppose you are given a piece of tubing that is 30.48 cm long. How many inches long is it? First, check the table for the appropriate conversion factor.

$$1 \text{ inch} = 2.54 \text{ cm}$$

Next, divide both sides by 2.54 cm to get the conversion factor for going from centimeters to an equivalent quantity of inches.

$$\left(\frac{1 \text{ inch}}{2.54 \text{ cm}}\right) = \left(\frac{2.54 \text{ cm}}{2.54 \text{ cm}}\right) = 1$$

Next, multiply 30.48 cm by the conversion factor for going from centimeters to inches.

$$(30.48 \text{ cm}) \times \left(\frac{1 \text{ inch}}{2.54 \text{ cm}}\right) = ?$$

Notice that "centimeters" is set up to cancel, leaving you with inches as your unit.

$$(30.48) \times \left(\frac{1 \text{ inch}}{2.54 \text{ cm}}\right) = 12 \text{ inches}$$

As before, two things tell you that this is probably the correct answer. First, unwanted units (cm) canceled to leave desired units (inches). Second, the number went down. The number is expected to go down because an inch is a larger unit than a centimeter.

## PRACTICE 13: Converting Between Different Units

Decide if each statement on the following page is true (**T**) or false (**F**). Write the correct letter on each line.

T 1. There are 2.54 cm in an inch.

T 2. One pound equals 0.4536 kg.

F 3. One foot equals 1 meter.

F 4. There are 1.057 quarts in 1 gallon.

F 5. There are 28.35 g in 1 pound.

T 6. If one liter equals 1.057 quarts, then a 2-liter bottle of soda equals 2.114 quarts.

T 7. If one kilometer equals 0.6214 miles, then a 10-kilometer run equals 6.214 miles.

T 8. If 1 gallon equals 3.785 L, then 15 gallons of gasoline equals 56.78 L.

TIP

Many modern calculators will do simple unit conversions for you. Examples include conversions between pounds and kilograms, inches and centimeters, and gallons and liters. All you need to do is enter the number in one unit (inches), push a button, and the calculator automatically converts it to the other unit (centimeters). Remember, though, that a calculator displays numbers only, not numbers and their units. You have to carry the units in your head. Therefore, you may want to learn how to do these calculations yourself before you grow to rely on a calculator. This way you will begin to develop the "feel" for numbers and units that may prevent you from making costly errors.

## Series of Unit Conversions

Suppose you were given two yards of fabric, and you were asked how many centimeters that was. If you looked at the table on page 29 for an appropriate conversion factor, you would find that there is not one listed for going from yards to centimeters. You can still do the conversion.

You just have to do it as a series of conversions. Each step in the series is done exactly like the one-step conversions done on page 29.

For example, you may know that 1 yard equals 36 inches. Once you know how many inches of fabric you have, you can convert inches to centimeters because you know that 1 inch equals 2.54 cm.

$$(2 \text{ yards}) \times \left(\frac{36 \text{ inches}}{1 \text{ yard}}\right) = (2) \times (36 \text{ inches}) = 72 \text{ inches}$$

$$(72 \text{ inches}) \times \left(\frac{2.54 \text{ cm}}{1 \text{ inch}}\right) = (72) \times (2.54 \text{ cm}) = 182.88 \text{ cm}$$

You may know that 1 yard equals 3 feet and that 1 foot equals 12 inches. Either way, you should end up with 182.88 cm of fabric.

$$(2 \text{ yards}) \times \left(\frac{3 \text{ feet}}{1 \text{ yard}}\right) = (2) \times (3 \text{ ft}) = 6 \text{ ft}$$

$$(6 \text{ ft}) \times \left(\frac{12 \text{ inches}}{1 \text{ ft}}\right) = (6) \times (12 \text{ inches}) = 72 \text{ inches}$$

$$(72 \text{ inches}) \times \left(\frac{2.54 \text{ cm}}{1 \text{ inch}}\right) = (72) \times (2.54 \text{ cm}) = 182.88 \text{ cm}$$

It is possible to do a series of conversions, because conversion factors change the units of the quantity but not the value of the quantity. In other words, the length of the fabric is the same whether you express it as 2 yards, 6 feet, 72 inches, or 182.88 cm. You do not even have to do the intermediate calculations that give you 6 feet or 72 inches. Instead, you can string together all of the conversions:

$$(2 \text{ yards}) \times \left(\frac{3 \text{ feet}}{1 \text{ yard}}\right) \times \left(\frac{12 \text{ inches}}{1 \text{ ft}}\right) \times \left(\frac{2.54 \text{ cm}}{1 \text{ inch}}\right) =$$

$$2 \times 36 \times 2.54 \text{ cm} = 182.88 \text{ cm}$$

Note that yards, feet, and inches all cancel when you do the conversion this way. You are left with centimeters, which was the desired unit.

## PRACTICE 14: Series of Unit Conversions

Decide if each statement on the following page is true (**T**) or false (**F**). Write the correct letter on each line. (*Hint:* You may want to refer to page 29 to answer some of these questions.)

_____ **1.** It is possible to do a series of conversions because conversion factors change the units of the quantity but not the value of the quantity.

_____ **2.** If there are 5280 feet in every mile, and Mount Everest is 29,141 feet high, then it is also 8.88 km high.

_____ **3.** Each step in a series of conversions is done exactly like a one-step conversion.

_____ **4.** One pound equals 453.6 g.

_____ **5.** If there are 32 ounces in a quart, then 8 ounces is the same as 236.6 mL.

_____ **6.** 3.785 mL is the same as 1 gallon.

## Mass and Weight

Most of us do not distinguish between "mass" and "weight" in ordinary conversation. To scientists, however, "mass" and "weight" are different. **Mass** is the amount of matter that an object possesses. The mass of an object does not change unless a physical or chemical change occurs to it. The metric unit for mass is grams (g).

**Weight** is the force that gravity exerts on the object. Therefore, the weight of an object depends on its mass and on the strength of the gravity pulling on it. The English unit for weight is pounds.

**TIP**

One way to try to remember the difference between mass and weight is to imagine an astronaut who has a mass of 100 kg. On the surface of Earth, the astronaut would weigh 220 pounds. On the surface of the Moon, however, the force of gravity is only about one sixth as strong as Earth's. As a result, the astronaut would still have a mass of 100 kg, but would weigh only about 37 pounds. This is why astronauts, such as Neil Armstrong and Edwin Aldrin, were able to move around so effortlessly on the surface of the Moon, despite their heavy space suits.

## ■ PRACTICE 15: Mass and Weight

Decide if each statement that follows is true (**T**) or false (**F**). Write the correct letter on each line.

__T__ **1.** To scientists, mass and weight are different.

__F__ **2.** Your weight will be the same whether you are standing on Earth or on the Moon.

__T__ **3.** Your mass will be the same whether you are standing on Earth or on the Moon.

__T__ **4.** The metric unit for mass is the gram (g).

__F__ **5.** The English unit for weight is the gram (g).

__T__ **6.** Mass is the amount of matter that an object possesses.

__F__ **7.** The weight of an object depends on its mass only.

__T__ **8.** Weight is the force that gravity exerts on an object.

## Volume and Density

**Volume** is the amount of space that an object occupies. Imagine a cube that measures 10 cm on each edge. The area of each side is 100 $cm^2$ (10 cm × 10 cm). The volume of the cube is 1000 $cm^3$ (10 cm × 10 cm × 10 cm). The metric unit for volume is liters (L). One liter is defined as 1000 $cm^3$. This means that 1 milliliter (mL) equals 1 $cm^3$. Thus, it is possible to use mL and $cm^3$ interchangeably.

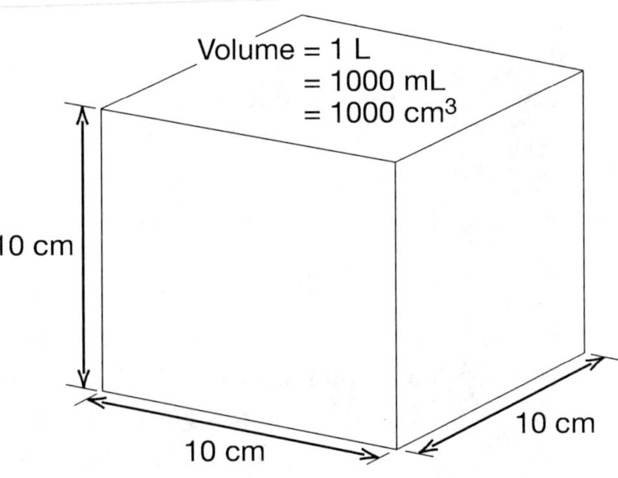


**Density** is the amount of mass in a given volume. A very dense object has a lot of mass in a given volume. One that is not very dense has only a little bit of mass in the same volume. For example, the density of water is 1.00 g/mL.

This means that every milliliter of water has a mass of 1.00 g. The density of gold, on the other hand, is 19.3 g/mL. This means that every milliliter of gold has a mass of 19.3 g. Gold is much more dense than water, so gold sinks in water. The density of cork is 0.24 g/mL. This means that every milliliter of cork has a mass of 0.24 g. Cork is much less dense than water, so cork floats on water.

## PRACTICE 16: Volume and Density

Decide if each statement that follows is true (**T**) or false (**F**). Write the correct letter on each line.

__T__ **1.** Density is the amount of mass in a given volume.

__F__ **2.** The density of water is 19.3 g/mL.

__T__ **3.** Volume is the amount of space that an object occupies.

__F__ **4.** Iron is much more dense than water, so iron floats on water.

__T__ **5.** One milliliter (mL) equals 1 $cm^3$.

__T__ **6.** The density of balsa wood is 0.12 g/mL, so balsa wood floats on water.

__T__ **7.** The density of mercury is 13.55 g/mL, so mercury sinks in water.

__F__ **8.** One liter is defined as 5000 $cm^3$.

## Temperature and Heat

**Temperature** is a measure of the average kinetic energy of the particles in a substance. The faster the particles move, the higher the temperature of the substance. Temperature can also be thought of as a relative measure of the hotness or coldness of an object, although temperature is not the feeling of hotness or coldness that an object has.

For example, if you take a cold shower before jumping into a heated swimming pool, the pool will probably feel warm to you. If you take a hot shower before jumping into the same pool, the pool will probably feel cold to you. The temperature of the pool has not changed, but your perception of its hotness or coldness has.

**Heat** is energy that flows between objects that are at different temperatures. Temperature measures the direction of the heat flow because heat always flows from a warm object to a cool object. Heat and temperature are not the same thing.

A thermometer is used to measure temperature. It contains a fluid (such as mercury) that expands when heated and contracts when cooled. If you place the thermometer in something hotter than itself (like boiling water), heat flows from the water to the mercury in the thermometer. The mercury expands and rises in the thermometer tube. If you place the thermometer in something colder than itself (like ice water), heat flows from the mercury. The mercury contracts and falls in the thermometer tube.

## PRACTICE 17: Temperature and Heat

Decide if each statement that follows is true (**T**) or false (**F**). Write the correct letter on each line.

__T__ **1.** Temperature is a measure of the hotness or coldness of an object relative to another object.

__F__ **2.** Heat always flows from a cool object to a warm object.

__T__ **3.** Heat always flows from a warm object to a cool object.

__T__ **4.** A thermometer is used to measure temperature.

__T__ **5.** Heat is energy that flows between objects that are at different temperatures.

__T__ **6.** Temperature is NOT the feeling of hotness or coldness that an object has.

__F__ **7.** The fluid in a thermometer contracts when heated and expands when cooled.

__F__ **8.** Temperature and heat are the same thing.

## Temperature Scales

The temperature scale used most commonly in the United States is the **Fahrenheit scale**. It is named for Gabriel D. Fahrenheit, the German physicist who invented it in 1709. On the Fahrenheit scale, the freezing point of water is 32°F, and the boiling point of water is 212°F. This means that there are 180 degrees between the freezing and boiling points of water on the Fahrenheit scale. The zero point on the Fahrenheit scale, 0°F, is the temperature of a mixture of equal parts salt and snow.

The temperature scale used most commonly in the rest of the world is the **Celsius scale.** It is named for Anders Celsius, the Swedish astronomer who invented it in 1742. The Celsius scale is also called the centigrade scale. On the Celsius scale, the freezing point of water is 0°C, and the boiling point of water is 100°C. This means there are only 100 degrees between the freezing and boiling points of water on the Celsius scale. Also, the zero point on the Celsius scale is the same as the freezing point of water, but different from the zero point on the Fahrenheit scale.

Another scale is the **Kelvin scale.** The Kelvin scale makes the lowest possible temperature zero. This is –273.15 on the Celsius scale and –459.67 on the Fahrenheit scale. This temperature is referred to as **absolute zero.** It is the theoretical point at which all particle motion stops. Because the Kelvin scale starts at zero, the degree symbol (°) is not needed. Celsius and Fahrenheit are only scales of measurement, but the Kelvin itself is the name of the scale and is a unit of measurement.

In order to convert from degrees Celsius to degrees Fahrenheit, you need to use the following formula:

$$°F = \left(\frac{9}{5}\right)°C + 32$$

For example, if you have a temperature of 10°C, then the temperature in °F is the following:

$$\left(\frac{9}{5}\right)(10°C) + 32 = 50°F$$

The "$\frac{9}{5}$" in the formula comes about because there are 180 Fahrenheit degrees but only 100 Celsius degrees between the freezing and boiling points of water. As a result, one degree on the Fahrenheit scale is smaller than one degree on the Celsius scale $\left(\frac{180}{100} = \frac{9}{5}\right)$. The "32" in the formula comes about because the zero points of the two scales differ by that amount.

In order to convert from degrees Fahrenheit to degrees Celsius, you need to use the following formula:

$$°C = (°F - 32)\left(\frac{5}{9}\right)$$

For example, if you have a temperature of 68°F, then the temperature in °C is the following:

$$(68°F - 32)\left(\frac{5}{9}\right) = 20°C$$

To convert a temperature from Celsius to Kelvin, you add 273.15 to the Celsius temperature.

For example, if you have a temperature of 55°C, then the temperature in Kelvin is the following:

$$55°C + 273.15 = 328.15 \text{ K}$$

To convert from Kelvin to Celsius, you would subtract 273.15 from the Kelvin temperature.

For example, if you have a temperature of 300 K, then the temperature in Celsius is the following:

$$300 \text{ K} - 273.15 = 26.85°C$$

## PRACTICE 18: Temperature Scales

Decide if each statement that follows is true (**T**) or false (**F**). Write the correct letter on each line.

_____ **1.** The Celsius temperature scale is named for Anders Celsius, the Swedish astronomer who invented it in 1742.

_____ **2.** The zero point on the Celsius scale is the same as the zero point on the Fahrenheit scale.

_____ **3.** On the Fahrenheit scale, the freezing point of water is 32°F and the boiling point of water is 212°F.

_____ **4.** On the Celsius scale, the freezing point of water is 32°C and the boiling point of water is 212°C.

_____ **5.** 233 K is the same temperature as 158.15°C.

_____ **6.** –221°C is the same temperature as 52.15 K.

_____ **7.** 212°C is the same temperature as 100°F.

_____ **8.** One degree on the Fahrenheit scale is smaller than one degree on the Celsius scale.

**THINK ABOUT IT**

Imagine that you are traveling in Europe, where all temperatures are reported in degrees Celsius. Before you head out for a day of sightseeing, you read in the newspaper that the high temperature for the day is expected to be 37°C. What kind of clothes should you wear? Write your answer on a separate sheet of paper.

## Scientific Notation

Many things that scientists measure are very large or very small. For example, the mass of the planet Jupiter is approximately 1,900,000,000,000,000,000,000,000,000 kg. The mass of an atom of lead is 0.000000000000000000000344 g. There are so many zeros in these two numbers that it is easy to make a mistake when using them. In order to make it easier to write very large or very small numbers, scientists use a shorthand called **scientific notation.** Scientific notation is also called exponential notation. Scientific notation does not change the value of a number. It just rewrites the number in a form that is easier to use and keep track of.

Scientific notation is possible because any number can be written as a number between 1 and 10, multiplied or divided by 10 the correct number of times. For example, 753,000 can be written as 7.53 multiplied by five 10s.

$$(7.53)(10)(10)(10)(10)(10)$$

The five 10s can be shortened to $10^5$, which means "multiply by 10, five times." You are then left with $(7.53)(10^5)$ which, in scientific notation, is written as $7.53 \times 10^5$. The mass of Jupiter can now be rewritten as $1.9 \times 10^{27}$ kg, which means that 1.9 should be multiplied by 10, 27 times.

Very small numbers can be written this way, too. For example, 0.0000033 can be written as 3.3 divided by six 10s:

$$3.3/(10)(10)(10)(10)(10)(10)$$

The six 10s can be shortened to $10^6$, so you are then left with $(3.3)/(10^6)$. In scientific notation, this is written as $3.3 \times 10^{-6}$. The negative sign is inserted between the "10" and the "6" to indicate that you should "divide by 10, six times" instead of "multiply by 10, six times." The mass of an atom of lead can now be rewritten as $3.44 \times 10^{-22}$ g, which means that 3.44 should be divided by 10, 22 times.

Now that you understand the basis for scientific notation, you can learn a simpler, more practical way to convert numbers to scientific notation, and to convert scientific notation to regular numbers. Begin with a number greater than 1, such as 12,000 miles. This is the average number of miles a person drives every year. Without saying so, it is implied that there is a decimal point to the right of the rightmost zero (that is, 12,000 miles = 12,000.0 miles). Move that decimal point to the left until you get a number that is between 1 and 10 (1.2). Next, multiply 1.2 by $10^n$, where $n$ is the number of places that you moved the decimal point to the left ($n = 4$). What you are left with, then, is $1.2 \times 10^4$ miles.

In order to convert a number less than 1 into scientific notation, you need to do the opposite of what you did for a number greater than 1. Use 0.0000037 m as an example. Move the decimal point to the right until you get a number between 1 and 10 (3.7). Next, multiply 3.7 by $10^{-n}$, where $n$ is the number of places you moved the decimal point to the right ($n = 6$). The negative sign is important because it means the number is less than 1. If it were positive, it would mean that the number is greater than 1. In fact, the number would be 3,700,000 m, which is much larger than 0.0000037 m. What you are left with, then, is $3.7 \times 10^{-6}$ m.

In order to convert a number in scientific notation to regular numbers, you do the opposite of what you did to convert a regular number into scientific notation. For example, the average distance of Earth from the Sun is $9.3 \times 10^7$ miles. Begin with 9.3, and move the decimal point to the right seven times. Fill in with zeros, as necessary. What you end up with is 93,000,000.0 miles. That is more miles than anyone will ever drive in a lifetime.

The average thickness of a human hair is about $1.0 \times 10^{-4}$ m. Begin with the 1.0, and move the decimal point to the left four times. Fill in with zeros, as necessary. What you end up with is 0.00010 m. That is not very wide, but you probably did not expect a human hair to be very wide.

**TIP**

When you convert regular numbers to scientific notation, or when you convert scientific notation to regular numbers, you need to make sure you do not move the decimal point in the wrong direction. If you think about what the numbers mean after you have converted them, you can avoid silly errors. For example, if you had taken $9.3 \times 10^7$ miles and moved the decimal point to the left seven times, you would have ended up with 0.00000093 miles as the average distance between Earth and the Sun. That is less than an inch. All the sunscreen ever made would not protect you from a sunburn if the sun were that close! Similarly, if you had taken $1.0 \times 10^{-4}$ m and moved the decimal point to the right four times, you would have ended up with 10,000 m as the average thickness of a human hair. Ten thousand meters is the same as 6.2 miles, which is one really thick hair. It should suggest to you that you have moved the decimal point the wrong way.

## PRACTICE 19: Scientific Notation

Decide if each statement that follows is true (**T**) or false (**F**). Write the correct letter on each line.

__T__ **1.** Scientific notation makes it easier to write very large and very small numbers.

__F__ **2.** Scientific notation changes the value of a number.

_____ 3. The negative sign in $3.27 \times 10^{-5}$ grams tells you that this number is greater than 1.

_____ 4. $3.27 \times 10^{-5}$ grams is the same as 0.0000327 grams.

_____ 5. $1.636 \times 10^{4}$ liters is the same as 16,360 liters.

_____ 6. $2.898 \times 10^{-3}$ m is the same as 2898 m.

_____ 7. 15,060,000 km can be written in scientific notation as $1.506 \times 10^{7}$ km.

_____ 8. 0.00000033 mL can be written in scientific notation as $3.3 \times 10^{-7}$ mL.

## UNIT 1 REVIEW

Circle the letter of the correct answer.

1. What is studied in chemistry?
   - **a.** the composition, structure, and properties of matter, but not the changes that matter undergoes
   - **b.** the composition, structure, and properties of matter, and the changes that matter undergoes
   - **c.** the properties of matter, but not its composition and structure

2. What is the scientific method?
   - **a.** the way scientists propose and test ideas
   - **b.** the way chemistry is done, but not physics
   - **c.** the way physics is done, but not chemistry

3. A mixture _____.
   - **a.** contains two or more substances that retain their individual identities
   - **b.** is the same as a substance
   - **c.** is not really matter at all

4. An element is _____.
   - **a.** the same as a chemical compound
   - **b.** a substance that cannot be broken down into simpler substances by chemical means
   - **c.** a special kind of heterogeneous mixture

5. A solid ______.
   a. has its own fixed shape and volume
   b. has the same physical properties as a liquid or a gas
   c. has a fixed shape but no fixed volume

6. A liquid ______.
   a. has a fixed volume but not a fixed shape
   b. has the same physical properties as a solid or a gas
   c. has both a fixed shape and a fixed volume

7. The burning of wood is a chemical change because ______.
   a. wood and ash are different forms of the same chemical substance
   b. wood is turned into ash, carbon dioxide, and water
   c. wood and ash have different physical properties, but the same chemical properties

8. When scientists measure something, they always report ______.
   a. a unit only
   b. a number only
   c. a number and a unit

9. Weight is ______.
   a. different from mass
   b. the force that gravity exerts on an object
   c. both a and b

10. 850 mL is the same as ______.
   a. 0.850 L
   b. 85.0 L
   c. 8.50 L

## UNIT 1 APPLICATION ACTIVITY 1

### Metric Calculation Versus English Calculation

Have you ever wondered why some people use the metric system? Try comparing the English system with the metric system.

Find the area (length × width) of five common objects—such as a tabletop, a window, a sheet of paper, a ruler, and a chalkboard—in inches (English measurement). Record your data in the chart below. Then find the area of each object in centimeters (metric measurement), and record your data.

| | English Measurement | | | Metric Measurement | | |
|---|---|---|---|---|---|---|
| **Object** | **Length** | **Width** | **Area** | **Length** | **Width** | **Area** |
| | | | | | | |
| | | | | | | |
| | | | | | | |
| | | | | | | |
| | | | | | | |

Which is easier to calculate, area in metric units or area in English units?

______________________________________________

Why?

______________________________________________

______________________________________________

______________________________________________

______________________________________________

______________________________________________

______________________________________________

______________________________________________

______________________________________________

______________________________________________

______________________________________________

______________________________________________

## UNIT 1 APPLICATION ACTIVITY 2

### Freshwater and Saltwater Boiling Points

Do you think there is a difference between the boiling points of freshwater and salt water? Here is a way to find out:

Place 150 mL of freshwater in a beaker. Put the beaker of water on a hot plate, and heat to boiling. When the water comes to a full boil, measure the temperature of the water. This will be the temperature at time = 0 minutes. Record your data in the chart. Then reduce the heat so the water is boiling gently. Record the temperature after 1, 2, 3, 4, and 5 minutes of boiling. Observe what happens to the water level in the beaker after each minute of boiling. Record your observations in the chart, in the Beaker 1 column. Remove the beaker from the hot plate, and empty the beaker.

**Caution:** Be careful when boiling water. You can easily burn yourself with the boiling water or steam. Be careful to use a hot pad when you remove the beaker from the heat.

Now fill the beaker with 150 mL of freshwater, and add 10 grams of salt to the water. Stir to dissolve the salt in the water. Put this second beaker of water on the hot plate, and bring the saltwater solution to a boil. Once it begins to boil, record temperatures at time = 0, 1, 2, 3, 4, and 5 minutes, as you did for the freshwater. Record your data in the chart, in the Beaker 2 column. Observe what happens to the water level in the beaker after each minute of boiling, and record your observations in the chart. Remove the beaker from the hot plate, and empty the beaker.

Run the experiment one more time, but this time dissolve 20 grams of salt in 150 mL of water. Record your data in the chart, in the Beaker 3 column.

| | Beaker 1 | | | | | | Beaker 2 | | | | | | Beaker 3 | | | | | |
|---|---|---|---|---|---|---|---|---|---|---|---|---|---|---|---|---|---|---|
| **Time (minutes)** | **0** | **1** | **2** | **3** | **4** | **5** | **0** | **1** | **2** | **3** | **4** | **5** | **0** | **1** | **2** | **3** | **4** | **5** |
| **Temperature of water (°C)** | | | | | | | | | | | | | | | | | | |
| **Water level** | | | | | | | | | | | | | | | | | | |

Graph all your data for the three experiments on one graph. You can use three different colors to represent each experiment. On the graph, write temperature (°C) on the vertical axis and time (minutes) on the horizontal axis.

What does adding salt do to the boiling point of water?

______________________________________________________________

______________________________________________________________

______________________________________________________________

______________________________________________________________

## UNIT 1 APPLICATION ACTIVITY 3

### Rubber Versus Mylar®

Rubber and Mylar® are both substances used to make balloons. Yet they are quite different.

Obtain one rubber balloon and one Mylar® balloon. Blow up each balloon, and tie off the open end securely. Observe the size, shape, and appearance of the balloon, and record your observations in the chart that follows on page 47.

Then cool the two balloons by placing them in a refrigerator for five minutes. Remove the balloons from the refrigerator, and record your observations in the chart below.

| | **Room Temperature** | | **Cool Temperature** | |
|---|---|---|---|---|
| | **Rubber** | **Mylar®** | **Rubber** | **Mylar®** |
| **Size** | | | | |
| **Shape** | | | | |
| **Appearance** | | | | |

How would you describe the size, shape, and appearance of the balloons before cooling?

_______________________________________________

_______________________________________________

_______________________________________________

_______________________________________________

How would you describe them after they were cooled?

_______________________________________________

_______________________________________________

_______________________________________________

_______________________________________________

How might you explain the differences?

_______________________________________________

_______________________________________________

_______________________________________________

_______________________________________________

# UNIT 2

## Properties of Matter

# LESSON 5: The Structure of Matter

GOAL: To learn about the internal structure of atoms

## WORDS TO KNOW

| | | |
|---|---|---|
| **atomic mass** | **coulombs** | **molecular mass** |
| **atomic mass unit** | **electrons** | **neutrons** |
| **atomic number** | **isotopes** | **protons** |
| **cathode-ray tube** | **mass number** | |

## Dalton's Atomic Theory

The ancient Greek philosopher Leucippus and his follower, Democritus, proposed more than 2000 years ago that matter is made up of extremely small particles that cannot be divided further. Democritus called these bits of matter *atomos*. *Atomos* means "indivisible" and is the source of our word *atoms* today.

Many contemporaries of Leucippus and Democritus, including Plato and Aristotle, did not accept the idea that matter was made up of particles that have distinct properties of their own. Instead, they believed that all matter was uniform in composition, no matter how small the piece of matter.

These two opposing ideas were not tested until the 1700s. That is when scientists began doing careful experiments on the changes that matter undergoes. In 1808, an English schoolteacher named John Dalton proposed his own atomic view of matter. It has since become known as Dalton's atomic theory.

Dalton's atomic theory can be summarized as follows:

1. All matter is composed of tiny particles called atoms.

2. All atoms of a given element are identical. They all have the same mass, size, and chemical properties.

3. All atoms of a given element are distinct from all atoms of any other element. The mass, size, and chemical properties of the atoms of one element are different from the mass, size, and chemical properties of the atoms of any other element.

4. Chemical compounds form when atoms combine in whole-number ratios. A pure compound has the same combination of atoms, no matter how it was prepared. For example, pure water always contains two hydrogen atoms chemically joined to one oxygen atom. If some compound contains a different combination of hydrogen and oxygen atoms, then it is not water. It is a different compound altogether.

5. Atoms cannot be created from nothing or destroyed in a chemical reaction. Instead, atoms retain their identities but change the way they are combined or arranged.

## PRACTICE 20: Dalton's Atomic Theory

Decide if each statement that follows is true (**T**) or false (**F**). Write the correct letter on each line.

__T__ **1.** The Greek word *atomos* means "indivisible" and is the source of the word *atoms* today.

__F__ **2.** Dalton's atomic theory is named for the ancient Greek philosopher Leucippus and his follower, Democritus.

__T__ **3.** According to Dalton's atomic theory, all atoms of a given element are identical.

__F__ **4.** According to Dalton's atomic theory, a pure compound has a different combination of atoms depending on how it was prepared.

__T__ **5.** According to Dalton's atomic theory, atoms cannot be created from nothing or destroyed in a chemical reaction.

__T__ **6.** According to Dalton's atomic theory, the mass, size, and chemical properties of the atoms of one element are different from the mass, size, and chemical properties of the atoms of any other element.

F 7. According to Dalton's atomic theory, atoms CAN be created or destroyed in a chemical reaction.

T 8. According to Dalton's atomic theory, chemical compounds form when atoms combine in whole-number ratios.

## Electrons, Protons, and Neutrons

Although matter is composed of atoms, atoms are not as indivisible as Democritus or Dalton suggested. Thanks to the careful experiments of physicists such as J. J. Thomson, Robert Millikan, Hans Geiger, Ernest Marsden, Ernest Rutherford, and James Chadwick, it is now known that atoms are made up of electrons, protons, and neutrons.

**Electrons** are negatively charged particles that have very little mass but take up most of the volume of an atom. **Protons** are positively charged particles that have more than 1800 times the mass of an electron, but take up very little of the volume of an atom. The charge on a proton is equal and opposite to the charge on an electron. **Neutrons** have no charge and have a mass that is only slightly greater than the mass of a proton. Electrons, protons, and neutrons are called subatomic particles because they are the building blocks of atoms. The mass of a subatomic particle is measured in kilograms. The charge of a subatomic particle is measured in units called **coulombs.**

| Name | Symbol | Charge | Mass |
|---|---|---|---|
| Electron | $e$ | $-1.6022 \times 10^{-19}$ coulomb | $9.1094 \times 10^{-31}$ kg |
| Proton | $p$ | $+1.6022 \times 10^{-19}$ coulomb | $1.6726 \times 10^{-27}$ kg |
| Neutron | $n$ | 0 | $1.6749 \times 10^{-27}$ kg |

J. J. Thomson's experiments in 1897 measured the ratio of the electron's mass to the electron's charge. Thomson was unable to determine the exact mass of an electron, but he estimated it to be less than $\frac{1}{1000}$ as much as hydrogen, the lightest element known. Thomson's experiments showed that atoms were divisible into smaller particles, after all.

Robert Millikan's experiments in 1909 determined the exact charge on an electron. From his value for the charge, and Thomson's value for the electron's mass-to-charge ratio, Millikan was able to determine the mass of an electron:

$$\text{Mass of electron} = \frac{\text{mass}}{\text{charge}} \times \text{charge}$$

$$= \left(5.686 \times \frac{10^{-12}\,\text{kg}}{\text{coulomb}}\right)(1.602 \times 10^{-19}\ \text{coulomb})$$

$$= 9.109 \times 10^{-31}\ \text{kg}$$

At this point, scientists knew two things about atoms. First, they knew that atoms are electrically neutral overall. Second, they knew that atoms contain negatively charged electrons. In order to be electrically neutral overall, atoms must also contain some positively charged particles (protons) to balance the negative charge of the electrons. Thomson proposed that atoms could be thought of as positively charged spheres of matter in which electrons are embedded like raisins in plum pudding.

Another way to think of Thomson's "plum pudding" model of the atom is to imagine a chocolate chip cookie. The chocolate chips are the electrons, and the cookie is the "positively charged sphere of matter." Together, the cookie and the chips make up an atom.

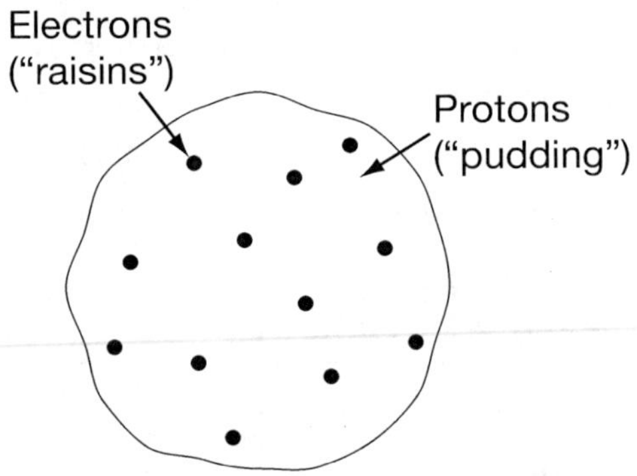


**Thomson's "Plum Pudding" Model**

The experiments of Hans Geiger and Ernest Marsden in Ernest Rutherford's lab in 1911 suggested, however, that the protons are concentrated in the core of the atom, not spread throughout the atom. Rutherford proposed that an atom consists of a positively charged nucleus surrounded by a cloud of electrons. The nucleus is the central core of the atom where most of the mass is. Thus, the protons of an atom are in the nucleus. Rutherford's theory is often called the nuclear model of the atom.

In the nuclear model of the atom, the volume of the cloud of electrons is huge compared to the volume of the nucleus. In fact, if a golf ball were the nucleus of an atom, the electron cloud would measure 3 miles across. The mass of an electron is so small compared to the mass of a proton that the electron cloud is mostly empty space.

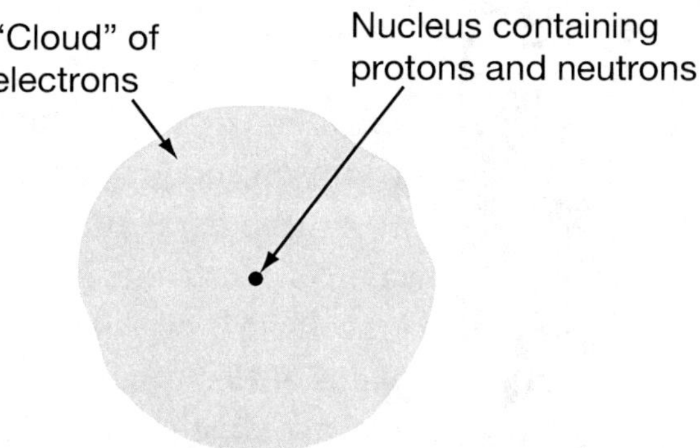

**Rutherford's Nuclear Model**

Finally, in 1932, James Chadwick conducted experiments that led to the discovery of the neutron. Because the mass of a neutron is slightly greater than the mass of a proton, neutrons must be located in the nucleus, too.

## ■ PRACTICE 21: Electrons, Protons, and Neutrons

Decide if each statement that follows is true (**T**) or false (**F**). Write the correct letter on each line.

____ **1.** The nucleus of an atom is where the electrons are.

____ **2.** The nucleus of an atom is where the protons and neutrons are.

____ **3.** The mass of a neutron is slightly greater than the mass of a proton, and the mass of a proton is more than 1800 times greater than the mass of an electron.

____ **4.** J. J. Thomson's experiments measured the ratio of the electron's mass to the electron's charge.

____ **5.** Hans Geiger proposed the "plum pudding" model of the atom.

____ **6.** James Chadwick discovered the electron.

____ **7.** In Rutherford's nuclear model of the atom, protons have most of the mass, but electrons have most of the volume of an atom.

____ **8.** Robert Millikan's experiments determined the exact charge on an electron.

IN REAL LIFE

There's no telling where scientific inquiry will take you or what kind of applications will come from your work. J. J. Thomson conducted his ground-breaking experiments with a cathode-ray tube. A **cathode-ray tube** consists of two metal electrodes in an evacuated glass tube. When a high voltage is applied between the electrodes, glowing streams of electrons are emitted from one of the electrodes. A more sophisticated version of the cathode-ray tube used by Thomson is used in television sets today. Hans Geiger moved on from Ernest Rutherford's labs to invent, with W. Müller, the Geiger counter. Geiger counters are used routinely to check for unsafe levels of radiation.

## Atomic Number and Mass Number

In Unit 1, page 11, you learned that each of the 115 known elements has unique physical and chemical properties. Remember also from Dalton's atomic theory (pages 51–52) that all atoms of a given element are identical, but all atoms of a given element are distinct from all atoms of any other element. The differences between elements are due to differences in their atoms.

An atom of hydrogen consists of one proton and one electron. An atom of helium consists of two protons, two neutrons, and two electrons. An atom of lithium consists of three protons, four neutrons, and three electrons. The differences between these atoms and the atoms of the other elements are the differences in the number of protons, neutrons, and electrons they contain. Each element has a unique combination of these three subatomic particles.

The **atomic number** of an element is the number of protons in the nucleus of each of its atoms. All of the atoms of an element have the same atomic number. All elements have atomic numbers that are different from all other elements. For example, the atomic number of hydrogen is 1, the atomic number of helium is 2, and the atomic number of lithium is 3.

A hydrogen atom cannot have an atomic number of 2 because an atom with an atomic number of 2 is a helium atom.

The symbol for atomic number is Z. Therefore, Z = 1 for hydrogen, Z = 2 for helium, and Z = 3 for lithium.

The **mass number** of an atom is the total number of protons and neutrons in its nucleus. The mass number for an atom of hydrogen with one proton and zero neutrons is 1. The mass number for an atom of helium with two protons and two neutrons is 4. The mass number for an atom of lithium with three protons and four neutrons is 7.

The symbol for mass number is A. Therefore, A = 1 for a hydrogen atom with one proton and zero neutrons, A = 4 for a helium atom with two protons and two neutrons, and A = 7 for a lithium atom with three protons and four neutrons.

The mass number of an atom is not unique to that element. As you will see in Lesson 6, atoms of the same element can have different mass numbers. Atoms of different elements can have the same mass numbers. It all depends on the number of neutrons.

## PRACTICE 22: Atomic Number and Mass Number

Decide if each statement that follows is true (**T**) or false (**F**). Write the correct letter on each line.

__T__ **1.** The atomic number of an element is the number of protons in the nucleus of each of its atoms.

__T__ **2.** The mass number of an atom is the total number of protons and neutrons in its nucleus.

__F__ **3.** If carbon atoms have six protons, then the atomic number of carbon is 12.

__T__ **4.** If uranium atoms have 92 protons, then the atomic number of uranium is 92.

__F__ **5.** A = 7 for a helium atom with two protons and two neutrons.

__F__ **6.** Some elements, but not all elements, have atomic numbers that are different from all other elements.

____ **7.** If a chlorine atom has 17 protons and 18 neutrons, then its mass number is 35.

____ **8.** The mass number of an atom is not unique to that element.

**THINK ABOUT IT**

If you know the atomic number (Z) and the mass number (A) of an atom, then you have a lot of information about that atom. The atomic number tells you how many protons the atom has and what element it is. It also tells you how many electrons the atom has because the number of electrons equals the number of protons. The mass number tells you the total number of protons and neutrons in the element. If you subtract the atomic number from the mass number, you will find out how many neutrons the atom has. For example, the atomic number for a fluorine atom is 9 and the mass number is 19. How many protons, electrons, and neutrons does the fluorine atom have? The number of protons equals the atomic number, so the fluorine atom has 9 protons. The number of electrons equals the number of protons, so the fluorine atom has 9 electrons. The number of neutrons equals A – Z, which is 19 – 9 = 10 neutrons. Now it is your turn. How many protons, electrons, and neutrons does a carbon atom have if Z = 6 and A = 12? Write your answer on a separate sheet of paper.

## Isotopes

On page 57, you learned that the mass number of an atom is not unique to that element. For example, atoms of the same element can have different numbers of neutrons. When that occurs, the mass numbers of the atoms are different, too, because the mass number is the total number of protons and neutrons that the atom has.

Atoms of the same element that have different numbers of neutrons are called **isotopes** of the element. Because isotopes have the same atomic number but different numbers of neutrons, isotopes have different mass numbers, too.

The element hydrogen has three isotopes. The isotopes are called protium, deuterium, and tritium. The protium isotope has one proton and zero neutrons. The deuterium isotope has one proton and one neutron. The tritium isotope has one proton and two neutrons. All three isotopes have one electron.

The isotopes of the other elements do not have unique names like protium, deuterium, and tritium. Instead, isotopes of any element can be identified by the elemental symbol, the mass number of the isotope, and the atomic number of the element.

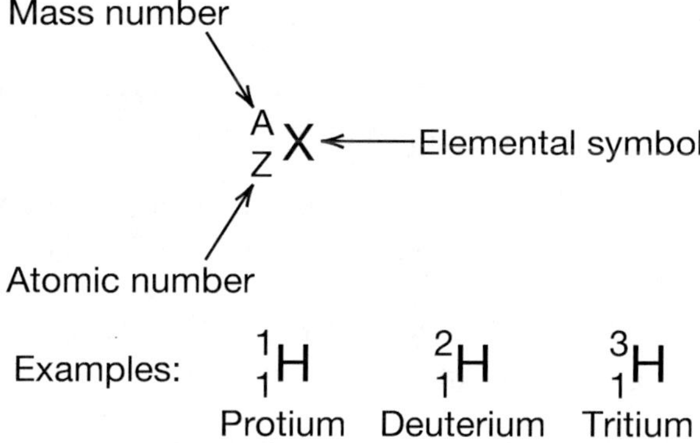


Another way to name isotopes is to use the name of the element with the mass number of the isotope. For example, the two most common isotopes of uranium are uranium-238 and uranium-235. These can also be written as $^{238}U$ and $^{235}U$, respectively.

Not every isotope of an element is present in equal amounts. For example, a sample of naturally occurring hydrogen contains 99.985% $^{1}H$, 0.015% $^{2}H$, and so little $^{3}H$ that it is difficult to measure. When chemists say "naturally occurring," they mean "as you would find it in nature." That is, the sample has not been changed in any way in a laboratory.

A naturally occurring sample of titanium (the metal used in jet engines) contains 8.0% $^{46}Ti$, 7.5% $^{47}Ti$, 73.7% $^{48}Ti$, 5.5% $^{49}Ti$, and 5.3% $^{50}Ti$. The percentage of each isotope is also called its natural abundance. Thus, the natural abundance of $^{46}Ti$ is 8.0%, the natural abundance of $^{47}Ti$ is 7.5%, the natural abundance of $^{48}Ti$ is 73.7%, the natural abundance of $^{49}Ti$ is 5.5%, and the natural abundance of $^{50}Ti$ is 5.3%.

The chemical properties of the isotopes of an element are so similar that the minute differences can be ignored in most common situations. That is, $^{46}Ti$ behaves in a chemical reaction the same way that $^{47}Ti$, $^{48}Ti$, $^{49}Ti$, and $^{50}Ti$ do. The chemical properties of isotopes are similar because chemical properties depend on electrons and protons much more than they depend on neutrons. And, all isotopes of an element have the same number of electrons and protons. If they did not, they would not be isotopes.

## PRACTICE 23: Isotopes

Decide if each statement that follows is true (**T**) or false (**F**). Write the correct letter on each line.

T **1.** Atoms of the same element that have different numbers of neutrons are called isotopes of the element.

T **2.** Isotopes have the same atomic number but different numbers of neutrons, so isotopes have different mass numbers, too.

T **3.** The element hydrogen has three isotopes named protium, deuterium, and tritium.

F **4.** The chemical properties of the various isotopes of an element are extremely different.

F **5.** Every isotope of an element is present in equal amounts in that element.

T **6.** When chemists say "naturally occurring," they mean "as you would find it in nature."

T **7.** The percentage of each isotope of an element is also called its natural abundance.

### Atomic Mass and Molecular Mass

So far you have learned the following:

- Atoms are made up of protons, neutrons, and electrons.
- The protons and neutrons are concentrated in the nucleus of the atom.
- The protons and neutrons are responsible for the mass of the atom.

- Atoms of the same element can have different numbers of neutrons (isotopes).

It stands to reason, then, that isotopes of an element have different masses. In fact, an atom of deuterium (one proton and one neutron) has a mass of $3.3475 \times 10^{-27}$ kg, and an atom of protium (one proton, zero neutrons) has a mass of $1.6726 \times 10^{-27}$ kg. The mass of deuterium is twice the mass of protium.

Numbers such as $3.3475 \times 10^{-27}$ kg and $1.6726 \times 10^{-27}$ kg are clumsy to work with and too small to measure conveniently. Instead, chemists measure the mass of an atom relative to the mass of an agreed-upon standard. The agreed-upon standard is the carbon-12 atom. It contains six protons and six neutrons. If you add the mass of six protons and six neutrons, you get $2.0085 \times 10^{-26}$ kg. This mass is defined as 12 atomic mass units. Therefore, one **atomic mass unit** (amu) is $\frac{1}{12}$ the mass of a carbon-12 atom.

Chemists rarely work with individual atoms. Instead, they work with small quantities of substances (usually less than a gram) that contain huge numbers of atoms. Furthermore, the samples of substances that chemists generally work with contain all of the naturally occurring isotopes. For example, a representative sample of the element boron contains 19.91% boron-10 and 80.09% boron-11. It would be too costly and take too much time to try to prepare a sample that contained 100% of either boron-10 or boron-11. Besides, the chemical properties of the mixture of the two isotopes would be almost identical to the chemical properties of either pure boron-10 or pure boron-11.

Chemists need to know the average mass of the atoms in their samples. The average mass of the naturally occurring isotopes in the sample of an element is called the **atomic mass** or the atomic weight of the element. The average is the weighted average of the natural isotopes in the sample. For example, the atomic mass of boron is 10.81 amu. This value is closer to the mass of a boron-11 atom (mass = 11.0093 amu) than it is to the mass of a boron-10 atom (mass = 10.0129 amu), because the natural abundance of boron-11 (80.09%) is higher than the natural abundance of boron-10 (19.91%).

TIP

Calculating atomic mass from the exact masses of isotopes is a lot like calculating an average grade from several test scores. Suppose you took five tests worth 100 points each. Suppose you scored 95 on three of the tests and 55 on the other two. Your average score would be 79.

$$\text{Average} = \frac{(95 + 95 + 95 + 55 + 55)}{5} = 79$$

This is no different from taking the weighted average of the abundances of the two test scores. That is, $\frac{3}{5}$ (or 0.6 or 60%) of the time you scored 95 and $\frac{2}{5}$ (or 0.4 or 40%) of the time you scored 55.

$$\text{Average} = \left(\frac{3}{5}\right)(95) + \left(\frac{2}{5}\right)(55) = (0.6)(95) + (0.4)(55) = 79$$

The average score is closer to 95 than it is to 55 because you received more scores of 95 than you did of 55. Now, for the atomic mass of boron, the calculation is as follows:

$$\text{Atomic mass} = \left(\frac{19.91}{100}\right)(10.0129 \text{ amu}) + \left(\frac{80.09}{100}\right)(11.0093 \text{ amu}) = 10.8109 \text{ amu}$$

When working with molecules, chemists need to know the average mass of the molecules in their samples. Chemists calculate the average mass of the molecules in their samples by adding the atomic masses of the atoms in their molecules. The sum of the atomic masses of the atoms in a molecule is called the **molecular mass** or the molecular weight of the molecule. For example, the molecular mass of water, $H_2O$, is 18.015 amu (1.008 amu for H + 1.008 amu for H + 15.999 amu for O).

## PRACTICE 24: Atomic Mass and Molecular Mass

Decide if each statement that follows is true (**T**) or false (**F**). Write the correct letter on each line.

__T__ **1.** The abbreviation for the atomic mass unit is amu.

__T__ **2.** One atomic mass unit is $\frac{1}{12}$ the mass of a carbon-12 atom.

_____ **3.** The different isotopes of an element have exactly the same masses.

_____ **4.** The mass of protium is twice the mass of deuterium.

_____ **5.** A representative sample of the element boron contains 19.91% boron-10 and 80.09% boron-11.

_____ **6.** The atomic mass of an element is different from the atomic weight of the same element.

_____ **7.** The average mass of the naturally occurring isotopes in a sample of an element is called the atomic mass or the atomic weight of the element.

_____ **8.** If the atomic mass of carbon is 12.011 amu and the atomic mass of hydrogen is 1.008 amu, then the molecular mass of $CH_4$ is 16.043 amu.

### THINK ABOUT IT

Recently, the atomic mass unit has been renamed the dalton. The abbreviation for a dalton is Da. Therefore, 1 amu = 1 Da. Also, the mass of a carbon-12 atom is 12 daltons, or 12 Da. Who do you think the dalton was named for? Why? Can you think of other people for whom the unit could be named? Write your answers below.

________________________________________

________________________________________

________________________________________

________________________________________

________________________________________

________________________________________

________________________________________

________________________________________

# LESSON 6: The Periodic Table

GOAL: To learn what the periodic table of the elements is and how it organizes chemical information

## WORDS TO KNOW

**actinides**

**alkali metals**

**alkaline earth metals**

**ductile**

**families**

**graphite**

**groups**

**halogens**

**heteronuclear diatomic molecule**

**homonuclear diatomic molecule**

**inner transition elements**

**lanthanides**

**luster**

**malleable**

**metalloids**

**metals**

**noble gases**

**nonmetals**

**periodic table**

**periods**

**transition metals**

## What Is the Periodic Table?

By 1870, 65 different elements were known. Nineteenth-century chemists studied the wide range of physical and chemical properties of these elements and the reactions they underwent. Then they began to notice that some elements behaved similarly to others. Many scientists attempted to organize the known elements according to one of these physical or chemical properties.

In 1871, the Russian chemist Dmitri Mendeleev published a table that organized the known elements according to their atomic masses. He also arranged the elements in the table so that elements with similar chemical properties would lie in the same column of the table. When he did this, gaps were left in the table. Mendeleev correctly predicted that the gaps would be filled in with elements that would be discovered later.

Mendeleev's table has been revised somewhat in the last 125 years, and many new elements have been added to it, but it remains a remarkable achievement in chemistry. The modern version of his table is called the periodic table of the elements, or just the **periodic table.**

The modern periodic table of the elements is organized according to atomic number (number of protons) instead of atomic mass (number of protons and neutrons). The first element in the table is hydrogen (Z = 1), the second element is helium (Z = 2), and so forth. (See Appendix A for a larger version of the table.)

### Periodic Table of the Elements

Key: 6 ← Atomic Number; C ← Element's Symbol; Carbon ← Name; 12.011 ← Atomic Weight

Transition Metals (groups 3–12); Nonmetals (groups 13–17); Metals

| | 1<br>IA | 2<br>IIA | 3<br>IIIB | 4<br>IVB | 5<br>VB | 6<br>VIB | 7<br>VIIB | 8 | 9<br>VIIIB | 10 | 11<br>IB | 12<br>IIB | 13<br>IIIA | 14<br>IVA | 15<br>VA | 16<br>VIA | 17<br>VIIA | 18<br>VIIIA |
|---|---|---|---|---|---|---|---|---|---|---|---|---|---|---|---|---|---|---|
| 1 | 1<br>**H**<br>Hydrogen<br>1.0079 | | | | | | | | | | | | | | | | | 2<br>**He**<br>Helium<br>4.003 |
| 2 | 3<br>**Li**<br>Lithium<br>6.941 | 4<br>**Be**<br>Beryllium<br>9.01218 | | | | | | | | | | | 5<br>**B**<br>Boron<br>10.811 | 6<br>**C**<br>Carbon<br>12.011 | 7<br>**N**<br>Nitrogen<br>14.0067 | 8<br>**O**<br>Oxygen<br>15.9994 | 9<br>**F**<br>Fluorine<br>18.998 | 10<br>**Ne**<br>Neon<br>20.180 |
| 3 | 11<br>**Na**<br>Sodium<br>22.98977 | 12<br>**Mg**<br>Magnesium<br>24.305 | | | | | | | | | | | 13<br>**Al**<br>Aluminum<br>26.982 | 14<br>**Si**<br>Silicon<br>28.086 | 15<br>**P**<br>Phosphorus<br>30.974 | 16<br>**S**<br>Sulfur<br>32.066 | 17<br>**Cl**<br>Chlorine<br>35.453 | 18<br>**Ar**<br>Argon<br>39.948 |
| 4 | 19<br>**K**<br>Potassium<br>39.0983 | 20<br>**Ca**<br>Calcium<br>40.078 | 21<br>**Sc**<br>Scandium<br>44.956 | 22<br>**Ti**<br>Titanium<br>47.88 | 23<br>**V**<br>Vanadium<br>50.942 | 24<br>**Cr**<br>Chromium<br>51.996 | 25<br>**Mn**<br>Manganese<br>54.938 | 26<br>**Fe**<br>Iron<br>55.847 | 27<br>**Co**<br>Cobalt<br>58.933 | 28<br>**Ni**<br>Nickel<br>58.69 | 29<br>**Cu**<br>Copper<br>63.546 | 30<br>**Zn**<br>Zinc<br>65.39 | 31<br>**Ga**<br>Gallium<br>69.723 | 32<br>**Ge**<br>Germanium<br>72.61 | 33<br>**As**<br>Arsenic<br>74.922 | 34<br>**Se**<br>Selenium<br>78.96 | 35<br>**Br**<br>Bromine<br>79.904 | 36<br>**Kr**<br>Krypton<br>83.80 |
| 5 | 37<br>**Rb**<br>Rubidium<br>85.4678 | 38<br>**Sr**<br>Strontium<br>87.62 | 39<br>**Y**<br>Yttrium<br>88.906 | 40<br>**Zr**<br>Zirconium<br>91.224 | 41<br>**Nb**<br>Niobium<br>92.906 | 42<br>**Mo**<br>Molybdenum<br>95.94 | 43<br>**Tc**<br>Technetium<br>(98) | 44<br>**Ru**<br>Ruthenium<br>101.07 | 45<br>**Rh**<br>Rhodium<br>102.906 | 46<br>**Pd**<br>Palladium<br>106.42 | 47<br>**Ag**<br>Silver<br>107.868 | 48<br>**Cd**<br>Cadmium<br>112.411 | 49<br>**In**<br>Indium<br>114.82 | 50<br>**Sn**<br>Tin<br>118.71 | 51<br>**Sb**<br>Antimony<br>121.75 | 52<br>**Te**<br>Tellurium<br>127.60 | 53<br>**I**<br>Iodine<br>126.906 | 54<br>**Xe**<br>Xenon<br>131.29 |
| 6 | 55<br>**Cs**<br>Cesium<br>132.905 | 56<br>**Ba**<br>Barium<br>137.327 | 71<br>**Lu**<br>Lutetium<br>174.967 | 72<br>**Hf**<br>Hafnium<br>178.49 | 73<br>**Ta**<br>Tantalum<br>180.948 | 74<br>**W**<br>Tungsten (Wolfram)<br>183.85 | 75<br>**Re**<br>Rhenium<br>186.207 | 76<br>**Os**<br>Osmium<br>190.2 | 77<br>**Ir**<br>Iridium<br>192.22 | 78<br>**Pt**<br>Platinum<br>195.08 | 79<br>**Au**<br>Gold<br>196.967 | 80<br>**Hg**<br>Mercury<br>200.59 | 81<br>**Tl**<br>Thallium<br>204.383 | 82<br>**Pb**<br>Lead<br>207.2 | 83<br>**Bi**<br>Bismuth<br>208.980 | 84<br>**Po**<br>Polonium<br>(209) | 85<br>**At**<br>Astatine<br>(210) | 86<br>**Rn**<br>Radon<br>(220) |
| 7 | 87<br>**Fr**<br>Francium<br>(223) | 88<br>**Ra**<br>Radium<br>226.025 | 103<br>**Lr**<br>Lawrencium<br>(260) | 104<br>**Rf**<br>Rutherfordium<br>(261) | 105<br>**Db**<br>Dubnium<br>(262) | 106<br>**Sg**<br>Seaborgium<br>(263) | 107<br>**Bh**<br>Bohrium<br>(264) | 108<br>**Hs**<br>Hassium<br>(265) | 109<br>**Mt**<br>Meitnerium<br>(266) | | | | | | | | | |

| | | | | | | | | | | | | | | |
|---|---|---|---|---|---|---|---|---|---|---|---|---|---|---|
| * Lanthanide series: | 57<br>***La**<br>Lanthanum<br>138.906 | 58<br>**Ce**<br>Cerium<br>140.115 | 59<br>**Pr**<br>Praseodymium<br>140.908 | 60<br>**Nd**<br>Neodymium<br>144.24 | 61<br>**Pm**<br>Promethium<br>(145) | 62<br>**Sm**<br>Samarium<br>150.36 | 63<br>**Eu**<br>Europium<br>151.965 | 64<br>**Gd**<br>Gadolinium<br>157.25 | 65<br>**Tb**<br>Terbium<br>158.925 | 66<br>**Dy**<br>Dysprosium<br>162.50 | 67<br>**Ho**<br>Holmium<br>164.93 | 68<br>**Er**<br>Erbium<br>167.26 | 69<br>**Tm**<br>Thulium<br>168.934 | 70<br>**Yb**<br>Ytterbium<br>173.04 |
| † Actinide series: | 89<br>**†Ac**<br>Actinium<br>227.028 | 90<br>**Th**<br>Thorium<br>232.038 | 91<br>**Pa**<br>Protactinium<br>231.036 | 92<br>**U**<br>Uranium<br>238.029 | 93<br>**Np**<br>Neptunium<br>237.048 | 94<br>**Pu**<br>Plutonium<br>(244) | 95<br>**Am**<br>Americium<br>(243) | 96<br>**Cm**<br>Curium<br>(247) | 97<br>**Bk**<br>Berkelium<br>(247) | 98<br>**Cf**<br>Californium<br>(251) | 99<br>**Es**<br>Einsteinium<br>(252) | 100<br>**Fm**<br>Fermium<br>(257) | 101<br>**Md**<br>Mendelevium<br>(258) | 102<br>**No**<br>Nobelium<br>(259) |

Note that in the drawing of the periodic table each element is given its own box. Each box contains the atomic number, symbol, name, and atomic mass of the element. For example, gold has atomic number 79, symbol Au, and atomic mass 196.967 amu. Aluminum, on the other hand, has atomic number 13, symbol Al, and atomic mass 26.982 amu. Not every version of the periodic table contains the same amount of information as this one. Some contain more, and some contain less. The basic shape of the periodic table, however, does not change.

The horizontal rows of the periodic table are called **periods.** The numbers down the left side of the periodic table indicate the period number. For example, the first period consists of hydrogen (H) and helium (He). The second period consists of Li, Be, B, C, N, O, F, and Ne. The third period consists of Na, Mg, Al, Si, P, S, Cl, and Ar, and so on.

The vertical columns of the periodic table are called **groups**. The numbers across the top of the periodic table indicate the group number. For example, Group 1 consists of H, Li, Na, K, Rb, Cs, and Fr. Group 2 consists of Be, Mg, Ca, Sr, Ba, and Ra. Group 3 consists of Sc, Y, Lu, and Lr, and so on. Groups of elements are sometimes called **families** because groups of elements tend to have similar properties.

## PRACTICE 25: What Is the Periodic Table?

Decide if each statement that follows is true (**T**) or false (**F**). Write the correct letter on each line.

__T__ **1.** The modern periodic table of the elements is based on the one proposed by Dmitri Mendeleev in 1871.

__T__ **2.** Mendeleev was able to use his table of elements to predict the existence of elements that would be discovered later.

__F__ **3.** The horizontal rows of the periodic table are called groups.

__T__ **4.** The vertical columns of the periodic table are called groups.

__T__ **5.** The horizontal rows of the periodic table are called periods.

__F__ **6.** On the periodic table, Group 14 consists of the elements Cr, Mo, W, and Sg.

__T__ **7.** On the periodic table, Group 14 consists of the elements C, Si, Ge, Sn, and Pb.

__T__ **8.** On the periodic table, Group 18 consists of the elements He, Ne, Ar, Kr, Xe, and Rn.

## Categories of the Elements

There are several ways to categorize the elements in the periodic table. One way is to divide them into main group elements, transition metals, and lanthanides and actinides. The elements in Groups 1, 2, 13, 14, 15, 16, 17, and 18 are called the main group elements. The elements in Groups 3–12 are called the **transition metals,** or the transition elements. The elements in the two rows below the periodic table are called the **lanthanides** and **actinides.** Elements 57–70 are the lanthanides, and elements 89–102 are the actinides. The lanthanides and actinides are sometimes called the **inner transition elements.**

The lanthanides and actinides actually fit in periods 6 and 7 between Ba and Lu (elements 56 and 71) and between Ra and Lr (elements 88 and 103). This arrangement would make periods 6 and 7 quite long, however. It would also make the periodic table awkward to use. Because of this, the lanthanide and actinide elements are usually separated from the rest of the periodic table, as shown in the table on page 65.

Another way to categorize the elements in the periodic table is to divide them into **metals, nonmetals,** and **metalloids.** The drawing of the periodic table on page 68 shows that most of the elements are metals. The metals are located on the left side of the periodic table and include the lanthanides and actinides. The nonmetals are located in the upper right corner of the periodic table. Hydrogen is a nonmetal, too. The metalloids are the six elements B (boron), Si (silicon), Ge (germanium), As (arsenic), Sb (antimony), and Te (tellurium). The metalloids hug the thick staircase line in the periodic table and separate the metals from the nonmetals. Metalloids are sometimes called semimetals. On page 69, you will learn about the properties of metals, nonmetals, and metalloids in more detail.

A third way to categorize some of the elements in the periodic table is by the name of their group. On page 66, you learned that the vertical columns in the periodic table are called groups. The Group 1 elements (except for hydrogen) are also called the **alkali metals.** Thus, Li, Na, K, Rb, Cs, and Fr are alkali metals. The Group 2 elements are also called the **alkaline earth metals.** Thus, Be, Mg, Ca, Sr, Ba, and Ra are alkaline earth metals.

The Group 17 elements are also called the **halogens.** Thus, F, Cl, Br, I, and At are halogens. Finally, the Group 18 elements are also called the **noble gases.** Thus, He, Ne, Ar, Kr, Xe, and Rn are noble gases. These are also sometimes called inert gases or rare gases.

| | | | | | | | | | | | | | | | | | |
|---|---|---|---|---|---|---|---|---|---|---|---|---|---|---|---|---|---|
| 1 **H** | | | | | | | | | | | | | | | | | 2 **He** |
| 3 **Li** | 4 **Be** | | | | | | | | | | | 5 **B** | 6 **C** | 7 **N** | 8 **O** | 9 **F** | 10 **Ne** |
| 11 **Na** | 12 **Mg** | | | | | | | | | | | 13 **Al** | 14 **Si** | 15 **P** | 16 **S** | 17 **Cl** | 18 **Ar** |
| 19 **K** | 20 **Ca** | 21 **Sc** | 22 **Ti** | 23 **V** | 24 **Cr** | 25 **Mn** | 26 **Fe** | 27 **Co** | 28 **Ni** | 29 **Cu** | 30 **Zn** | 31 **Ga** | 32 **Ge** | 33 **As** | 34 **Se** | 35 **Br** | 36 **Kr** |
| 37 **Rb** | 38 **Sr** | 39 **Y** | 40 **Zr** | 41 **Nb** | 42 **Mo** | 43 **Tc** | 44 **Ru** | 45 **Rh** | 46 **Pd** | 47 **Ag** | 48 **Cd** | 49 **In** | 50 **Sn** | 51 **Sb** | 52 **Te** | 53 **I** | 54 **Xe** |
| 55 **Cs** | 56 **Ba** | 71 **Lu** | 72 **Hf** | 73 **Ta** | 74 **W** | 75 **Re** | 76 **Os** | 77 **Ir** | 78 **Pt** | 79 **Au** | 80 **Hg** | 81 **Tl** | 82 **Pb** | 83 **Bi** | 84 **Po** | 85 **At** | 86 **Rn** |
| 87 **Fr** | 88 **Ra** | 103 **Lr** | 104 **Rf** | 105 **Db** | 106 **Sg** | 107 **Bh** | 108 **Hs** | 109 **Mt** | | | | | | | | | |

| | | | | | | | | | | | | | |
|---|---|---|---|---|---|---|---|---|---|---|---|---|---|
| 57 **La** | 58 **Ce** | 59 **Pr** | 60 **Nd** | 61 **Pm** | 62 **Sm** | 63 **Eu** | 64 **Gd** | 65 **Tb** | 66 **Dy** | 67 **Ho** | 68 **Er** | 69 **Tm** | 70 **Yb** |
| 89 **Ac** | 90 **Th** | 91 **Pa** | 92 **U** | 93 **Np** | 94 **Pu** | 95 **Am** | 96 **Cm** | 97 **Bk** | 98 **Cf** | 99 **Es** | 100 **Fm** | 101 **Md** | 102 **No** |

Nonmetal

Metalloid

Metal

## PRACTICE 26: Categories of the Elements

Decide if each statement that follows is true (**T**) or false (**F**). Write the correct letter on each line.

_____ **1.** The elements in Groups 1, 2, 13, 14, 15, 16, 17, and 18 are called the main group elements.

_____ **2.** The Group 1 elements (except for hydrogen) are also called the halogens.

_____ **3.** The Group 1 elements (except for hydrogen) are also called the alkali metals.

_____ **4.** Hydrogen can be classified as a metalloid.

_____ **5.** Most of the elements in the periodic table are metals.

_____ **6.** The metalloids are the six elements B (boron), Si (silicon), Ge (germanium), As (arsenic), Sb (antimony), and Te (tellurium).

____F 7. The noble gases are sometimes called the transition elements.

____T 8. The Group 18 elements are also called the noble gases.

## Metals, Nonmetals, and Metalloids

Metals have certain characteristic properties that distinguish them from nonmetals and metalloids.

- Metals are good conductors of heat and electricity.
- Metals have metallic **luster**, which means they have a shiny appearance and reflect light well.
- Metals are **malleable**, which means they can be hammered into thin sheets.
- Metals are **ductile**, which means they can be drawn into wires.

Aluminum (Al) is malleable enough to be used for soft drink cans and aluminum foil. Gold (Au) is so malleable that one gram of it can be pounded into a sheet that is one meter on a side. Copper (Cu) is ductile enough and such a good conductor of electricity that it is used for electrical wiring.

All metals, except for mercury (Hg), are solids at normal room temperature (77°F or 25°C). Mercury is a liquid at 25°C. Because it is a liquid and has such a silvery, shiny appearance, it is sometimes called quicksilver.

Nonmetals have certain characteristic properties, too.

- Nonmetals are poor conductors of heat and electricity.
- Nonmetals do not have a shiny appearance or reflect light well.
- Nonmetals are brittle in the solid form, which means they crack and break easily when placed under stress.

There are a few exceptions to these properties. For example, **graphite** is a pure form of carbon (C) that does conduct electricity.

Although all metals except mercury are solids at 25°C, nonmetals may be solids, liquids, or gases at that temperature. Sulfur (S), selenium (Se), phosphorus (P), and iodine (I) are nonmetals that are solids at 25°C. Bromine (Br) is a nonmetal that is a liquid at 25°C. Hydrogen (H), helium (He), fluorine (F), chlorine (Cl), oxygen (O), nitrogen (N), neon (Ne), argon (Ar), krypton (Kr), xenon (Xe), and radon (Rn) are nonmetals that are gases at 25°C.

**IN REAL LIFE**

Have you ever noticed at a cookout that if you burn the outside of the hamburgers, it takes forever for them to cook on the inside? The burned outer layer of the hamburger is essentially carbon (C). All organic material is based on carbon, which results after organic material is burned. Carbon is a nonmetal, so it is a poor conductor of heat. As a result, the layer of carbon slows the flow of heat to the middle of the hamburgers, and it takes a long time for them to finish cooking.

The six elements classified as metalloids have properties that are somewhere in between the properties of metals and the properties of nonmetals.

- Metalloids are poor conductors of heat.
- Metalloids are semiconductors of electricity, which means they conduct electricity better than nonmetals, but not as well as metals.
- Metalloids are dull-appearing and do not reflect light well.
- Metalloids are brittle solids at 25°C.

The most important modern use of metalloids is the manufacture of computer chips from highly purified silicon (Si).

## PRACTICE 27: Metals, Nonmetals, and Metalloids

Decide if each statement that follows is true (**T**) or false (**F**). Write the correct letter on each line.

__F__ **1.** Metals are poor conductors of heat and electricity.

__T__ **2.** Metals like aluminum and gold are malleable, which means they can be hammered into thin sheets.

__T__ **3.** Metalloids are semiconductors of electricity, which means they conduct electricity better than nonmetals, but not as well as metals.

__F__ **4.** Metalloids have a shiny appearance and reflect light well.

__T__ **5.** All metals, except for mercury (Hg), are solids at 25°C.

__T__ **6.** Nonmetals may be solids, liquids, or gases at 25°C.

__F__ **7.** Nonmetals are ductile and malleable, just like metals.

__T__ **8.** Nonmetals are brittle in solid form, which means they crack and break easily when placed under stress.

## Alkali Metals and Alkaline Earth Metals

On page 67, you learned that the alkali metals are the elements in Group 1 (Li, Na, K, Rb, Cs, and Fr, but not H). Like most metals, the alkali metals are shiny solids that conduct heat and electricity very well. They are very soft, too. In fact, they are so soft that they can be cut with an ordinary kitchen knife.

The alkali metals are very reactive, which means they readily combine with other elements. For example, they react violently with chlorine gas ($Cl_2$) to form compounds with the general formula MCl. In this general formula, M stands for any of the alkali metals (Li, Na, K, Rb, Cs, or Fr). Table salt is NaCl.

The alkali metals also react violently with water to form hydrogen gas ($H_2$) and compounds with the general formula MOH. In this general formula, M stands for any of the alkali metals, too. So much heat is given off in one of these reactions that the hydrogen gas ignites. As a result, it looks as if the water is burning.

On page 67, you also learned that the alkaline earth metals are the elements in Group 2 (Be, Mg, Ca, Sr, Ba, and Ra). Like the alkali metals, the alkaline earth metals are shiny solids that conduct heat and electricity well. The alkaline earth metals are harder than the alkali metals, though.

The alkaline earth metals are reactive, though not as reactive as the alkali metals. For example, the alkaline earth metals react with chlorine gas ($Cl_2$), but the reaction is not as violent as the reaction of an alkali metal with $Cl_2$. The general formula of the compound that is formed is $MCl_2$. In this general formula, M stands for any of the alkaline earth metals.

The alkaline earth metals also react with water to form hydrogen gas and compounds with the general formula $M(OH)_2$. In this general formula, M stands for any of the alkaline earth metals. The reaction to form $Mg(OH)_2$ illustrates how much less violent the reaction is for Mg than it is for any of the alkali metals. Sodium (Na) reacts with water at room temperature, but magnesium (Mg) will not react with water unless the water is boiling.

**IN REAL LIFE**

Alkali metals and alkaline earth metals are used for many everyday items. For example, you may have heard about the use of "lithium" to treat people with bipolar (manic-depressive) disorders. The "lithium" used to treat bipolar disorders contains the alkali metal lithium, but it is not pure lithium metal. Instead, it is a compound called lithium carbonate. The formula for lithium carbonate is $Li_2CO_3$. As a matter of fact, the soft drink 7-Up used to contain lithium carbonate. Magnesium metal (Mg) burns in air to produce an intensely bright white light. It is so bright that it is used for the disposable flashbulbs that are attached to cameras. Finally, limestone, marble, chalk, and coral are all calcium carbonate. The formula for calcium carbonate is $CaCO_3$.

## ■ PRACTICE 28: Alkali Metals and Alkaline Earth Metals

Decide if each statement that follows is true (**T**) or false (**F**). Write the correct letter on each line.

___T___ **1.** The alkali metals are so soft that they can be cut with an ordinary kitchen knife.

___F___ **2.** The alkaline earth metals are more reactive than the alkali metals.

___F___ **3.** The formula for calcium carbonate is $Li_2CO_3$.

___T___ **4.** Sodium (Na) reacts with water at room temperature, but magnesium (Mg) will not react with water unless the water is boiling.

___T___ **5.** The alkali metals are the elements in Group 1 (Li, Na, K, Rb, Cs, and Fr, but not H).

___F___ **6.** Table salt is $MgCl_2$.

___T___ **7.** Like the alkali metals, the alkaline earth metals are shiny solids that conduct heat and electricity well.

___T___ **8.** The alkaline earth metals are the elements in Group 2 (Be, Mg, Ca, Sr, Ba, and Ra).

## The Halogens and the Noble Gases

On page 67, you learned that the halogens are the elements in Group 17 (F, Cl, Br, I, and At). The information provided here about the halogens really applies only to fluorine (F), chlorine (Cl), bromine (Br), and iodine (I). Astatine (At) is so rare that its chemical properties are not well known.

The halogens are nonmetals and exist as diatomic molecules: $F_2$, $Cl_2$, $Br_2$, and $I_2$. A diatomic molecule is one that contains two atoms. If both atoms in a molecule are the same element, then it is a **homonuclear diatomic molecule.** $F_2$, $Cl_2$, $Br_2$, and $I_2$ are homonuclear diatomic molecules. If both atoms in a molecule are different elements, then it is a **heteronuclear diatomic molecule**. CO (carbon monoxide) is a heteronuclear diatomic molecule because carbon (C) and oxygen (O) are different elements. NO (nitrogen oxide) is a heteronuclear diatomic molecule, too.

$F_2$, $Cl_2$, $Br_2$, and $I_2$ have different physical states at 25°C. For example, fluorine ($F_2$) is a pale yellow gas, chlorine ($Cl_2$) is a pale green gas, bromine ($Br_2$) is a reddish-brown liquid that easily turns into an orange-red gas, and iodine ($I_2$) is a bluish-black solid that gives off purple fumes when heated.

**THINK ABOUT IT**

Recall from Unit 1 that the process of going from a solid to a liquid is called melting, and the process of going from a liquid to a solid is called freezing. Also, the process of going from a liquid to a gas is called evaporation, and the process of going from a gas to a liquid is called condensation. Finally, the process of going from a solid directly to a gas is called sublimation, and the process of going from a gas directly to a solid is called deposition. Which of these processes describes what happens to iodine ($I_2$) when it is heated? Write your answer on a separate sheet of paper.

$F_2$, $Cl_2$, $Br_2$, and $I_2$ are quite reactive. They react with hydrogen gas ($H_2$) to form compounds that have the general formula HX. In this general formula, X stands for F, Cl, Br, or I. HF is used to etch glass in the manufacture of lightbulbs and television tubes. HCl is one of the components of the juices in the human stomach that digests food.

The noble gases are the elements in Group 18 (He, Ne, Ar, Kr, Xe, and Rn), as you learned on page 67. All are colorless gases at 25°C, and all are remarkably unreactive. This means that they are very stable and do not react with other elements or compounds in almost all cases. A few compounds have been prepared with xenon (Xe) and krypton (Kr), but none has been prepared with helium (He), neon (Ne), argon (Ar), or radon (Rn). The "neon" in neon signs is gaseous Ne that has been excited by electricity so that it glows.

**IN REAL LIFE**

Helium-filled balloons are a common sight at parties and fairs. Helium causes balloons to float because it is less dense (lighter) than air. Helium is even less dense when it is heated. Helium was used in the hot-air balloon that took Steve Fossett on his solo, around-the-world voyage in 2002. An ordinary hot-air balloon simply heats the regular air inside of it. Fossett's balloon contained special, closed-off sections filled with helium. When the helium was heated, it expanded, becoming even less dense. This expansion created the "lift" that took the balloon around the world high up in the atmosphere.

## PRACTICE 29: The Halogens and the Noble Gases

Decide if each statement that follows is true (**T**) or false (**F**). Write the correct letter on each line.

_____ **1.** A diatomic molecule is one that contains two atoms.

_____ **2.** The noble gases are unreactive.

_____ **3.** $F_2$, $Cl_2$, $Br_2$, and $I_2$ are homonuclear diatomic molecules.

_____ **4.** $F_2$, $Cl_2$, $Br_2$, and $I_2$ are all solids at 25°C.

_____ **5.** The noble gases are all liquids at 25°C.

_____ **6.** The "neon" in neon signs is really a mixture of helium (He) and astatine (At).

_____ **7.** HCl is one of the components of the juices in the human stomach that is responsible for digesting food.

_____ **8.** HF is used to etch glass in the manufacture of lightbulbs and television tubes.

# LESSON 7: Atoms, Molecules, Ions, and the Mole

GOAL: To learn about ions, different chemical formulas, and how chemists count using the mole

## WORDS TO KNOW

| | | |
|---|---|---|
| **anions** | **empirical formula** | **molecular formula** |
| **Avogadro's number** | **ionic compound** | **single bonds** |
| **bonds** | **ions** | **structural formula** |
| **cations** | **molar mass** | **triple bond** |
| **double bond** | **mole** | |

## Anions and Cations

Atoms are electrically neutral. This means that atoms have the same number of electrons as they do protons in their nucleus. Thus, the positive charge of the protons in the nucleus is exactly balanced by the negative charge of the electrons that surround the nucleus. For example, a hydrogen atom has one electron and one proton, an oxygen atom has eight electrons and eight protons, and a chlorine atom has 17 electrons and 17 protons.

Molecules are electrically neutral, too. This means that the total number of electrons in the molecule equals the number of protons in all of the atoms of the molecule. For example, a water molecule ($H_2O$) has 10 electrons to balance its 10 protons. The oxygen atom provides eight of the protons, and each of the two hydrogen atoms provides one proton. A carbon monoxide molecule (CO) contains 14 electrons to balance its 14 protons (six from carbon and eight from oxygen).

**Ions** are charged particles that form when an atom or a molecule gains or loses one or more electrons. Ions are not electrically neutral. Ions that have a net negative charge are called **anions.** Anions have more electrons than they have protons. Chloride ($Cl^-$), hydroxide ($OH^-$), and sulfate ($SO_4^{2-}$) are examples of anions.

Note that a net negative charge of 1 on an anion is indicated by a superscript negative sign. Chloride and hydroxide both have net negative charges of 1. If the anion has a net negative charge greater than 1, a superscript number precedes the negative sign. Sulfate has a net negative charge of 2. The subscript 4 in the formula for the sulfate anion indicates that it contains four oxygen atoms, and has nothing to do with the negative charge on the sulfate anion.

Ions that have a net positive charge are called **cations.** Cations have more protons than they have electrons. Examples of cations include sodium ($Na^+$), magnesium ($Mg^{2+}$), and ammonium ($NH_4^+$). Note that a net positive charge of 1 is indicated by a superscript plus sign. Sodium and ammonium have net positive charges of 1. The subscript 4 in the formula for the ammonium cation indicates that it contains four hydrogen atoms, and has nothing to do with the positive charge on the ammonium cation. If the cation has a net positive charge greater than 1, a superscript number precedes the plus sign. Magnesium has a net positive charge of 2.

## PRACTICE 30: Anions and Cations

Decide if each statement that follows is true (**T**) or false (**F**). Write the correct letter on each line.

F **1.** Cations and anions are both ions with a net negative charge.

T **2.** Ions are charged particles that form when an atom or a molecule gains or loses one or more electrons.

T **3.** Atoms and molecules are electrically neutral.

T **4.** Ions that have a net positive charge are called cations.

F **5.** Chloride ($Cl^-$) is an example of a cation.

T **6.** The magnesium cation ($Mg^{2+}$) has a net positive charge of 2.

F **7.** Cations have more electrons than they have protons.

T **8.** Anions have more electrons than they have protons.

## Ionic Compounds

Large groups of cations or anions do not exist in nature. In fact, electrical charges that are alike repel each other. That is, a positive charge repels another positive charge, and a negative charge repels another negative charge. As a result, large groups of cations or anions are highly unstable.

On the other hand, opposite electrical charges attract each other. That is, a positive charge attracts a negative charge, and a negative charge attracts a positive charge. As a result, a large group of cations and anions can be highly stable. It will be stable if the group of cations and anions is electrically neutral overall. In order to be electrically neutral, the total positive charge of the cations must be exactly balanced by the total negative charge of the anions.

An **ionic compound** forms when cations and anions combine to make an electrically neutral compound. Sodium chloride, NaCl, is a good example of an ionic compound. It is a compound because it is made up of two different elements. It is ionic because it contains sodium cations, $Na^+$, and chloride anions, $Cl^-$. There is one $Na^+$ for each $Cl^-$, so sodium chloride is electrically neutral overall.

Other examples of ionic compounds include magnesium chloride, $MgCl_2$, calcium sulfate, $CaSO_4$, and potassium sulfide, $K_2S$. In magnesium chloride, the positive charge on each magnesium cation, $Mg^{2+}$, is balanced by the negative charge on two chloride anions, $Cl^-$. In calcium sulfate, the positive charge on each calcium cation, $Ca^{2+}$, is balanced by the negative charge on a sulfate anion, $SO_4^{2-}$. In potassium sulfide, the positive charge on two potassium cations, $K^+$, is balanced by the negative charge on one sulfide anion, $S^{2-}$.

The elements in Group 1 of the periodic table (the alkali metals) form stable ionic compounds in which they appear as cations with +1 charges. Examples include NaCl, LiCl, KBr, RbBr, and CsI. The cations in these ionic compounds are $Na^+$, $Li^+$, $K^+$, $Rb^+$, and $Cs^+$, respectively. The anions are $Cl^-$, $Br^-$, and $I^-$. These ionic compounds also point out that the elements in Group 17 of the periodic table (the halogens) form stable ionic compounds in which they appear as anions with –1 charges. Finally, the elements in Group 2 of the periodic table (the alkaline earth metals) form stable ionic compounds in which they appear as cations with +2 charges. Examples include $MgCl_2$, $CaSO_4$, $BeCl_2$, $SrI_2$, and $BaSO_4$. The cations in these ionic compounds are $Mg^{2+}$, $Ca^{2+}$, $Be^{2+}$, $Sr^{2+}$, and $Ba^{2+}$, respectively.

Ionic compounds such as NaCl, KBr, and $BaSO_4$ are also known as salts.

**IN REAL LIFE**

Barium sulfate, $BaSO_4$, is opaque to X-rays. That means that $BaSO_4$ will show up on an X-ray film in much the same way that your bones will. As a result, doctors use $BaSO_4$ to get an X-ray picture of a patient's intestines. The patient is given a "barium cocktail" to swallow and then X-rays of the patient's intestines are taken.

## PRACTICE 31: Ionic Compounds

Decide if each statement that follows is true (**T**) or false (**F**). Write the correct letter on each line.

T **1.** Ionic compounds such as NaCl, KBr, and $BaSO_4$ are also known as salts.

F **2.** Large groups of cations or anions exist in nature.

T **3.** A positive charge repels another positive charge and a negative charge repels another negative charge.

T **4.** Opposite electrical charges attract each other, so a large group of cations and anions can be highly stable.

F **5.** NaCl, LiCl, KBr, and CsI are NOT ionic compounds.

F **6.** NaCl, KBr, and $BaSO_4$ are ionic compounds, but they are NOT salts.

F **7.** The elements in Group 1 of the periodic table (the alkali metals) form stable ionic compounds in which they appear as anions with –2 charges.

T **8.** An ionic compound forms when cations and anions combine to make an electrically neutral compound.

## Molecular Formulas and Empirical Formulas

In Unit 1, page 16, you learned that a chemical formula uses numbers and symbols for the elements. These indicate which elements are present in a substance and how many of each element are present in the substance. The chemical formula for water, for example, is $H_2O$ because every water molecule consists of two atoms of hydrogen and one atom of oxygen chemically bound together.

Actually, there are three different kinds of chemical formulas: molecular formulas, empirical formulas, and structural formulas (discussed on page 81). $H_2O$ is an example of a molecular formula. A **molecular formula** shows the actual number of atoms of each element in a compound.

An **empirical formula**, on the other hand, shows the relative number of atoms of each element in a compound. For example, the molecular formula for hydrogen peroxide is $H_2O_2$ because each molecule of hydrogen peroxide consists of two hydrogen atoms chemically bound to two oxygen atoms. The empirical formula for hydrogen peroxide is HO, however, because the relative number of atoms of hydrogen and oxygen is one each. That is, for every hydrogen atom, there is an oxygen atom.

If there were compounds whose molecular formulas were $H_3O_3$, $H_4O_4$, $H_5O_5$, and so forth, they would all have the empirical formula HO because the relative number of hydrogen atoms and oxygen atoms is one each. Because two compounds with very different molecular formulas can have the same empirical formulas, you will use molecular formulas whenever possible.

For many compounds, the molecular formula is the empirical formula. In fact, $H_2O$ is both the molecular formula and the empirical formula for water. The molecular formula for methane, $CH_4$, is also the empirical formula for methane. The molecular formula for ammonia, $NH_3$, is also the empirical formula.

### ■ PRACTICE 32: Molecular Formulas and Empirical Formulas

Decide if each statement on the following page is true (**T**) or false (**F**). Write the correct letter on each line.

_____ **1.** Empirical formulas are never the same as molecular formulas.

_____ **2.** A molecular formula shows the actual number of atoms of each element in a compound.

_____ **3.** If a molecule of caffeine contains 8 carbon atoms, 10 hydrogen atoms, 4 nitrogen atoms, and 2 oxygen atoms, then the molecular formula for caffeine is $C_8H_{10}N_4O_2$.

_____ **4.** If the molecular formula for carbon dioxide is $CO_2$, then the empirical formula for carbon dioxide is CO.

_____ **5.** The empirical formula for hydrogen peroxide is HO because the relative number of atoms of hydrogen and oxygen is one each.

_____ **6.** If the molecular formula for acetylene is $C_2H_2$, then the empirical formula for acetylene is CH.

_____ **7.** If the molecular formula for hydrazine is $N_2H_4$, then the empirical formula for hydrazine is $NH_2$.

_____ **8.** If the molecular formula for ethylene is $C_2H_4$, then the empirical formula for ethylene is $C_2H_4$, also.

## Structural Formulas and Chemical Bonds

A **structural formula** shows the number and kind of atoms present in the compound as well as the way the atoms are connected to one another. For example, the structural formula of hydrogen peroxide is H–O–O–H. This structural formula shows that hydrogen peroxide consists of two hydrogen atoms chemically bound to two oxygen atoms. The oxygen atoms are chemically bound to each other, too. The hydrogen atoms are not chemically bound to each other.

In Unit 1, on page 15, you learned that a molecule is a combination of two or more atoms that are chemically bound together in a specific shape. The atoms in a molecule are bound together in a specific shape because they are held together by attractive forces called **bonds.** Bonds occur when an attraction develops between the positively charged nucleus of one atom and the negatively charged electron cloud of another atom. For now, you should think of a bond as a pair of electrons shared between two atoms.

A structural formula, therefore, shows the number and kind of atoms present as well as the bonds between them. The bonds are represented by lines. Each line represents one bond or one pair of shared electrons. Thus, the structural formula for hydrogen peroxide shows bonds between the hydrogen atoms and the oxygen atoms, as well as bonds between the oxygen atoms.

The bonds in hydrogen peroxide are called **single bonds** because each represents one pair of shared electrons. Some atoms can also share two pairs of electrons. When two atoms share four electrons (two pairs), the bond is called a **double bond.** A double bond is represented by two lines in a structural formula. Finally, some atoms can share three pairs of electrons. When two atoms share six electrons (three pairs), the bond is called a **triple bond.** A triple bond is represented by three lines in a structural formula.

The table on the right shows molecular, empirical, and structural formulas for water, hydrogen peroxide, ethane, ethylene (used to ripen fruit), acetylene (used in welding), and dimethyl ether. Notice the double bond in the structural formula of ethylene and the triple bond in the structural formula of acetylene.

| Name of Compound | Molecular Formula | Empirical Formula | Structural Formula |
|---|---|---|---|
| Water | $H_2O$ | $H_2O$ | $H\diagup\overset{O}{}\diagdown H$ |
| Hydrogen peroxide | $H_2O_2$ | $HO$ | $H-O-O-H$ |
| Ethane | $C_2H_6$ | $CH_3$ | $H-\overset{H}{\underset{H}{C}}-\overset{H}{\underset{H}{C}}-H$ |
| Ethylene | $C_2H_4$ | $CH_2$ | $\overset{H}{\underset{H}{}}\!>C=C<\!\overset{H}{\underset{H}{}}$ |
| Acetylene | $C_2H_2$ | $CH$ | $H-C\equiv C-H$ |
| Dimethyl ether | $C_2H_6O$ | $C_2H_6O$ | $H-\overset{H}{\underset{H}{C}}-O-\overset{H}{\underset{H}{C}}-H$ |

## PRACTICE 33: Structural Formulas and Chemical Bonds

Decide if each statement that follows is true (**T**) or false (**F**). Write the correct letter on each line.

F **1.** A structural formula shows the relative number of atoms of each element in a compound.

T **2.** The atoms in a molecule are bound together in a specific shape because they are held together by attractive forces called bonds.

T **3.** A structural formula shows the number and kind of atoms present as well as the bonds between them.

F **4.** When two atoms share six electrons (three pairs), the bond is called a single bond.

T **5.** When two atoms share four electrons (two pairs), the bond is called a double bond.

T **6.** In a structural formula, each line represents one bond, or one pair, of shared electrons.

T **7.** A triple bond is represented by three lines in a structural formula.

F **8.** The structural formula for hydrogen peroxide is H–H–O–O.

## The Mole and Avogadro's Number

Remember from the discussion of atomic mass and molecular mass in Lesson 5, on page 61, that chemists rarely work with individual atoms or molecules. Instead, they work with small quantities of substances (usually less than a gram) that contain huge numbers of atoms, molecules, or ions. For example, a speck of dust contains approximately $1 \times 10^{18}$ atoms.

Chemists want to know how many atoms, molecules, or ions they are working with, but they do not want to have to work with such huge numbers. So, chemists use a unit called the **mole** to make it easier to count atoms, molecules, or ions. One mole is defined as the number of atoms in exactly 12 grams of pure carbon-12 (the isotope of carbon that has six protons and six neutrons). The abbreviation for a mole is mol.

The number of atoms in exactly 12 grams of pure carbon-12 is $6.022137 \times 10^{23}$ atoms. Thus, chemists say that one mole of carbon-12 contains $6.022137 \times 10^{23}$ atoms, or there are $6.022137 \times 10^{23}$ atoms per mole of carbon-12. This number is known as **Avogadro's number.** Avogadro's number is named after Amedeo Avogadro, a nineteenth-century Italian physicist. The symbol for Avogadro's number is $N_A$.

The mole does not just apply to the carbon-12 isotope. In fact, a mole of anything contains $6.022137 \times 10^{23}$ items. For example, a mole of water molecules contains $6.022137 \times 10^{23}$ water molecules. A mole of sodium chloride contains $6.022137 \times 10^{23}$ NaCl units. A mole of electrons is $6.022137 \times 10^{23}$ electrons.

## PRACTICE 34: The Mole and Avogadro's Number

Decide if each statement that follows is true (**T**) or false (**F**). Write the correct letter on each line.

T **1.** One mole is defined as the number of atoms in exactly 12 grams of pure carbon-12.

T **2.** The abbreviation of the mole is mol.

T **3.** A mole of anything contains $6.022137 \times 10^{23}$ items.

T **4.** Avogadro's number is named after Amedeo Avogadro, a nineteenth-century Italian physicist.

F **5.** The symbol for Avogadro's number is mol.

F **6.** A mole of water molecules contains six or seven water molecules.

F **7.** The mole applies only to the carbon-12 isotope. The number of atoms in a mole of any other isotope is different.

T **8.** If one mole of carbon monoxide has a mass of 28.01 grams, then 28.01 grams of carbon monoxide contain $6.022137 \times 10^{23}$ molecules of carbon monoxide.

TIP

One mole of marbles would cover the earth with a layer 3 miles thick, or the United States with a layer 70 miles thick. The sheer size of Avogadro's number may make it seem different from anything you have ever faced before. However, to help you understand Avogadro's number, think about other ways to measure quantities every day. For example, eggs are sold by the dozen, not individually. Paper is packaged by the ream of 500 sheets, not individually. You measure your age in years, but you measure cooking times in hours or minutes. A dozen, a ream, and a year are convenient ways to measure eggs, paper, and age. Each unit is well suited for what it measures. The same is true of the mole. It conveniently measures huge quantities of atoms, molecules, or ions. For example, a cup of water contains slightly less than five moles of water molecules.

## Molar Mass

In the discussion of atomic mass and molecular mass in Lesson 5, you learned that individual isotopes of an element have slightly different masses because of the different number of neutrons the isotopes contain. As a result, the atomic mass of an element is the weighted average of the masses of the naturally occurring isotopes of that element.

For example, a naturally occurring sample of carbon contains 98.89% carbon-12 (atomic mass = 12.0000 amu) and 1.11% carbon-13 (atomic mass = 13.00335 amu). Therefore, the atomic mass of naturally occurring carbon is 12.0111 amu. For the purposes of measuring, all atoms of carbon are treated as if they have this average atomic mass.

When all atoms of carbon are treated as if they have this average atomic mass, one mole of naturally occurring carbon atoms has a mass of 12.0111 grams, too. That is, the atomic mass of an element expressed in amu is the same number as the mass of one mole of the element expressed in grams. For example, the atomic mass of fluorine is 18.998 amu, and the mass of one mole of fluorine is 18.998 grams. This means that the values given in the periodic table in Lesson 6, page 65, for the atomic masses of the elements also work for the mass of one mole of each of the elements. You just have to be careful to use amu units for atomic masses and gram units for the mass of a mole.

When you add atomic masses to get molecular masses of molecules, you are once again treating all of the atoms of each element in the molecule as if they have the weighted average of the mass of each naturally occurring isotope. For example, the molecular mass of water ($H_2O$) is 18.015 amu (1.008 amu for H + 1.008 amu for H + 15.999 amu for O). The mass of one mole of water is 18.015 grams. Thus, the molecular mass of a molecule expressed in amu is the same number as the mass of one mole of the molecule expressed in grams.

Chemists call the mass of one mole of any substance the **molar mass.** The substance may be an atom or a molecule or an ion. Molar mass is measured in grams per mole, which can be abbreviated as g/mol. The molar mass of a substance is sometimes called the gram-molecular weight, or the molecular weight, or the atomic weight. The symbol for molar mass is MM.

## PRACTICE 35: Molar Mass

Decide if each statement that follows is true (**T**) or false (**F**). Write the correct letter on each line.

____ **1.** The mass of one mole of a substance is the molar mass of that substance.

____ **2.** Molar mass applies to atoms, but not molecules or ions.

____ **3.** The molar mass of a substance is sometimes called the gram-molecular weight.

____ **4.** The molecular mass of a molecule expressed in amu is the same number as the mass of one mole of the molecule expressed in grams.

____ **5.** If the atomic mass of sulfur is 32.066 amu, then the molar mass of sulfur is 32.066 g/mol.

____ **6.** The abbreviation for grams per mole is gpm.

# LESSON 8: Periodic Trends

GOAL: To learn how the properties of atoms vary across the periodic table

## WORDS TO KNOW

**atomic radius**
**effective nuclear charge, $Z_{eff}$**
**ionic radius**
**shielding**
**valence electrons**

## The Shell Model of the Atom

You learned that each element in the periodic table has unique physical and chemical properties. These properties are due to the unique physical and chemical properties of the atoms that make up the elements. The unique properties of the atoms, in turn, are due to the differences in the number of electrons that the atoms of different elements have.

Recall, also, that elements within the same group in the periodic table have similar properties. They have similar properties even though they have very different numbers of protons, neutrons, and electrons. For example, lithium and cesium are both Group 1 elements. The most abundant isotope of lithium has 3 protons, 4 neutrons, and 3 electrons. The most abundant isotope of cesium has 55 protons, 78 neutrons, and 55 electrons.

Nevertheless, both lithium and cesium react with water to produce MOH compounds, where M is either Li or Cs. They both react with halogens ($F_2$, $Cl_2$, $Br_2$, and $I_2$) to form MX compounds, too, where M is either Li or Cs and X is either F, Cl, Br, or I. Finally, they both react with hydrogen to form MH compounds, where M is either Li or Cs.

The electrons in an atom act as if they occupy shells or layers around the nucleus. All of the elements in a period of the periodic table have the same number of shells. For example, hydrogen and helium have the same number of shells. So do Li, Be, B, C, N, O, F, and Ne, which are the elements of the second period. So do Na, Mg, Al, Si, P, S, Cl, and Ar, and so on. Furthermore, the elements in the first period have their electrons in one shell, the elements in the second period have their electrons in two shells, the elements in the third period have their electrons in three shells, and so on.

The table below lists the first 18 elements of the periodic table and the shell or shells in which their electrons can be found.

| Atomic Number | Element | Electrons in First Shell | Electrons in Second Shell | Electrons in Third Shell | Group Number (Name) |
|---|---|---|---|---|---|
| 1 | Hydrogen | 1 | | | 1 |
| 2 | Helium | 2 | | | 18 (Noble gas) |
| 3 | Lithium | 2 | 1 | | 1 (Alkali metal) |
| 4 | Beryllium | 2 | 2 | | 2 (Alkaline earth metal) |
| 5 | Boron | 2 | 3 | | 13 |
| 6 | Carbon | 2 | 4 | | 14 |
| 7 | Nitrogen | 2 | 5 | | 15 |
| 8 | Oxygen | 2 | 6 | | 16 |
| 9 | Fluorine | 2 | 7 | | 17 (Halogen) |
| 10 | Neon | 2 | 8 | | 18 (Noble gas) |
| 11 | Sodium | 2 | 8 | 1 | 1 (Alkali metal) |
| 12 | Magnesium | 2 | 8 | 2 | 2 (Alkaline earth metal) |
| 13 | Aluminum | 2 | 8 | 3 | 13 |
| 14 | Silicon | 2 | 8 | 4 | 14 |
| 15 | Phosphorus | 2 | 8 | 5 | 15 |
| 16 | Sulfur | 2 | 8 | 6 | 16 |
| 17 | Chlorine | 2 | 8 | 7 | 17 (Halogen) |
| 18 | Argon | 2 | 8 | 8 | 18 (Noble gas) |

Note in the table above that the first shell holds two electrons and the second and third shells hold eight electrons each. Note that the first shell is filled at helium, the second shell is filled at neon, and the third shell is filled at argon. All three elements are noble gases. Recall that the noble gases are virtually unreactive. There must be something particularly stable about a completely filled shell of electrons.

The electrons in the outermost occupied shell of an atom are called **valence electrons.** For example, the electron in the second shell is the valence electron for Li, and the electron in the third shell is the valence electron for Na. It is not a coincidence that Li and Na, both Group 1 elements, have the same number of valence electrons. All members of a group in the periodic table have the same number of valence electrons.

For the main group elements (Groups 1, 2, 13, 14, 15, 16, 17, and 18), the valence electrons are the only ones that take part in chemical reactions. If all members of a group have the same number of valence electrons, then it stands to reason that they will have similar chemical properties.

**TIP**

The group number of an element makes it easy to remember how many valence electrons it has. Except for He (Group 18, two valence electrons), the number of valence electrons that an element has equals the last number in its group number. For example, the Group 1 elements all have one valence electron, the Group 2 elements have two valence electrons, the Group 13 elements have three valence electrons, the Group 14 elements have four valence electrons, and so on.

## PRACTICE 36: The Shell Model of the Atom

Decide if each statement that follows is true (**T**) or false (**F**). Write the correct letter on each line.

__T__ **1.** The electrons in an atom act as if they occupy shells, or layers, around the nucleus.

__T__ **2.** The electrons in the outermost occupied shell of an atom are called valence electrons.

__F__ **3.** Carbon, a Group 14 element, has seven valence electrons.

__T__ **4.** The elements in the first period have their electrons in one shell, the elements in the second period have their electrons in two shells, the elements in the third period have their electrons in three shells, and so on.

T 5. The noble gases are stable because they have completely filled electron shells.

F 6. All members of a group in the periodic table have different numbers of valence electrons.

## Shielding and Effective Nuclear Charge

On page 88, you learned that lithium has two inner shell electrons and one outer shell (valence) electron. The nuclear charge on a lithium atom is +3 because it has three protons in its nucleus. However, the nuclear charge felt by the valence electron is less than +3. This is because the two inner shell electrons shield the valence electron from the full attractive effect of the nuclear charge.

How do inner shell electrons shield valence electrons? **Shielding** occurs because inner shell electrons reside between the valence electron and the positively-charged nucleus. The attractive force between oppositely charged particles decreases with distance, so the inner shell electrons are held more tightly than the valence electron.

Shielding also occurs because like charges repel each other. That is, repulsion between the inner shell electrons and the valence electron reduces the attraction between the positively charged nucleus and the valence electron.

The nuclear charge that an electron actually experiences is called the **effective nuclear charge**. The symbol for effective nuclear charge is $\mathbf{Z_{eff}}$. The effective nuclear charge for the valence electron in lithium is only +1. This can be calculated by adding the nuclear charge (+3) and the negative charge on the inner shell electrons. There are two inner shell electrons, so they have a total charge of –2. Thus, $+3 + (-2) = 3 - 2 = +1$.

The effective nuclear charge on the rest of the elements in Group 1 of the periodic table is also +1. For example, sodium has a nuclear charge of +11 and ten inner shell electrons that give a charge of –10. Similarly, cesium has a nuclear charge of +55 and 54 inner shell electrons. All elements in a group have the same effective nuclear charge on their valence electrons.

Beryllium (Group 2) has two inner shell electrons and two valence electrons. The $Z_{eff}$ on the valence electrons is +2. This is because the nuclear charge is +4, and the charge on the inner shell electrons is –2. If you continue calculating $Z_{eff}$ for the valence electrons on boron (Group 13), carbon (Group 14), nitrogen (Group 15), oxygen (Group 16), and fluorine (Group 17), you should get +3, +4, +5, +6, and +7, respectively. In fact, $Z_{eff}$ for any main group element equals the last number in its group number.

## PRACTICE 37: Shielding and Effective Nuclear Charge

Decide if each statement that follows is true (**T**) or false (**F**). Write the correct letter on each line.

T **1.** Inner shell electrons shield valence electrons from the full attractive effect of the nuclear charge.

F **2.** The effective nuclear charge on an outer shell electron is always the same as the nuclear charge on the atom.

T **3.** Shielding occurs because inner shell electrons reside between the valence electrons and the positively charged nucleus, and because like charges repel each other.

T **4.** The nuclear charge that an electron actually experiences is called the effective nuclear charge.

F **5.** All elements in a group have different effective nuclear charges on their valence electrons.

T **6.** The symbol for effective nuclear charge is $Z_{eff}$.

T **7.** $Z_{eff}$ for any main group element equals the last number in its group number.

F **8.** Bromine is in Group 17, so $Z_{eff}$ should be +2.

## Atomic and Ionic Radii

The size of an atom is difficult to define because it is difficult to tell exactly where the edge of the electron cloud is. Thus, chemists define the size of an atom in terms of its **atomic radius.** For metals, the atomic radius is one half the distance between the nuclei of adjacent atoms in a crystal of the element. For nonmetals that form homonuclear diatomic molecules, such as $Cl_2$ or $N_2$, the atomic radius is one half the distance between the nuclei of the two atoms. The drawing on the right may help you visualize how the atomic radius of an element is measured.

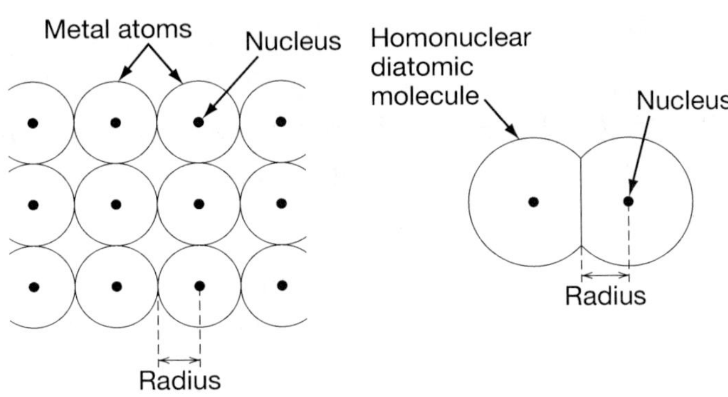


The atomic radius increases as you go down the elements in a group. For example, Na is larger than Li, K is larger than Na, Rb is larger than K, Cs is larger than Rb, and Fr is larger than Cs. Atomic radius increases down a group because the number of electron shells is greater for Fr than it is for Cs and is greater for Cs than it is for K, and so forth. Another way of saying this is that the valence electrons of Fr are farther from the nucleus than the valence electrons of Cs, and so on. Effective nuclear charge does not affect atomic radius within a group because $Z_{eff}$ remains constant as you go down a column of the periodic table.

As you go from left to right across a row of the periodic table, the number of electron shells remains constant. The number of electrons increases from left to right, but so does the effective nuclear charge. As $Z_{eff}$ increases from Li, to Be, to B, to C, to N, to O, to F, the valence electrons are pulled closer to the nucleus and held more tightly. When this happens, the atomic radius decreases. Thus, the atomic radius decreases as you go from left to right within a period of the periodic table.

**Ionic radius** is the radius of a cation or an anion. The radius of a cation is smaller than the radius of the corresponding neutral atom. For example, the ionic radius of $Na^+$ is smaller than the atomic radius of Na. The radius of an anion is larger than the radius of the corresponding neutral atom. For example, the ionic radius of $Cl^-$ is larger than the atomic radius of Cl.

The radius of a cation is smaller than the radius of the corresponding neutral atom because the cation has fewer electrons. The loss of an electron to form a cation does not affect $Z_{eff}$ because the electrons lost are valence electrons. What is affected, though, is the number of electrons over which that nuclear charge is spread. In a cation, it is spread over fewer electrons. As a result, the remaining electrons are held tighter and closer to the nucleus. This is another way of saying the radius of the cation is smaller than the radius of the neutral atom.

The radius of an anion is larger than the radius of the corresponding neutral atom because the anion has more electrons. As with the formation of a cation, the gain of an electron to form an anion does not affect $Z_{eff}$. What is affected, though, is the number of electrons over which the nuclear charge is spread. In an anion, it is spread over more electrons than in the neutral atom. As a result, the valence electrons are held less tightly and farther from the nucleus.

## PRACTICE 38: Atomic and Ionic Radii

Decide if each statement that follows is true (**T**) or false (**F**). Write the correct letter on each line.

_T_ **1.** For nonmetals that form homonuclear diatomic molecules, such as $Cl_2$ or $N_2$, the atomic radius is one half the distance between the nuclei of the two atoms.

_T_ **2.** Ionic radius is the radius of a cation or an anion.

_F_ **3.** The atomic radius decreases as you go down the elements in a group.

_T_ **4.** The radius of a cation is smaller than the radius of the corresponding neutral atom because the cation has fewer electrons.

_F_ **5.** The radius of an anion is smaller than the radius of the corresponding neutral atom.

## UNIT 2 REVIEW

Circle the letter of the correct answer.

1. Atoms are made up of _______.
   a. electrons only
   b. neutrons only
   c. electron, protons, and neutrons

2. Electrons are _______.
   a. negatively charged particles that have very little mass but take up most of the volume of an atom
   b. positively charged particles that have a lot of mass but very little volume
   c. particles that have no charge but have a mass that is only slightly greater than the mass of a proton

3. The atomic mass of an element is _______.
   a. the average mass of the naturally occurring isotopes in the sample
   b. also called the atomic weight of the element
   c. both *a* and *b*

4. The periodic table of the elements is organized _______.
   a. by atomic number
   b. by color
   c. by density

5. The main group elements _______.
   a. are the same as the lanthanides and actinides
   b. are the elements in Groups 1, 2, 13, 14, 15, 16, 17, and 18 of the periodic table
   c. are sometimes called the inner transition elements

6. The elements Be, Mg, Ca, Sr, Ba, and Ra are _______.
   a. the noble gases
   b. the alkaline earth metals
   c. the metalloids

7. Ions are _______.
   a. neutral particles that form when an atom or a molecule gains or loses one or more electrons
   b. not electrically neutral
   c. both *a* and *b*

8. Molar mass is _______.
   a. the same as the empirical formula of the compound
   b. the mass of one mole of any substance
   c. neither *a* nor *b*

9. The electrons in the outermost occupied shell of an atom are called _______.
   a. valence electrons
   b. protons
   c. core electrons

10. All members of a group in the periodic table have _______.
   a. different numbers of valence electrons
   b. the same number of valence electrons
   c. no valence electrons

## UNIT 2 APPLICATION ACTIVITY 1

### Finding the Density of an Irregular Solid

The density of an object is equal to the object's mass divided by its volume. Density is usually expressed in units, such as grams per milliliter. Obtain a sample of sand for this experiment from your instructor. Using a gram scale, find the mass of the sand in grams, and record your findings in the chart at the right. Follow the method on page 96 to find the volume of the sand alone and its density. Record your findings in the chart.

| | |
|---|---|
| **Mass of sand (g)** | |
| **Original volume of water alone in graduated cylinder (ml)** | |
| **Volume of sand and water (ml)** | |
| **Volume of sand alone (ml)** | |
| **Density of sand (g/ml)** | |

1. Place 50 ml of water in a 100-ml graduated cylinder.
2. Add the sand to the water. Gently tap the cylinder, and agitate the sand to release any trapped air bubbles.
3. Measure the volume of the sand and water. Record the data in the chart.
4. Determine the volume of the sand alone by subtracting the volume of the water alone from the volume of the sand and water—that is, (volume of sand and water) – (volume of water) = (volume of sand).
5. Determine the density of the sand in grams/milliliter by dividing the mass of the sand by the volume of the sand.

Compare your density measurement with that of others in your learning group. How do the densities compare?

________________________________________________

________________________________________________

If there are differences between your results and those of others, how can you account for those differences?

________________________________________________

________________________________________________

________________________________________________

________________________________________________

________________________________________________

________________________________________________

________________________________________________

________________________________________________

________________________________________________

________________________________________________

________________________________________________

# UNIT 2 APPLICATION ACTIVITY 2

## Comparing Atomic Radii

Use the data and grids provided to graph atomic radius against atomic number for elements in the third period and for elements in Group 2A of the periodic table. The first two elements in the third period, sodium (Na) and magnesium (Mg), have been graphed for you. Plot the remaining elements, and connect the points with a line to make your graphs.

**Third Period**

| Element | Number | Atomic Radius ($\times 10^{-10}$) |
|---|---|---|
| Na | 11 | 1.86 |
| Mg | 12 | 1.60 |
| Al | 13 | 1.43 |
| Si | 14 | 1.17 |
| P | 15 | 1.10 |
| S | 16 | 1.04 |
| Cl | 17 | .99 |
| Ar | 18 | .94 |

Atomic Radii (x10−10)
2.0
1.5
1.0
0.5
Na
Mg
11 12 13 14 15 16 17 18
Atomic number

**Group 2A**

| Element | Number | Atomic Radius ($\times 10^{-10}$) |
|---|---|---|
| Be | 4 | 1.11 |
| Mg | 12 | 1.60 |
| Ca | 20 | 1.97 |
| Sr | 38 | 2.15 |
| Ba | 56 | 2.17 |

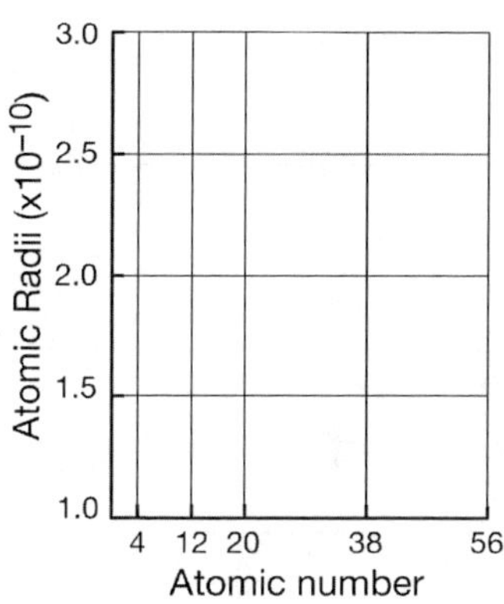

For the graph of elements in the third period, what trend do you observe?

For the graph of elements in the Group 2A, what trend do you observe?

How might you explain the trend in each group of elements?

# UNIT 3

## Transformations of Matter

# LESSON 9: Chemical Reactions

GOAL: To learn how to write and balance chemical equations

## WORDS TO KNOW

**chemical equation**
**law of mass conservation**
**products**
**reactants**
**stoichiometric coefficients**

## Writing Chemical Equations

In Unit 1, page 20, you learned that a chemical change occurs when the chemical properties of matter change. New substances are formed in a chemical change. One example was burning propane in a camp stove to form carbon dioxide and water. Another example was the reaction of sodium metal with chlorine gas to form sodium chloride. In both cases, a chemical reaction occurred in which certain substances became new substances. A chemical reaction is another name for a chemical change.

Suppose you want to tell another chemist how to mix propane and oxygen to get carbon dioxide and water. You could write it in words in a sentence such as the following: burn 1 mole of propane with 5 moles of oxygen to form 3 moles of carbon dioxide and 4 moles of water. Or, you could write it as a chemical equation:

$$C_3H_8 + 5\,O_2 \longrightarrow 3\,CO_2 + 4\,H_2O$$

A **chemical equation** uses formulas to identify the substances involved in a chemical reaction and numbers to identify the amounts of those substances. Chemical equations are a kind of chemist's shorthand for describing chemical reactions.

TIP

One way to think of a chemical equation is as a chemical sentence. If the equation is the sentence, then the chemical formulas are the words in the sentence. If the formulas are the words, then the elemental symbols are the letters used to form the words.

The substances that react with one another in a chemical reaction are called the **reactants.** In a chemical equation, the reactants are written on the left side of the arrow. In the equation for the reaction of propane with oxygen, the reactants are $C_3H_8$ (propane) and $O_2$ (oxygen).

The substances formed in a chemical reaction are called the **products.** In a chemical equation, the products are written on the right side of the arrow. In the equation for the reaction of propane with oxygen, the products are $CO_2$ (carbon dioxide) and $H_2O$ (water).

The arrow in the chemical equation connects the reactants to the products. The arrow indicates the direction in which the reaction proceeds. In the reaction of propane with oxygen, carbon dioxide and water form from propane and oxygen, not the other way around. In words, the arrow means "yields," "forms," "gives," or "produces." The arrow is sometimes called a yield arrow or a reaction arrow.

The numbers to the left of the chemical formulas of the reactants and products are called **stoichiometric coefficients,** or just coefficients. In almost all cases, the coefficients are whole numbers (1, 2, 3, and so forth, instead of 0.33, 0.5, or 0.86, and so forth). The coefficients indicate how many moles of each reactant are consumed or how many moles of each product are produced in the reaction. When the coefficient is 1, no number is written. In the reaction of propane with oxygen, 1 mole of $C_3H_8$ reacts with 5 moles of $O_2$ to form 3 moles of $CO_2$ and 4 moles of $H_2O$. Note that no coefficient is given for $C_3H_8$.

The coefficients also indicate how many *molecules* of the substances are consumed or produced in the reaction. This is because, at the atomic/molecular level, the reaction is occurring between individual molecules. This will be particularly important later, when you learn how to balance chemical equations.

One of the most important things to remember about stoichiometric coefficients is that the coefficient applies to every atom in the formula. Thus, "3 $CO_2$" means "3 moles (or molecules) of $CO_2$," which have a total of 3 moles (or atoms) of carbon and 6 moles (or atoms) of oxygen.

## PRACTICE 39: Writing Chemical Equations

Decide if each statement that follows is true (**T**) or false (**F**). Write the correct letter on each line.

__T__ **1.** The substances that react with one another in a chemical reaction are called the reactants.

__T__ **2.** A chemical equation uses formulas to identify the substances involved in a chemical reaction and numbers to identify the amounts of those substances.

__F__ **3.** In the reaction $2\ Na + 2\ H_2O \longrightarrow 2\ NaOH + H_2$, the reactants are 2 moles of NaOH and 1 mole of $H_2$.

__T__ **4.** The substances formed in a chemical reaction are called the products.

__T__ **5.** In the reaction $N_2 + 3\ H_2 \longrightarrow 2\ NH_3$, the stoichiometric coefficient of $NH_3$ is 2.

__T__ **6.** In the reaction $N_2 + O_2 \longrightarrow 2\ NO$, the reactants are 1 mole of $N_2$ and 1 mole of $O_2$.

__F__ **7.** A chemical reaction is not the same as a chemical change.

__T__ **8.** In the reaction $CH_4 + 2\ O_2 \longrightarrow CO_2 + 2\ H_2O$, the products are 1 mole of $CO_2$ and 2 moles of $H_2O$.

## Balanced Versus Unbalanced Chemical Equations

A chemical equation is balanced when the number of atoms of each element in the reactants *equals* the number of atoms of that same element in the products. The elements will be arranged into different compounds in the products, but the number of atoms of each element is the same as in the reactants.

Remember the equation from page 101.

$$C_3H_8 + 5\,O_2 \longrightarrow 3\,CO_2 + 4\,H_2O$$

This is a balanced chemical equation. On the reactants side of the equation, there are 3 C atoms and 8 H atoms from $C_3H_8$, and 10 O atoms from the 5 $O_2$ molecules. On the products side, there are 3 C atoms from the 3 $CO_2$ molecules, 8 H atoms from the 4 $H_2O$ molecules, and 10 O atoms (6 from the 3 $CO_2$ molecules and 4 from the 4 $H_2O$ molecules). Thus, the number of C atoms, the number of H atoms, and the number of O atoms are the same on both sides of the equation. There are no other elements to consider, so this equation is balanced.

A chemical equation is unbalanced when the number of atoms of each element in the reactants does *not* equal the number of atoms of that same element in the products. An example of an unbalanced equation is as follows:

$$N_2 + H_2 \longrightarrow NH_3$$

In this equation, there are 2 N atoms and 2 H atoms in the reactants. But there is 1 N atom and 3 H atoms in the product.

An unbalanced equation usually tells all of the compounds involved in the reaction. However, it does not tell the ratios of the amounts of all of the reactants and products. You get these ratios from the stoichiometric coefficients of the balanced equation.

A balanced chemical equation fulfills a scientific principle called the **law of mass conservation.** The law of mass conservation says that the total mass of matter does not change during a chemical reaction. Another way of saying this is that the atoms in a chemical reaction are conserved. Thus, the atoms present in the reactants must be present in the products, too.

You learned in Unit 2, page 52, that the fifth point in Dalton's atomic theory was that matter is neither created nor destroyed by chemical reactions. Instead, atoms retain their identities but change the way they are combined or arranged. This is Dalton's way of saying that mass is conserved during chemical reactions.

**IN REAL LIFE**

Trying to do chemistry using unbalanced chemical equations is a little like trying to pay your bills with an unbalanced checkbook. Everything might turn out fine. On the other hand, you might bounce a few checks and ruin your credit rating. The only way you will know for sure whether or not you have enough money is by balancing your checkbook before you write the checks. In chemistry, everything might turn out fine, too. On the other hand, you might run out of one reactant before you have turned it into enough of some product to do all the tests you need to do. Throughout Lesson 10, you will see that the only way you will know for sure is by starting with a balanced chemical equation.

## PRACTICE 40: Balanced Versus Unbalanced Chemical Equations

Decide if each chemical equation below is balanced (**B**) or unbalanced (**U**). Write the correct letter on the line.

__U__ **1.** $N_2 + H_2 \longrightarrow NH_3$

__B__ **2.** $N_2 + 3\ H_2 \longrightarrow 2\ NH_3$

__B__ **3.** $N_2 + O_2 \longrightarrow 2\ NO$

__B__ **4.** $2\ Mg + O_2 \longrightarrow 2\ MgO$

__U__ **5.** $Na + Cl_2 \longrightarrow NaCl$

__B__ **6.** $Fe + 2\ HCl \longrightarrow FeCl_2 + H_2$

__U__ **7.** $C_8H_{18} + O_2 \longrightarrow CO_2 + H_2O$

__B__ **8.** $C_6H_{12}O_6 + 6\ O_2 \longrightarrow 6\ CO_2 + 6\ H_2O$

## Balancing Chemical Equations

To balance a chemical equation, you must be able to adjust the stoichiometric coefficients so that mass is conserved. That is, the number and kind of atoms present in the reactants must be present in the products, too.

TIP

You must adjust only the stoichiometric coefficients of the reactants and products. You must NOT change the chemical formulas of the reactants or of the products. If you change the chemical formulas, then you are changing the chemical reaction, not balancing it. Suppose you took the unbalanced equation, $H_2 + O_2 \longrightarrow H_2O$, and changed it to $H_2 + O_2 \longrightarrow H_2O_2$ in order to balance the number of oxygen atoms in the reactants and products. You now have a balanced equation. But, the product is now hydrogen peroxide, not water. Hydrogen peroxide and water are very different chemical compounds. Hydrogen peroxide is used as a bleaching agent and as an antiseptic. You would not want to drink a glass of it when you are thirsty.

The method that is used to balance chemical equations is called balancing by inspection. It is a trial-and-error approach that can be summarized in the following four steps.

**Step 1.** Write the complete unbalanced equation. You must write the correct chemical formulas for all of the reactants and all of the products. For example, here is the reaction of propane with oxygen to give carbon dioxide and water.

$$C_3H_8 + O_2 \longrightarrow CO_2 + H_2O$$

**Step 2.** Change the stoichiometric coefficients to balance one element at a time. It is usually easiest to begin with an element that appears in only one substance on each side of the reaction arrow. In the example on the previous page, you can begin with either carbon or hydrogen. Carbon appears only in propane in the reactants and only in carbon dioxide in the products. Similarly, hydrogen appears only in propane in the reactants and only in water in the products. Oxygen, on the other hand, appears in the reactants ($O_2$). It also appears in both carbon dioxide and water in the products.

In order to balance carbon, you must count up the carbon atoms in the reactants (there are three of them) and in the products (there is only one of them). Therefore, you need to change the stoichiometric coefficient of $CO_2$ from 1 to 3.

$$C_3H_8 + O_2 \longrightarrow 3\ CO_2 + H_2O$$

Carbon is now balanced. Do the same for hydrogen. There are eight hydrogen atoms in the reactants and only two in the products. You need to change the stoichiometric coefficient of $H_2O$ from 1 to 4.

$$C_3H_8 + O_2 \longrightarrow 3\ CO_2 + 4\ H_2O$$

Hydrogen is now balanced, too. Only oxygen remains to be balanced. There are two oxygen atoms in the reactants. But there are now ten oxygen atoms in the products (six from the three molecules of $CO_2$ and four from the four molecules of $H_2O$). You need to change the stoichiometric coefficient of oxygen from 1 to 5.

$$C_3H_8 + 5\ O_2 \longrightarrow 3\ CO_2 + 4\ H_2O$$

**Step 3.** Change the stoichiometric coefficients to eliminate any fractional coefficients. Remember that whole number coefficients are important. This is because equations can be interpreted as the ratio of either molecules or moles. Fractions of a mole are fine, but fractions of a molecule are meaningless.

If you end up with a balanced equation that contains a coefficient that is a fraction, multiply all of the coefficients by the denominator of the fractional coefficient. This will give you coefficients that are all whole numbers. Suppose, for example, that you end up with a coefficient of $\frac{5}{2}$ for $O_2$. You would need to multiply the coefficients for $C_3H_8$, $O_2$, $CO_2$, and $H_2O$ by 2 (the denominator) to eliminate the fractional coefficient for $O_2$.

**Step 4.** Check to make sure that the equation is balanced. Count the total number of atoms of each element on both sides of the equation. Make sure they are the same. In the example, the balanced equation has 3 C, 8 H, and 10 O in the reactants and 3 C, 8 H, and 10 O in the products. The totals on both sides are the same. So, the equation is balanced.

TIP

You've seen that a chemical equation is sort of like a recipe. The idea of a balanced equation is also similar to a recipe. For example, suppose you have a recipe that makes 1 dozen (12) brownies. The recipe calls for 2 eggs, 1 cup butter, 1 cup sugar, $\frac{1}{2}$ cup cocoa, and $\frac{1}{2}$ cup flour. If you were having a party and wanted to make 6 dozen brownies, you would have to increase all the ingredients by a factor of 6. So, you would need 12 eggs, 6 cups butter, 6 cups sugar, 3 cups cocoa, and 3 cups flour.

## PRACTICE 41: Balancing Chemical Equations

Decide if each statement that follows is true (**T**) or false (**F**). Write the correct letter on each line.

T **1.** In order to balance a chemical equation, you must adjust the stoichiometric coefficients so that mass is conserved.

T **2.** The unbalanced equation $Fe + HCl \longrightarrow FeCl_2 + H_2$ can be balanced by changing the stoichiometric coefficient of HCl from 1 to 2.

F **3.** The unbalanced equation $H_2 + O_2 \longrightarrow H_2O$ can be balanced by changing $H_2O$ to $H_2O_2$.

T **4.** The unbalanced equation $H_2 + O_2 \longrightarrow H_2O$ can be balanced by changing the stoichiometric coefficients of both $H_2$ and $H_2O$ from 1 to 2.

F **5.** The unbalanced equation $C_3H_8 + O_2 \longrightarrow CO_2 + H_2O$ can be balanced by changing the stoichiometric coefficient of $CO_2$ from 1 to 3.

T **6.** The unbalanced equation $SO_2 + O_2 \longrightarrow SO_3$ can be balanced by changing the stoichiometric coefficients of both $SO_2$ and $SO_3$ from 1 to 2.

F **7.** Step 1 of the balancing by inspection method of equation balancing is to eliminate fractional coefficients.

T **8.** All of the coefficients in the reaction $K + \frac{1}{2} Cl_2 \longrightarrow KCl$ should be multiplied by 2 in order to eliminate the fractional coefficient for $Cl_2$.

# LESSON 10: Stoichiometry

GOAL: To learn how to calculate amounts of reactants and products using balanced chemical equations; to understand the concepts of stoichiometry

## WORDS TO KNOW

| | | |
|---|---|---|
| **actual yield** | **percent yield** | **stoichiometry** |
| **limiting reactant** | **reversible reaction** | **theoretical yield** |
| **molar ratio** | **side reactions** | **yield** |

## Molar Ratios

**Stoichiometry** is the study of the quantitative relationships between the amounts of reactants and products in a chemical reaction. Stoichiometry is quantitative because it can be used to calculate how much of one substance reacts with another substance. You can also use it to calculate how much of a product can form from a known amount of a reactant.

The key to understanding stoichiometry is a balanced chemical equation. A balanced chemical equation is important because the stoichiometric coefficients establish the molar relationships between the various reactants and products. Consider the following equation as an example:

$$2\,H_2 + O_2 \longrightarrow 2\,H_2O$$

This balanced equation tells you that for each mole of $O_2$ that you have, you need 2 moles of $H_2$ for a complete reaction. Alternatively, for every 2 moles of $H_2$, you need 1 mole of $O_2$ for a complete reaction. Additionally, for every 2 moles of $H_2$, you get 2 moles of $H_2O$. Or, for every 2 moles of $H_2O$ formed, you need 2 moles of $H_2$. Similarly, for every 1 mole of $O_2$, you get 2 moles of $H_2O$. Or, for every 2 moles of $H_2O$ formed, you need 1 mole of $O_2$.

You can also write these relationships as molar ratios. A **molar ratio** shows the relationship between the number of moles of one reactant or product and the number of moles of a different reactant or product. For example, the molar ratio between water and oxygen in the equation on page 110 is as follows:

$$\frac{2 \text{ mol } H_2O}{1 \text{ mol } O_2}$$

This is the same as saying that for every 2 moles of $H_2O$ formed, you need 1 mole of $O_2$. The molar ratios for the other five relationships mentioned previously are as follows:

$$\frac{1 \text{ mol } O_2}{2 \text{ mol } H_2} \quad \frac{2 \text{ mol } H_2}{1 \text{ mol } O_2} \quad \frac{2 \text{ mol } H_2}{2 \text{ mol } H_2O} \quad \frac{2 \text{ mol } H_2O}{2 \text{ mol } H_2} \quad \frac{1 \text{ mol } O_2}{2 \text{ mol } H_2O}$$

Not every chemical equation has six molar ratios. Some have more, and some have fewer. The number of molar ratios depends on how many different reactants and products there are in the balanced chemical equation. There is one molar ratio between each reactant and every other reactant and product. There is also one molar ratio between each product and every other product and reactant.

**TIP**

Molar ratios may remind you of the conversion factors used to convert between different units that you learned about in Unit 1. Molar ratios are, in fact, very much like the conversion factors between units, such as centimeters and inches or grams and kilograms. Molar ratios are the conversion factors between the number of moles of one reactant or product and the number of moles of another reactant or product. Although you may need to look up the conversion factor between centimeters and inches, you can figure out the molar ratios between reactants and products by balancing the chemical equation.

## PRACTICE 42: Molar Ratios

Decide if each statement that follows is true (**T**) or false (**F**). Write the correct letter on each line.

__T__ **1.** Stoichiometry is the study of the quantitative relationships between the amounts of reactants and products in a chemical reaction.

__T__ **2.** According to the balanced chemical equation $2\ NO_2 \longrightarrow N_2O_4$, for every 1 mole of $N_2O_4$ formed, you need 2 moles of $NO_2$.

__F__ **3.** According to the balanced chemical equation $2\ Al + 3\ S \longrightarrow Al_2S_3$, for every 2 moles of aluminum (Al), you need 1 mole of sulfur (S) for a complete reaction.

__F__ **4.** According to the balanced chemical equation $HCl + NaOH \longrightarrow NaCl + H_2O$, for every 1 mole of NaCl formed, you need 2 moles of NaOH.

__T__ **5.** Molar ratios show the relationship between the number of moles of one reactant or product and the number of moles of a different reactant or product.

__F__ **6.** Every chemical reaction has six molar ratios.

__T__ **7.** The number of molar ratios depends on how many different reactants and products there are in the balanced chemical equation.

__T__ **8.** The key to understanding stoichiometry is a balanced chemical equation.

## Mole–Mole Conversions

So far you have learned how to balance chemical equations and set up molar ratios. These two skills can now be used to do mole–mole conversions. Mole–mole conversions allow you to calculate the number of moles of a product you should obtain from a known number of moles of a reactant. Mole–mole conversions also make it possible to calculate the number of moles of reactants you will need in order to make a known number of moles of a product.

Suppose you have 5 moles of propane to burn. You want to know how many moles of carbon dioxide you will form. Mole–mole conversions always begin with a balanced chemical equation.

$$C_3H_8 + 5\ O_2 \longrightarrow 3\ CO_2 + 4\ H_2O$$

Next, figure out the molar ratio between $CO_2$ formed and $C_3H_8$ burned. According to the balanced equation, 3 moles of $CO_2$ form from every 1 mole of $C_3H_8$ burned.

$$\frac{3\text{ mol }CO_2}{1\text{ mol }C_3H_8}$$

Next, multiply the amount of $C_3H_8$ that you have (5 mol) by the molar ratio. Note that moles of $C_3H_8$ cancel and leave you with moles of $CO_2$:

$$(5\text{ mol }C_3H_8)\left(\frac{3\text{ mol }CO_2}{1\text{ mol }C_3H_8}\right) = 15\text{ mol }CO_2$$

So, 15 moles of carbon dioxide ($CO_2$) will form when you burn 5 moles of propane ($C_3H_8$).

Suppose, instead, that you want to know how many moles of water you will form in the same reaction. In this case, you multiply the amount of $C_3H_8$ that you have (5 mol) by the molar ratio between $H_2O$ formed and $C_3H_8$ burned.

$$(5\text{ mol }C_3H_8)\left(\frac{4\text{ mol }H_2O}{1\text{ mol }C_3H_8}\right) = 20\text{ mol }H_2O$$

Burning 5 moles of $C_3H_8$ will produce 20 moles of $H_2O$.

The two mole–mole conversions described so far have followed a three-step pattern. Step 1 is to write a balanced chemical equation. Step 2 is to figure out the molar ratio between the reactant and product in question. Step 3 is to multiply the number of moles of reactant by the molar ratio to get the moles of product. The same method can be used to determine the number of moles of $O_2$ needed to burn the 5 moles of $C_3H_8$. How many moles of $O_2$ is it? By following the steps described on page 113, you should get the following equation:

$$(5 \text{ mol } C_3H_8)\ \frac{5 \text{ mol } O_2}{1 \text{ mol } C_3H_8} = 25 \text{ mol } O_2$$

These calculations show that you need 25 moles of $O_2$ to burn 5 moles of $C_3H_8$. Now, suppose you want to make 12 moles of $CO_2$ from this reaction. How many moles of $C_3H_8$ would you need? How many moles of $O_2$ would you need? The general method does not change. Begin with the balanced chemical equation given previously. Next, figure out the molar ratios between $CO_2$ and $C_3H_8$ and between $CO_2$ and $O_2$.

$$\frac{1 \text{ mol } C_3H_8}{3 \text{ mol } CO_2} \text{ and } \frac{5 \text{ mol } O_2}{3 \text{ mol } CO_2}$$

Finally, multiply the amount of $CO_2$ that you want to make (12 mol) by the molar ratios.

$$(12 \text{ mol } CO_2)\left(\frac{1 \text{ mol } C_3H_8}{3 \text{ mol } CO_2}\right) = 4 \text{ mol } C_3H_8$$

$$(12 \text{ mol } CO_2)\left(\frac{5 \text{ mol } O_2}{3 \text{ mol } CO_2}\right) = 20 \text{ mol } O_2$$

These calculations show that you need 4 moles of $C_3H_8$ and 20 moles of $O_2$ to make 12 moles of $CO_2$.

Suppose you find that the units do not cancel properly in these calculations to give you the answer you are looking for. You are probably doing one of two things incorrectly. First, you may have chosen the molar ratio between the wrong two reactants and/or products. For example, choosing a molar ratio between $CO_2$ and $H_2O$ is not going to help you figure out how many moles of $O_2$ are needed to form 12 moles of $CO_2$. Second, you may have chosen the correct reactants and/or products, but you may have inverted the molar ratio.

$$(12 \text{ mol } CO_2)\left(\frac{3 \text{ mol } CO_2}{1 \text{ mol } C_3H_8}\right) = \frac{36 \text{ mol}^2 \ CO_2}{1 \text{ mol } C_3H_8}$$

The odd units obtained from this calculation should tip you off that something is wrong.

The following flowchart summarizes the relationship between moles of one substance and moles of any other substance in a chemical reaction. You can move back and forth between the two boxes by using the information over the arrow as a conversion factor.

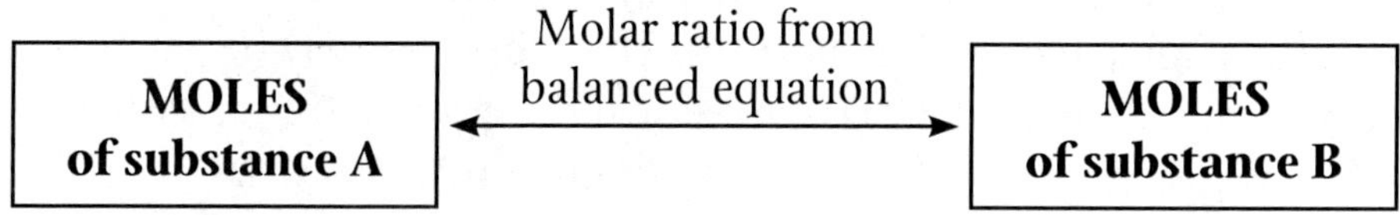


## PRACTICE 43: Mole–Mole Conversions

Decide if each statement that follows is true (**T**) or false (**F**). Write the correct letter on each line.

__T__ **1.** Mole–mole conversions allow you to calculate the number of moles of product you should obtain from a known number of moles of a reactant.

__T__ **2.** Mole–mole conversions always begin with a balanced chemical equation.

__F__ **3.** According to the balanced chemical equation 2 HgO $\longrightarrow$ 2 Hg + $O_2$, you should expect to get 2 moles of Hg for every 2 moles of HgO that you start with.

__T__ **4.** According to the balanced chemical equation HCl + NaOH $\longrightarrow$ NaCl + $H_2O$, you should expect to get 5 moles of NaCl for every 1 mole of HCl that you start with.

__T__ **5.** According to the balanced chemical equation $H_2$ + $I_2$ $\longrightarrow$ 2 HI, you need 1 mole of $H_2$ in order to make 2 moles of HI.

__F__ **6.** It does not matter whether the chemical equation you are using for a mole–mole conversion is balanced or unbalanced.

__T__ **7.** If you find that the units do not cancel properly in a mole–mole conversion, then you may have chosen the molar ratio between the wrong two reactants and/or products.

## Mass–Mole Conversions

Often, a chemist knows the mass of a substance but wants to know how many moles it is. Or, a chemist knows the number of moles but wants to know the mass of the substance. Mass–mole conversions make it possible to do both of these calculations. The key to mass–mole conversions is the molar mass of the substance in question.

In Unit 2, page 86, you learned that chemists call the mass of one mole of any substance the molar mass. The substance may be an atom, a molecule, or an ion. Molar mass uses the units grams per mole, which can be abbreviated as g/mol. The symbol for molar mass is MM.

The molar masses of the elements can be found in the periodic table of the elements on page 65. The molar mass of a molecule can be calculated by adding the molar masses of its constituent atoms. For example, the molar mass of KI is 166.0043 g/mol because the molar mass of potassium (K) is 39.0983 g/mol, and the molar mass of iodine (I) is 126.906 g/mol. The molar mass of $H_2O$ is 18.0152 g/mol because the molar mass of each hydrogen atom is 1.0079 g/mol, and the molar mass of oxygen is 15.9994 g/mol.

Suppose you have 100.00 grams of KI and need to know how many moles that is. The equation for finding moles from mass is as follows:

$$\text{moles} = \frac{\text{mass (in grams)}}{\text{MM (in g/mol)}}$$

If you divide 100.00 grams (mass) by 166.00 g/mol (MM of KI), then the units of grams cancel and leave you with units of mole.

$$\frac{(100.00\text{ g})}{(166.0043\text{ g/mol})} = (100.00\text{ g})\left(\frac{1\text{ mol}}{166.0043\text{ g}}\right) = 0.6024\text{ mol KI}$$

Suppose, instead, that you have 3.250 moles of water and need to know how many grams that is. If you multiply 3.250 moles by 18.0152 g/mol (MM of $H_2O$), then the units of moles cancel and leave you with units of grams.

$$(3.250\text{ mol } H_2O)(18.0152\text{ g/mol}) = 58.5494\text{ g } H_2O$$

## PRACTICE 44: Mass–Mole Conversions

Decide if each statement that follows is true (**T**) or false (**F**). Write the correct letter on each line.

___F___ **1.** If the molar mass of NaCl is 58.44277 g/mol, then 1.000 mole of NaCl equals 29.22139 grams of NaCl.

___T___ **2.** If the molar mass of NaCl is 58.44277 g/mol, then 0.500 mole of NaCl equals 29.22139 grams of NaCl.

___T___ **3.** If the molar mass of $H_2O_2$ is 34.0146 g/mol, then 11.9051 grams of $H_2O_2$ equals 0.350 moles of $H_2O_2$.

___F___ **4.** If the molar mass of $H_2O_2$ is 34.0146 g/mol, then 34.0146 grams of $H_2O_2$ equals 0.350 moles of $H_2O_2$.

___T___ **5.** If the molar mass of $Na_2O$ is 61.97894 g/mol, then 4.50 moles of $Na_2O$ equals 278.9052 grams of $Na_2O$.

___T___ **6.** If the molar mass of $Na_2O$ is 61.97894 g/mol, then 185.93682 grams of $Na_2O$ equals 3.00 moles of $Na_2O$.

## Mass–Mass Conversions

Now that you have learned how to do mole–mole conversions and mass–mole conversions, you are ready to learn how to combine them to do mass–mass conversions. Mass–mass conversions allow you to calculate the mass of product you should obtain from a known mass of a reactant. Mass–mass conversions also make it possible to calculate the mass of reactants you will need in order to make a known mass of a product.

Suppose you have 100.00 grams of HgO, and you want to know how many grams of mercury (Hg) you can form from heating the HgO. Mass–mass conversions, like mole–mole conversions, always begin with a balanced chemical equation.

$$2\ HgO \longrightarrow 2\ Hg + O_2$$

Once you have a balanced equation, you can use the following three-step method.

**Step 1.** Convert the given mass to moles. You do this by dividing the mass (in grams) by the molar mass of the substance. This is nothing more than a mass–mole conversion. In the example, the molar mass of HgO is 216.5894 g/mol, so 100.00 g HgO is 0.4617 mol HgO.

**Step 2.** Convert the moles of the given substance to moles of the desired substance. You do this by choosing the appropriate molar ratio from the balanced chemical equation. This is nothing more than a mole–mole conversion. In the example, you need the molar ratio between the Hg formed and the HgO heated. According to the balanced equation, 2 moles of Hg form from every 2 moles of HgO heated.

$$(0.4617 \text{ mol HgO})\left(\frac{2 \text{ mol Hg}}{2 \text{ mol HgO}}\right) = 0.4617 \text{ mol Hg}$$

**Step 3.** Convert the moles of the desired substance to mass (in grams). You do this by multiplying the number of moles of the desired substance by the molar mass of the desired substance. This is nothing more than another mass–mole conversion. In the example, the molar mass of Hg is 200.59 g/mol, so 0.4617 mol Hg is 92.6124 g Hg.

The following flowchart summarizes the relationships between masses and moles in a chemical reaction. You can start at any box in the flowchart and end up at any other box by using the information over the arrows as conversion factors.

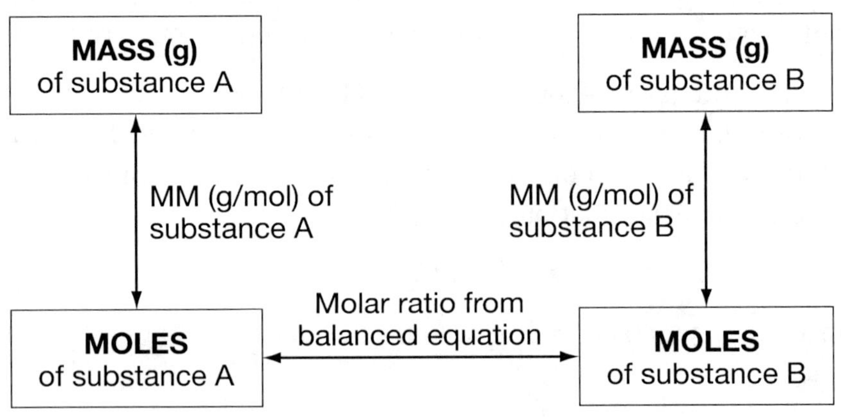

THINK ABOUT IT

Use the three-step method outlined in the text or the flowchart to figure out how many grams of HgO you will need to heat in order to make 150 g Hg. (*Hint:* If you use the flowchart, call the 150 g Hg the "mass of substance B" and the unknown mass of HgO the "mass of substance A." Work from "mass of substance B" back to "mass of substance A," using the conversion factors over the arrows.) Write your answer on a separate sheet of paper.

## PRACTICE 45: Mass–Mass Conversions

Decide if each statement that follows is true (**T**) or false (**F**). Write the correct letter on each line.

T **1.** Mass–mass conversions allow you to calculate the mass of product you should obtain from a known mass of a reactant.

T **2.** According to the balanced chemical equation $2\ H_2 + O_2 \longrightarrow 2\ H_2O$, 6.000 g $H_2$ should produce 53.6220 g $H_2O$. (The molar mass of H is 1.0079, O is 15.9994.)

F **3.** According to the balanced chemical equation $2\ H_2 + O_2 \longrightarrow 2\ H_2O$, 53.6220 g $H_2O$ should be produced from 6.000 g $O_2$.

F **4.** Mass–mass conversions never begin with a balanced chemical equation.

F **5.** According to the balanced chemical equation $2\ Al + 3\ S \longrightarrow Al_2S_3$, 13.491 g Al (0.500 mol) should produce 3.754 g $Al_2S_3$. (The molar mass of Al is 26.982; S is 32.066).

T **6.** According to the balanced chemical equation $2\ Al + 3\ S \longrightarrow Al_2S_3$, 37.541 g $Al_2S_3$ (0.250 mol) should be produced from 24.0495 g S.

T **7.** Mass–mass conversions make it possible to calculate the mass of reactants you will need in order to make a known mass of a product.

T **8.** Mass–mass conversions combine mass–mole conversions and mole–mole conversions.

## Mass–Mole–Number Conversions

Sometimes a chemist may know the mass or number of moles of a substance and may want to know how many atoms or molecules it contains. Or, a chemist may be given a certain number of atoms or molecules and may need to know the number of moles or the mass of the substance. Mass–mole–number conversions make it possible to do both of these calculations. The key to mass–mole–number conversions is Avogadro's number.

In Unit 2, page 84, you learned that Avogadro's number is the number of items in a mole of the item. The item may be an atom, a molecule, an ion, an electron, a proton, and so forth. Avogadro's number has the value of $6.022137 \times 10^{23}$ items/mol. The symbol for Avogadro's number is $N_A$. From now on, you will use Avogadro's number rounded off to $6.022 \times 10^{23}$ items/mol.

Strictly speaking, a mass–mole–number conversion does not require a balanced chemical equation. In fact, it does not require a chemical equation at all. Suppose, for example, that you have 50.02 g of $Br_2$ and you want to know how many molecules of $Br_2$ that is. Use the following two-step method.

**Step 1.** Convert the given mass to moles. You do this by dividing the mass (in grams) by the molar mass of the substance. This is nothing more than a mass–mole conversion. In the example, the molar mass of $Br_2$ is 159.808 g/mol, so 50.02 g $Br_2$ is 0.313 mol $Br_2$.

**Step 2.** Convert the moles of the given substance to the number of items of that substance. You do this by multiplying the number of moles by Avogadro's number. In the example, the items are molecules of $Br_2$. Thus, Avogadro's number is $6.022 \times 10^{23}$ molecules of $Br_2$ per mole of $Br_2$.

$$(0.313 \text{ mol } Br_2)\left(\frac{6.022 \times 10^{23} \text{ molecules of } Br_2}{1 \text{ mol } Br_2}\right) =$$

$$1.885 \times 10^{23} \text{ molecules of } Br_2$$

Suppose, instead, that someone told you that they had $1.506 \times 10^{23}$

atoms of gold (Au). You want to find out how much mass that is in order to determine whether or not it is worth very much. In order to do this calculation, you must retrace the steps you took to convert the mass of $Br_2$ to the number of molecules of $Br_2$. First, convert the number of atoms of Au to moles of Au. You do this by dividing the number of atoms of Au by Avogadro's number.

$$\frac{(1.506 \times 10^{23} \text{ Au atoms})}{\left(\frac{6.022 \times 10^{23} \text{ Au atoms}}{\text{mol Au}}\right)} = 0.250 \text{ mol Au}$$

Next, convert moles to mass. You do this by multiplying the number of moles of Au by the molar mass of Au. This is nothing more than a mass–mole conversion. In the example, the molar mass of Au is 196.967 g/mol, so 0.250 mol is 49.242 g Au. This is a little more than an ounce of gold.

Mass–mole–number conversions are summarized in the flowchart below. The flowchart on the right shows how mass–mole–number conversions fit into the mass–mass conversions flowchart from page 115. Thus, the flowchart on the right summarizes the relationships between masses, moles, and numbers in a chemical reaction. With both of the following flowcharts, you can start at any box and end up at any other box. Do this by using the information beside the arrows as conversion factors.

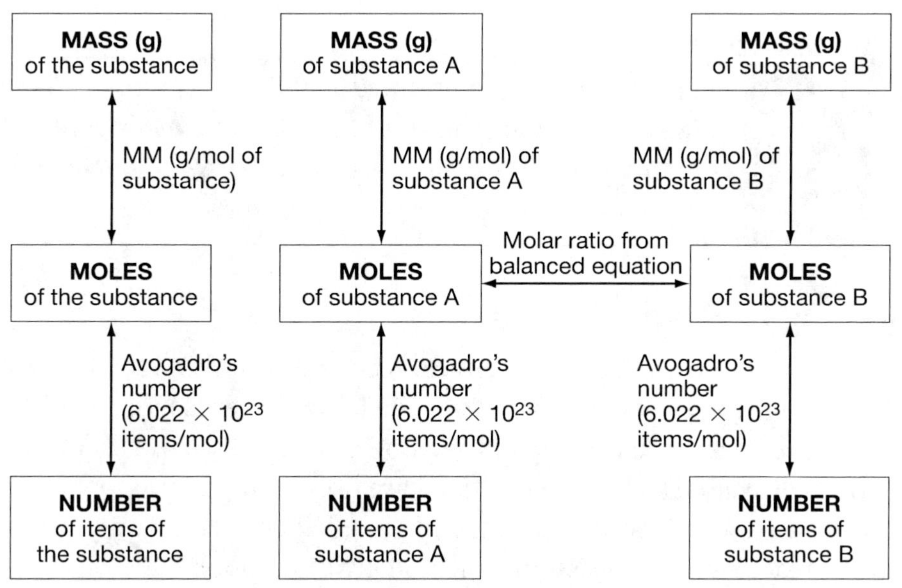

## PRACTICE 46: Mass–Mole–Number Conversions

Decide if each statement that follows is true (**T**) or false (**F**). Write the correct letter on each line.

____ **1.** Mass–mole–number conversions make it possible to calculate the number of atoms or molecules contained in a known mass of a substance.

____ **2.** 40.00 g of $AgNO_3$ (MM = 169.8729 g/mol) contains $1.4180 \times 10^{23}$ molecules of $AgNO_3$.

____ **3.** $2.8360 \times 10^{23}$ molecules of $AgNO_3$ has a mass of 20.00 g.

____ **4.** A mass–mole–number conversion does NOT require a balanced chemical equation.

____ **5.** $3.011 \times 10^{23}$ molecules of $F_2$ equals 1.50 mol of $F_2$.

____ **6.** 1.50 mol of $F_2$ contains $9.033 \times 10^{23}$ molecules of $F_2$.

____ **7.** Mass–mole–number conversions work fine for molecules but not for atoms or ions.

____ **8.** The key to mass–mole–number conversions is Avogadro's number, $6.022 \times 10^{23}$ items/mol.

**THINK ABOUT IT**

On page 120, you determined that 50.02 g of $Br_2$ contains $1.885 \times 10^{23}$ molecules of $Br_2$. How many *atoms* of Br are contained in 50.02 g $Br_2$? Write your answer on a separate sheet of paper.

## Limiting Reactants

So far, you have learned about chemical reactions as if the reactants were always present in the exact amounts needed. You have also assumed that the reactants would be used up at the same time. In other words, in the reactions discussed so far, the reactants are present in the proportions indicated by the balanced chemical equation. When this is true, you say that the reactants are present in stoichiometric amounts.

Sometimes, however, chemists run reactions in which one or more of the reactants exceeds the stoichiometric amount. Reactants that exceed their stoichiometric amounts are said to be in excess. They are called excess reactants because they will not be used up completely in the reaction.

When a reaction is run with one or more excess reactants, some other reactant will be used up in the chemical reaction before the excess reactants. The reactant used up first in the reaction is called the **limiting reactant.** It is called the limiting reactant because it limits the amount of product that can be made. Once the limiting reactant is used up, no more product can be made. It does not matter how much the other reactant or reactants are in excess.

It might help you to think about this process in another way. Suppose you are assembling cars. Each car needs 1 engine, 1 car body, and 4 wheels with tires. If your inventory contains 10 engines, 8 car bodies, and 24 wheels with tires, then the most cars you can assemble is 6. The 6 cars will use up all 24 wheels with tires, 6 of the 8 car bodies, and 6 of the 10 engines. Wheels with tires are the limiting reactant. Car bodies and engines are excess reactants.

Now, suppose you are given 64.132 g of sulfur (S) and 379.96 g of $F_2$. You want to determine how much $SF_6$ you can form from S and $F_2$. First, determine whether S or $F_2$ is the limiting reactant. In order to do that, begin with a balanced chemical equation.

$$S + F_2 \longrightarrow SF_6 \text{ (unbalanced)}$$

$$S + 3\,F_2 \longrightarrow SF_6 \text{ (balanced)}$$

Once you have a balanced equation, you can determine the limiting reactant and the amount of product that can be formed by using the following four-step method.

**Step 1.** Convert masses of reactants to moles of reactants. The molar mass of S is 32.066 g/mol. The molar mass of $F_2$ is 37.996 g/mol. So, you have 2.00 mol S and 10.00 mol $F_2$.

**Step 2.** Compare the number of moles of the reactants you are given to the number of moles required by the balanced chemical equation. According to the equation, 1 mol S reacts with 3 mol $F_2$ to form 1 mol $SF_6$. Thus, the 2.00 mol S you are given require 6.00 mol $F_2$ to completely form $SF_6$.

$$(2.00 \text{ mol S})\left(\frac{3 \text{ mol } F_2}{1 \text{ mol S}}\right) = 6.00 \text{ mol } F_2$$

You have 10.00 mol $F_2$, however. This is more than enough to react with the given amount of S. Thus, S must be the limiting reactant. That means that $F_2$ is the excess reactant.

You could also have figured out the limiting reactant from the perspective of $F_2$. In other words, 3 mol $F_2$ reacts with 1 mol S to form 1 mol $SF_6$. So, 10.00 mol $F_2$ requires 3.33 mol S to react completely. You have only 2.00 mol S, not 3.33 mol S. So, S must be the limiting reactant.

TIP

In step 2, you must *not* compare the masses (number of grams) of the reactants you are given. Masses are meaningless in this conversion because the number of grams in a mole of a substance varies according to the chemical formula of the substance. For example, 20 g $H_2$ has the same mass as 20 g $N_2$, but 20 g $H_2$ is almost 10 mol $H_2$ and 20 g $N_2$ only about 0.7 mol $N_2$.

**Step 3.** Convert the moles of the limiting reactant to moles of product. You do this by choosing the appropriate molar ratio from the balanced chemical equation. This is nothing more than a mole–mole conversion. In the example, you need the molar ratio between $SF_6$ formed and S consumed. According to the balanced equation, 1 mol $SF_6$ forms from every 1 mol S consumed.

$$(2.00 \text{ mol S})\left(\frac{1 \text{ mol } SF_6}{1 \text{ mol S}}\right) = 2.00 \text{ mol } SF_6$$

**Step 4.** Convert the moles of product to mass (in grams). You do this by multiplying the number of moles of the product by the molar mass of the product. This is nothing more than a mass–mole conversion. In the example, the molar mass of $SF_6$ is 146.054 g/mol. So, 2.00 mol $SF_6$ is 292.108 g $SF_6$.

**IN REAL LIFE**

One of the more annoying examples of the limiting reactant concept in real life is the way the number of hot dogs in a package never equals the number of hot dog rolls in a package. Typically, you get eight hot dogs in a package but only six hot dog rolls. If you like to eat your hot dog with a roll, then hot dog rolls are the limiting reactant.

## PRACTICE 47: Limiting Reactants

Decide if each statement that follows is true (**T**) or false (**F**). Write the correct letter on each line.

__T__ **1.** The reactant used up first in the reaction is called the limiting reactant because it limits the amount of product that can be made.

__F__ **2.** Once the limiting reactant is used up, more product can be made if you just wait long enough.

__T__ **3.** Reactants that exceed their stoichiometric amounts are said to be in excess, or are called excess reactants, because they will not be used up completely in the reaction.

__T__ **4.** If you have 15 slices of bread and 15 slices of cheese, and each grilled cheese sandwich uses up 2 slices of bread and 1 slice of cheese, then bread is the limiting reactant.

__F__ **5.** If you have 7 T-shirts, 6 pairs of pants, and 5 pairs of socks, and each day you wear a different shirt, pair of pants, and pair of socks, then you can go 7 days before wearing any of the same clothes again.

__T__ **6.** If you have 3 mol $H_2$ and 5 mol $Cl_2$, and you are making HCl according to the balanced chemical equation $H_2 + Cl_2 \longrightarrow 2\ HCl$, then $H_2$ is the limiting reactant.

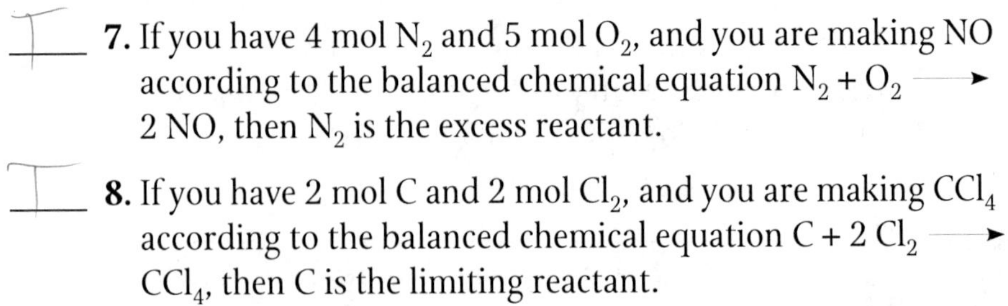

T 7. If you have 4 mol $N_2$ and 5 mol $O_2$, and you are making NO according to the balanced chemical equation $N_2 + O_2 \longrightarrow 2\ NO$, then $N_2$ is the excess reactant.

T 8. If you have 2 mol C and 2 mol $Cl_2$, and you are making $CCl_4$ according to the balanced chemical equation $C + 2\ Cl_2 \longrightarrow CCl_4$, then C is the limiting reactant.

## Reaction Yields

The amount of product obtained from a chemical reaction is called the **yield** of the reaction. The yield is typically expressed as mass (in grams, for instance). But it can also be expressed in moles or numbers of atoms, molecules, ions, and so forth.

When you do chemistry on paper, the limiting reactant always reacts completely with the excess reactant or reactants. According to the balanced chemical equation, all of the product, as predicted by stoichiometry, is formed. The amount of product predicted by stoichiometry is called the **theoretical yield** of the reaction.

The theoretical yield is the *maximum* amount of product that is obtainable from a reaction. In fact, if you ever perform chemistry experiments in a laboratory and obtain more product than the theoretical yield, then you should recognize that something is wrong. Perhaps your product is mixed with one of the excess reactants. Maybe your product is wet, or contains a piece of broken glass from the apparatus used to prepare it.

When you do chemistry in the laboratory, you rarely, if ever, obtain the theoretical yield. The amount of product you actually obtain from a reaction is called the **actual yield.**

The actual yield differs from the theoretical yield for many reasons. Sometimes reactions stop before the limiting reactant is used up. Sometimes reactions are reversible. A **reversible reaction** means that the reactants react with one another to form the products. Also, the products react with one another to re-form the reactants. Sometimes there are **side reactions.** That is, sometimes small amounts of the products may react with one another or with some of the reactants to form different products.

Finally, when you try to isolate your product at the end of the reaction, it is impossible to recover every last bit of it, no matter how careful you are. Some always sticks to the glassware or the filter paper, or whatever materials you are using.

The yield of a reaction can also be reported as a **percent yield**. A percent yield is the actual yield expressed as a percentage of the theoretical yield.

$$\text{Percent yield} = \left(\frac{\text{Actual yield}}{\text{Theoretical yield}}\right)(100\%)$$

For example, suppose you run the reaction of 64.132 g of sulfur (S) and 379.96 g of $F_2$ described on page 123. As calculated on pages 123 to 125, the maximum amount of $SF_6$ that can form is 292.108 g. Thus, the theoretical yield of $SF_6$ is 292.108 g. If the actual yield of $SF_6$ is 224.92 g, then the percent yield is 76.999%.

$$\text{Percent yield} = \left(\frac{224.92\text{ g}}{292.11\text{ g}}\right)(100\%) = 77.0\%$$

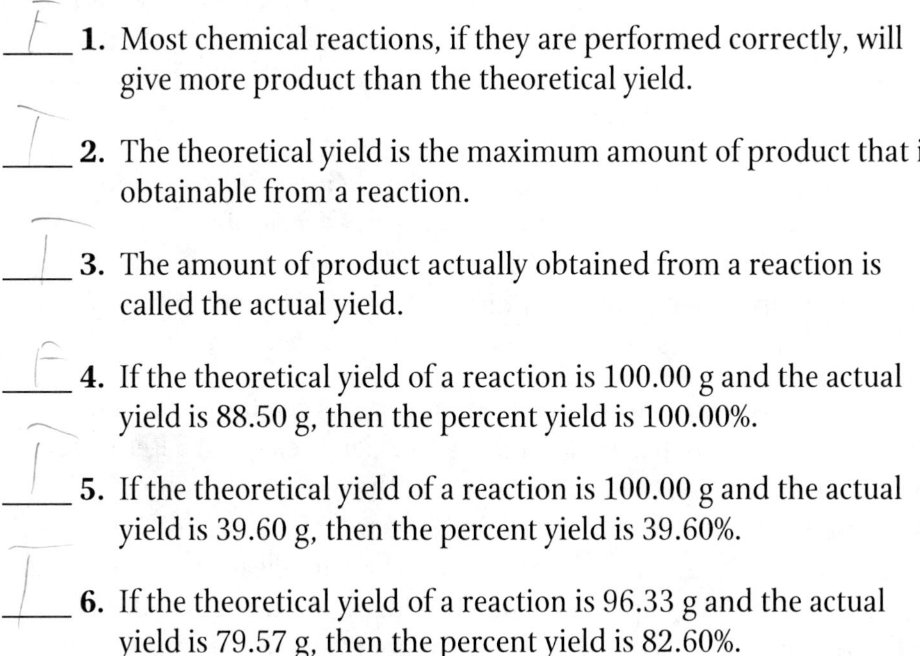

## PRACTICE 48: Reaction Yields

Decide if each statement that follows is true (**T**) or false (**F**). Write the correct letter on each line.

__F__ **1.** Most chemical reactions, if they are performed correctly, will give more product than the theoretical yield.

__T__ **2.** The theoretical yield is the maximum amount of product that is obtainable from a reaction.

__T__ **3.** The amount of product actually obtained from a reaction is called the actual yield.

__F__ **4.** If the theoretical yield of a reaction is 100.00 g and the actual yield is 88.50 g, then the percent yield is 100.00%.

__T__ **5.** If the theoretical yield of a reaction is 100.00 g and the actual yield is 39.60 g, then the percent yield is 39.60%.

__T__ **6.** If the theoretical yield of a reaction is 96.33 g and the actual yield is 79.57 g, then the percent yield is 82.60%.

# LESSON 11: Types of Chemical Bonds

GOAL: To understand the similarities and differences of ionic bonding, covalent bonding, and metallic bonding

## WORDS TO KNOW

**bond distance**
**chemical bonds**
**covalent bond**
**electronegativity**
**ionic bond**
**metallic bonds**
**polar covalent bonds**

## Ionic Bonding

You learned in Unit 2, page 81, that the atoms in a molecule are bound together in a specific shape. They are held together by attractive forces called bonds. At the time, you were asked to think of bonds as pairs of electrons shared between two atoms. It is now time to discuss chemical bonds in greater detail.

**Chemical bonds** are the forces that hold atoms or ions together in compounds. In sodium chloride (NaCl), the forces that hold sodium cations ($Na^+$) together with chloride anions ($Cl^-$) are the attractions of opposite charges. A bond that forms when oppositely charged ions attract each other is called an **ionic bond**.

In Unit 2, page 78, an ionic compound is defined as one that forms when cations and anions combine to make an electrically neutral compound. Alternatively, you can now say that compounds containing ionic bonds are called ionic compounds. You will remember that ionic compounds are also known as salts.

Ionic bonds tend to form between metals that readily lose valence electrons and nonmetals that readily gain valence electrons. Remember from Unit 2, page 89, that the electrons in the outermost occupied shell of an atom are called valence electrons. The metals in Groups 1 and 2 of the periodic table readily lose one and two valence electrons, respectively. The nonmetals in Group 17, on the other hand, readily gain one valence electron. Thus, NaCl forms because each neutral Na atom gives up one valence electron to each neutral Cl atom. The resulting $Na^+$ cations and $Cl^-$ anions then attract each other because they have opposite charges.

The drawing on the right shows the structure of NaCl. The structure of a compound is the three-dimensional arrangement of the atoms or ions in the compound. The structure of a compound is the direct result of the kind of bonding in the compound. In the case of NaCl, the ionic bonds between $Na^+$ cations and $Cl^-$ anions create a structure in which $Na^+$ cations alternate with $Cl^-$ anions. This pattern extends in all three directions.

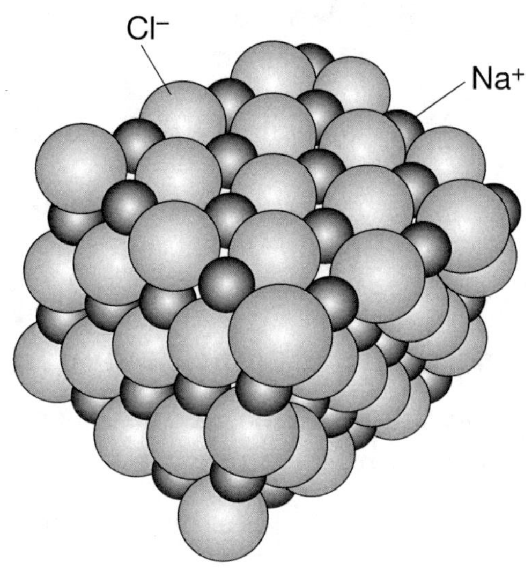


It is difficult to see in the drawing, but each $Na^+$ cation is surrounded by six $Cl^-$ anions. Also, each $Cl^-$ anion is surrounded by six $Na^+$ cations. This occurs because the attraction of oppositely charged ions occurs in all directions. That is, if a $Na^+$ cation is attracted to a $Cl^-$ anion on one side, it can be attracted to another $Cl^-$ anion on the other side. The same is true of the $Cl^-$ anions in NaCl.

Not every ionic compound has *exactly* the same structure as NaCl. There is one reason why the structure of NaCl is representative of all ionic compounds, however. Cations and anions alternate in such a way that the entire substance is held together by the attraction of the opposite charges.

## PRACTICE 49: Ionic Bonding

Decide if each statement that follows is true (**T**) or false (**F**). Write the correct letter on each line.

_T_ **1.** Chemical bonds are the forces that hold atoms or ions together in compounds.

_F_ **2.** A bond that forms when similarly charged ions attract each other is called an ionic bond.

T 3. A bond that forms when oppositely charged ions attract each other is called an ionic bond.

T 4. The structure of a compound is the three-dimensional arrangement of the atoms or ions in the compound.

F 5. Compounds that contain ionic bonds are called metalloids.

T 6. The structure of a compound is the direct result of the kind of bonding in the compound.

## Properties of Ionic Compounds

Ionic compounds have certain characteristic properties that particularly contrast with the properties of metals.

- Ionic compounds are hard, which means they do not dent.
- Ionic compounds are rigid, which means they do not bend.
- Ionic compounds are brittle, which means they crack when struck forcefully enough.
- Ionic compounds have high melting points and high boiling points (though not as high as many metals).
- Most ionic compounds do not conduct electricity in the solid state. However, they do conduct electricity when melted or dissolved in water.

The properties of ionic compounds can be explained by their ionic bonds. NaCl will be used as an example again. You may want to refer to the structure of NaCl shown on page 129.

The alternating arrangement of $Na^+$ and $Cl^-$ in NaCl means that the forces that hold the ions in place (the ionic bonds) are strong and extend in all directions. As a result, it is difficult to move the ions out of their places in the crystal. In other words, NaCl resists denting and bending the way a metal would.

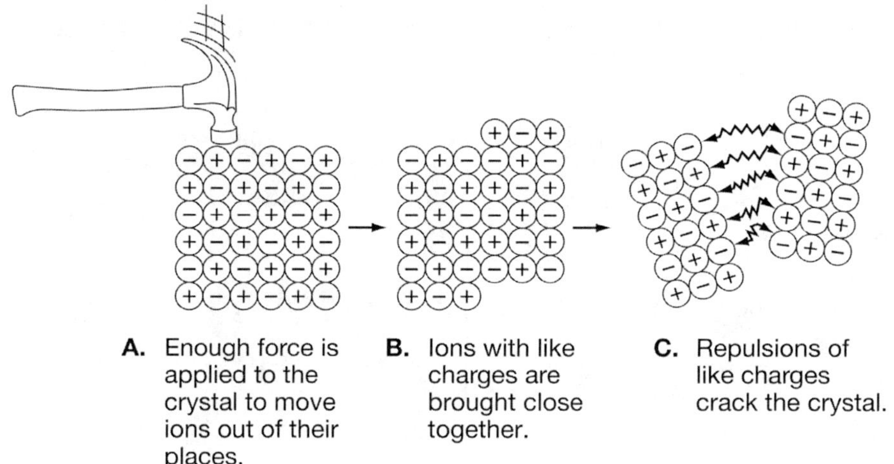

**A.** Enough force is applied to the crystal to move ions out of their places.

**B.** Ions with like charges are brought close together.

**C.** Repulsions of like charges crack the crystal.

If enough force *is* applied to move the ions out of their places in the crystal, then ions with like charges are brought close together. When this happens, their repulsions crack the crystal. This is shown in the drawing above.

In Unit 1, page 22, you learned that melting occurs when a solid changes to a liquid. At the atomic/molecular level, melting occurs when enough energy is added to the solid to free the atoms or molecules or ions of the solid from their fairly rigid positions in the solid. They then have enough energy to begin to slide past one another. Ionic compounds have high melting points. That is because it takes a lot of energy to free the ions from their positions in the solid. In other words, it takes a lot of energy to overcome the attraction between the opposite charges (the ionic bonds).

Remember, also, that boiling occurs when a liquid changes to a gas. At the atomic/molecular level, boiling occurs when enough energy is added to the liquid to completely separate the atoms or molecules or ions from the rest of the liquid. Ionic compounds have high boiling points. This is because it takes even more energy to vaporize them than it does to melt them.

The following table lists melting points and boiling points for some ionic compounds.

| Compound | Melting Point (°C) | Boiling Point (°C) | Compound | Melting Point (°C) | Boiling Point (°C) |
|---|---|---|---|---|---|
| LiI | 449 | 1180 | $CaCl_2$ | 782 | >1600 |
| CsBr | 636 | 1300 | $CaI_2$ | 784 | 1100 |
| CsCl | 645 | 1290 | NaCl | 801 | 1413 |
| NaI | 661 | 1304 | LiF | 845 | 1676 |
| KI | 681 | 1330 | KF | 858 | 1505 |
| $MgCl_2$ | 714 | 1412 | NaF | 993 | 1695 |
| RbCl | 718 | 1390 | $MgF_2$ | 1261 | 2239 |
| KBr | 734 | 1435 | MgO | 2852 | 3600 |

In order to conduct electricity, a substance must have mobile electrons or mobile ions. Ionic compounds have ions. But the ions are not mobile in the solid state. Thus, ionic compounds do not conduct electricity in the solid state. Once the ionic solid is melted, however, its ions are able to move enough to carry an electric current. Furthermore, when an ionic solid is dissolved in water, individual ions are separated from one another by water molecules. These ions are incredibly mobile. They conduct electricity very well.

## PRACTICE 50: Properties of Ionic Compounds

Decide if each statement that follows is true (**T**) or false (**F**). Write the correct letter on each line.

____ **1.** Ionic compounds are brittle, which means they crack when struck forcefully enough.

____ **2.** Ionic compounds dent and bend, just like metals.

____ **3.** Ionic compounds have high melting points because it takes a lot of energy to free the ions from their positions in the solid.

____ **4.** The properties of ionic compounds can be explained by their ionic bonds.

T 5. Ionic compounds have high boiling points because it takes even more energy to vaporize them than it does to melt them.

T 6. Ionic compounds crack when ions with like charges are brought close together.

## Covalent Bonding

The bond that holds two hydrogen atoms together in $H_2$ is very different from the forces that hold $Na^+$ and $Cl^-$ together in NaCl. Consider what happens when two separate hydrogen atoms approach each other.

As the two hydrogen atoms get closer to each other, the nucleus of each atom attracts the electron of the other atom. This pulls the two hydrogen atoms even closer to each other. There are repulsions between the two nuclei and between the two electrons. But, at some optimum distance, the net attractions exceed the net repulsions. The distance at which the attractions exceed the repulsions is called the **bond distance** or the bond length of the molecule. If the two atoms are pushed closer together than the bond distance, then net repulsions will exceed net attractions.

At the bond distance, the nuclei of the two hydrogen atoms attract the two electrons equally. The two hydrogen atoms share the pair of electrons. A bond that forms when two atoms share a pair of electrons is called a **covalent bond.** Compounds that contain covalent bonds are called covalent compounds.

In theory, Na and Cl atoms have electrons to share, also. Instead, Na completely gives up its valence electron to Cl. Thus, ionic bonds and covalent bonds are very different interactions.

Covalent bonds tend to form between nonmetals. That is, they tend to form between the atoms of elements that have similar properties. In contrast, ionic bonds form between metals that tend to lose valence electrons and nonmetals that tend to gain valence electrons.

Covalent bonds that form between identical atoms are also called nonpolar covalent bonds. The electron pairs in nonpolar covalent bonds are shared equally. The covalent bond in $H_2$ is a nonpolar covalent bond. The covalent bonds in $N_2$, $O_2$, $F_2$, $Cl_2$, $Br_2$, and $I_2$ are also nonpolar.

Covalent bonds also form between different atoms. When this happens, the electron pairs are not shared equally. That is, one atom attracts the electron pair more strongly than the other atom. The atom that attracts the electron pair more strongly ends up with a partial negative charge on it. Therefore, the other atom ends up with a partial positive charge on it. The partial charges are not nearly as strong as the charges on cations and anions. So, atoms with partial charges are not ions.

In HCl, for example, the Cl atom attracts the electron pair more strongly than the H atom. As a result, the electrons spend more time closer to Cl than they do to H. The Cl atom has a partial negative charge. The H atom has a partial positive charge. Covalent bonds that form between different atoms are called **polar covalent bonds.** Polar covalent bonds can be found in molecules such as HBr, HI, $PCl_3$, $SF_4$, $H_2O$ and $NH_3$.

**TIP**

> One way to help you remember the differences between ionic and covalent bonds is to think about the amount of electron sharing that takes place in each. At one extreme, there are ionic bonds. There is no electron sharing in ionic bonds. Instead, an electron has been transferred from one atom to the other. At the other extreme, there are nonpolar covalent bonds. There is complete electron sharing in nonpolar covalent bonds. Both atoms share the electron pair equally. In between the two extremes, there are polar covalent bonds. The electrons are shared, but they are shared unequally.

## PRACTICE 51: Covalent Bonding

Decide if each statement that follows is true (**T**) or false (**F**). Write the correct letter on each line.

_____ **1.** A bond that forms when two atoms share a pair of electrons is called a covalent bond.

_____ **2.** Covalent bonds that form between identical atoms are also called nonpolar covalent bonds.

T 3. Polar covalent bonds can be found in molecules, such as HCl, HBr, HI, and $PCl_3$.

F 4. The covalent bonds in $SF_4$ are nonpolar covalent bonds.

T 5. Covalent bonds tend to form between nonmetals.

## Electronegativity

You just learned that polar covalent bonds form when different atoms share electrons. At the time, you did not learn how to determine which atoms attract electron pairs more strongly than other atoms. One way to tell which atom in a covalent bond attracts the bonding electrons more strongly is to compare the electronegativities of the two atoms.

**Electronegativity** is the ability of an atom to attract bonding electrons to itself in a chemical compound. Elements with high electronegativities attract bonding electrons more strongly than elements with low electronegativities. On page 134, you learned that the Cl atom in HCl attracts the bonding pair of electrons more strongly than the H atom. Now, you can also say that the electronegativity of Cl is greater than the electronegativity of H.

Electronegativity values are relative estimates based on factors such as effective nuclear charge ($Z_{eff}$). Electronegativity values have no units because they are relative to one another, not measured experimentally. The following version of the periodic table lists the electronegativity values for all of the elements except for the noble gases and elements 103–112. These electronegativity values were determined in the early twentieth century by the American chemist Linus Pauling. Values for the noble gases are not included because they do not form bonds except in a few cases. Values are not included for elements 103–112 because they are not currently known.

In the periodic table, note that the electronegativity values increase from the lower left of the table to the upper right of the table. Francium (Fr) and cesium (Cs) have the lowest values (0.7). Fluorine (F) has the highest value (4.0). Additionally, values tend to decrease down a column. They also tend to increase across a row of the periodic table.

| 1 H 2.1 | | | | | | | | | | | | | | | | | 2 He |
|---|---|---|---|---|---|---|---|---|---|---|---|---|---|---|---|---|---|
| 3 Li 1.0 | 4 Be 1.5 | | | | | | | | | | | 5 B 2.0 | 6 C 2.5 | 7 N 3.0 | 8 O 3.5 | 9 F 4.0 | 10 Ne |
| 11 Na 0.9 | 12 Mg 1.2 | | | | | | | | | | | 13 Al 1.5 | 14 Si 1.8 | 15 P 2.1 | 16 S 2.5 | 17 Cl 3.0 | 18 Ar |
| 19 K 0.8 | 20 Ca 1.0 | 21 Sc 1.3 | 22 Ti 1.5 | 23 V 1.6 | 24 Cr 1.6 | 25 Mn 1.5 | 26 Fe 1.8 | 27 Co 1.8 | 28 Ni 1.8 | 29 Cu 1.9 | 30 Zn 1.6 | 31 Ga 1.6 | 32 Ge 1.8 | 33 As 2.0 | 34 Se 2.4 | 35 Br 2.8 | 36 Kr |
| 37 Rb 0.8 | 38 Sr 1.0 | 39 Y 1.2 | 40 Zr 1.4 | 41 Nb 1.6 | 42 Mo 1.8 | 43 Tc 1.9 | 44 Ru 2.2 | 45 Rh 2.2 | 46 Pd 2.2 | 47 Ag 1.9 | 48 Cd 1.7 | 49 In 1.7 | 50 Sn 1.8 | 51 Sb 1.9 | 52 Te 2.1 | 53 I 2.5 | 54 Xe |
| 55 Cs 0.7 | 56 Ba 0.9 | 71 Lu 1.3 | 72 Hf 1.3 | 73 Ta 1.5 | 74 W 1.7 | 75 Re 1.9 | 76 Os 2.2 | 77 Ir 2.2 | 78 Pt 2.2 | 79 Au 2.4 | 80 Hg 1.9 | 81 Tl 1.8 | 82 Pb 1.9 | 83 Bi 1.9 | 84 Po 2.0 | 85 At 2.2 | 86 Rn |
| 87 Fr 0.7 | 88 Ra 0.9 | 103 Lr | 104 Rf | 105 Db | 106 Sg | 107 Bh | 108 Hs | 109 Mt | | | | | | | | | |

| 57 La 1.1 | 58 Ce 1.1 | 59 Pr 1.1 | 60 Nd 1.1 | 61 Pm 1.2 | 62 Sm 1.2 | 63 Eu 1.1 | 64 Gd 1.2 | 65 Tb 1.2 | 66 Dy 1.2 | 67 Ho 1.2 | 68 Er 1.2 | 69 Tm 1.2 | 70 Yb 1.2 |
|---|---|---|---|---|---|---|---|---|---|---|---|---|---|
| 89 Ac 1.1 | 90 Th 1.3 | 91 Pa 1.5 | 92 U 1.7 | 93 Np 1.3 | 94 Pu 1.3 | 95 Am 1.3 | 96 Cm 1.3 | 97 Bk 1.3 | 98 Cf 1.3 | 99 Es 1.3 | 100 Fm 1.3 | 101 Md 1.3 | 102 No 1.5 |

Electronegativity differences between the two atoms in a bond can be used to determine the relative ionic character of a series of bonds. Ionic character means the degree to which a bond is purely ionic. A series of strong ionic bonds has a strong ionic character. A series of weak ionic bonds has a weak ionic character. The Greek symbol Δ (delta) is used as an abbreviation to mean "change in" or "difference between." Here, ΔEN is the difference between the electronegativities of two elements. The greater the ΔEN, the greater the ionic character of the bond.

For example, the ΔEN for the bond in $F_2$ is zero, because both fluorine atoms have the same electronegativity. Thus, $F_2$ has a nonpolar covalent bond, and the pair of electrons is shared equally between both F atoms. At the other extreme is NaF. In NaF, ΔEN is 3.1, so NaF is an ionic compound in which sodium metal has completely transferred its valence electron to fluorine to form $Na^+$ and $F^-$. Finally, HF ($\Delta EN = 1.9$) falls somewhere in between $F_2$ and NaF. Thus, HF may be a polar covalent compound, but it has a certain amount of ionic character, too. HF demonstrates how difficult it is to classify compounds that fall in between the obvious extremes of ionic compounds and nonpolar covalent compounds.

## ■ PRACTICE 52: Electronegativity

Decide if each statement that follows is true (**T**) or false (**F**). Write the correct letter on each line.

__T__ **1.** Electronegativity is the ability of an atom to attract bonding electrons to itself in a chemical compound.

__T__ **2.** Elements with high electronegativities attract bonding electrons more strongly than elements with low electronegativities.

__F__ **3.** Electronegativity values decrease from the lower left of the periodic table to the upper right of the table.

__T__ **4.** Electronegativity values tend to decrease down a column and to increase across a row of the periodic table.

__F__ **5.** According to the periodic table on page 136, the electronegativity of iodine (I) is greater than the electronegativity of bromine (Br).

__F__ **6.** The Greek symbol Δ means "ionic bond."

__T__ **7.** Electronegativity values are not included for the noble gases because they do not form bonds.

## Properties of Covalent Compounds

You just learned that covalent bonds tend to form between nonmetals. As a result, the properties of covalent compounds are the properties of nonmetals. You learned in Unit 2, pages 69–70, that the characteristic properties of nonmetals are the following:

- Nonmetals are poor conductors of heat and electricity.

- Nonmetals are brittle in the solid form, which means they crack and break easily when placed under stress.

- Some nonmetals are solids, some are liquids, and some are gases at 25°C.

As with ionic compounds, the properties of covalent compounds can be explained by their covalent bonds. For example, covalent compounds are poor conductors of heat and electricity for two reasons. First, they do not contain ions. Second, their electrons are not mobile enough to carry heat or a current. Instead, the electrons in covalent compounds are localized around individual atoms. Or, they are shared between two atoms in a covalent bond.

Covalent compounds are brittle in the solid form. This is because their atoms are held rigidly in place by the covalent bonds. If a force is placed on the solid, the atoms can move only if covalent bonds are broken. When the bonds break, the solid crumbles.

Covalent bonds are very strong. In fact, they are stronger than ionic bonds. That is, they are stronger than the attractions of opposite charges in ionic compounds. Why, then, are covalent compounds like $H_2$ or $CH_4$ gases at 25°C? Why, then, are covalent compounds like $H_2O$ or $C_6H_{14}$ (hexane) liquids at 25°C? Why, finally, are covalent compounds like stearic acid ($C_{18}H_{36}O_2$, a fatty acid in beef) and sulfur ($S_8$) such low-melting-point solids at 25°C? If covalent bonds are so strong, why don't covalent compounds all have high melting points and high boiling points like ionic compounds?

The covalent bonds between the atoms of covalent compounds are very strong. The forces that hold individual molecules near one another in the bulk sample, however, are very weak. So it takes very little energy to separate molecules of $H_2$ or $H_2O$ or $S_8$ from other molecules of $H_2$ or $H_2O$ or $S_8$. It does take considerable energy, however, to separate the two hydrogen atoms in $H_2$, the hydrogen atoms and the oxygen atom in $H_2O$, or the sulfur atoms in $S_8$.

## IN REAL LIFE

Two covalent compounds are graphite and diamond. Most people have more daily encounters with graphite (used in pencils and as a lubricant) than with diamonds. Both substances, however, are covalent compounds made up solely of carbon atoms. Graphite and diamond have very different properties. But their differences can be traced to the way in which the carbon atoms are bonded to one another. That is, graphite and diamond have different structures. The structure of graphite consists of flat sheets of carbon atoms. The carbon atoms within each sheet are covalently bonded to one another. But there are no covalent bonds between sheets. Thus, graphite is soft and slippery. The sheets can slide past one another without breaking the covalent bonds within the sheets. This is why graphite is used as a lubricant for locks and other instruments with lots of moving parts. The structure of diamond, on the other hand, consists of a vast three-dimensional network of covalently bonded carbon atoms. The only way to move carbon atoms in diamond is to break the covalent bonds. This takes so much energy that diamond is one of the hardest materials known. As a result, it is used in industrial cutting tools. You may prize diamond as a gemstone, but remember that it is just another form of carbon, just like the graphite in your pencil.

## PRACTICE 53: Properties of Covalent Compounds

Decide if each statement that follows is true (**T**) or false (**F**). Write the correct letter on each line.

__T__ **1.** The properties of covalent compounds are the properties of nonmetals.

__F__ **2.** Covalent compounds are malleable and ductile, just like metals.

__T__ **3.** Covalent compounds are poor conductors of heat and electricity.

F **4.** Both graphite and diamond are covalent compounds made up solely of uranium atoms.

T **5.** The forces that hold individual molecules near one another in the bulk sample of a covalent compound are very weak.

F **6.** Unlike properties of ionic compounds, the properties of covalent compounds cannot be explained by their covalent bonds.

T **7.** Covalent compounds are brittle in the solid form because their atoms are held rigidly in place by the covalent bonds.

T **8.** Graphite and diamond have very different properties, but their differences can be traced to the way in which their carbon atoms are bonded to one another.

## Metallic Bonding

So far you have learned that ionic bonds form when oppositely charged ions attract each other. The metal gives up its valence electrons to the nonmetal to form a cation and an anion, respectively. Furthermore, you have learned that covalent bonds form when nonmetals share pairs of electrons. The pairs of electrons are localized (confined to a bond between two atoms) between the two nonmetals.

The bonds that hold metal atoms together are called **metallic bonds.** Metallic bonds are different from ionic bonds and covalent bonds. To understand metallic bonds, you must understand that the positively charged nuclei of metal atoms attract their inner shell electrons very strongly. But they attract their valence electrons weakly. This is why metals, such as Na or Mg, readily form cations that participate in ionic bonds.

The atoms in a sample of a metal such as Na, Mg, Cu, or Al contribute their weakly-held valence electrons to a vast electron "sea." This "sea" surrounds all of the metal atoms in the sample. That is, the valence electrons are delocalized throughout the sample. They are shared by all of the metal atoms in the sample.

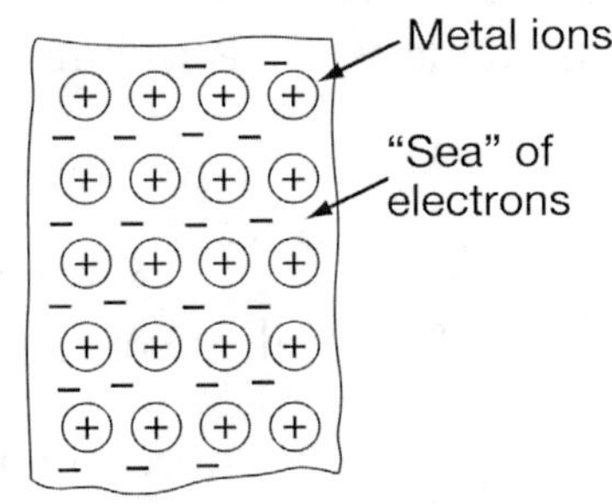

The metal atoms in a sample of a metal can be viewed as cations immersed in a "sea" of valence electrons. Similarly, the metallic bonds can be viewed as the result of the mutual attraction of the metal cations for the mobile, delocalized electrons. The drawing on page 140 may help you visualize metallic bonding.

## ■ PRACTICE 54: Metallic Bonding

Decide if each statement that follows is true (**T**) or false (**F**). Write the correct letter on each line.

T **1.** The bonds that hold metal atoms together are called metallic bonds.

T **2.** The atoms in a sample of a metal, such as Na, Mg, Cu, or Al, contribute their weakly-held valence electrons to a vast electron "sea" that surrounds all of the metal atoms in the sample.

F **3.** Metallic bonds are no different from ionic bonds and covalent bonds.

F **4.** Metallic bonds can be viewed as the result of the mutual attraction of metal anions for mobile, delocalized electrons.

T **5.** The valence electrons in a metal sample are delocalized throughout the sample and are shared by ALL of the metal atoms in the sample.

T **6.** The positively charged nuclei of metal atoms attract their inner shell electrons very strongly, but attract their valence electrons only weakly.

T **7.** The metal atoms in a sample of a metal can be viewed as cations immersed in a "sea" of valence electrons.

F **8.** Metallic bonds are really just covalent bonds between metals.

## Properties of Metals

You have learned that the ions in ionic compounds are held rigidly in place by the attraction of oppositely charged ions. This affects the properties of ionic compounds. You have learned that the localized electron-pair sharing in covalent compounds affects the properties of covalent compounds.

It stands to reason, then, that the properties of metallic bonds should greatly affect the properties of metals, too. In order to understand how the properties of metallic bonds influence the properties of metals, you need to keep in mind two things. First, the metal ions in a metal sample are held in an orderly fashion by the sea of valence electrons. But metal ions are not held as rigidly as the ions in ionic compounds. Second, the metal ions share electrons. But they share electrons with *all* of the other metal ions in the sample. Unlike covalent compounds, they do not share individual electron pairs with any other particular atom or ion.

You learned in Unit 2, page 69, that metals have certain characteristic properties.

- Metals are good conductors of heat and electricity.
- Metals are malleable, which means they can be hammered into thin sheets.
- Metals are ductile, which means they can be drawn into wires.
- Metals have moderately high melting points, but very high boiling points.

As with ionic compounds and covalent compounds, the properties of metals can be explained by their metallic bonds. For example, metals are good conductors of electricity because they contain metal ions that are not held rigidly in place. They are also good conductors because the sea of valence electrons is mobile enough to carry a current. Metals are good conductors of heat for the same reason. The delocalized electrons are mobile enough to carry heat away from whatever the metal comes in contact with.

Metals are malleable and ductile. They can be bent or dented without cracking or shattering because the metal ions are not held rigidly in place. If you hit the metal with a hammer, the metal ions slide past one another in the sea of electrons and assume new positions in the now dented sample. Metal ions are never forced up against one another, as they are in ionic compounds. So, the metal deforms instead of cracking or shattering. The drawing on the next page illustrates this concept.

Most metals have only moderately high melting points. This is because the attractions between the metal ions and the valence electrons are not severed when the solid metal becomes a liquid. In the liquid, the metal ions still swim in a sea of electrons. They just swim more quickly. Their positions in the sample are less regular. Most metals have very high boiling points, however. This is because vaporizing a metal means that the attractions between the metal ions and the valence electrons do have to be severed.

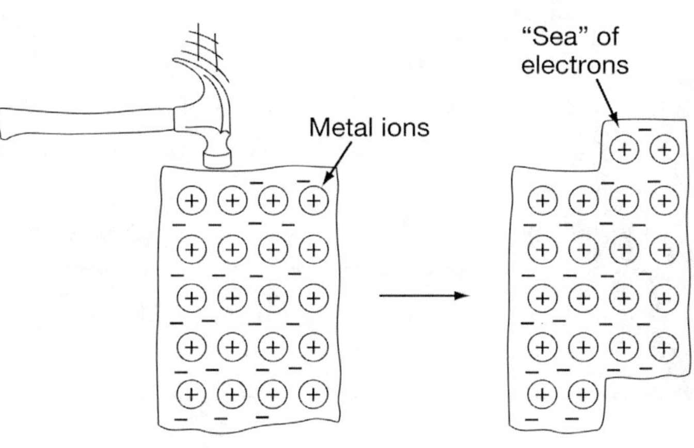

**A.** A force is applied to the metal.
**B.** The metal deforms without cracking or shattering.

The following table lists melting points and boiling points for several metals.

| Element | Melting Point (°C) | Boiling Point (°C) | Element | Melting Point (°C) | Boiling Point (°C) |
|---|---|---|---|---|---|
| Mercury (Hg) | –38.9 | 357 | Copper (Cu) | 1083 | 2570 |
| Gallium (Ga) | 29.8 | 2403 | Uranium (U) | 1130 | 3930 |
| Sodium (Na) | 97.8 | 883 | Nickel (Ni) | 1453 | 2732 |
| Lithium (Li) | 180 | 1347 | Iron (Fe) | 1535 | 2750 |
| Tin (Sn) | 232 | 2623 | Platinum (Pt) | 1772 | 3827 |
| Aluminum (Al) | 660 | 2467 | Ruthenium (Ru) | 2310 | 3900 |
| Barium (Ba) | 727 | 1850 | Tantalum (Ta) | 2996 | 5425 |
| Silver (Ag) | 961 | 2155 | Osmium (Os) | 3045 | 5027 |
| Gold (Au) | 1064 | 3080 | Tungsten (W) | 3407 | 5660 |

THINK ABOUT IT

Most of the elements in the periodic table are metals. So, metals show a wide range of melting points, boiling points, hardnesses, and abilities to conduct heat and electricity. For example, tungsten (W) is not very ductile and has a very high melting point (3407°C). The melting point of gallium (Ga), however, is only 29.8°C, which is less than normal human body temperature (37°C). Which metal, W or Ga, do you think is used for the filament in lightbulbs? Why?

## PRACTICE 55: Properties of Metals

Decide if each statement that follows is true (**T**) or false (**F**). Write the correct letter on each line.

_____ **1.** The properties of metals can be explained by their metallic bonds.

_____ **2.** Metals are good conductors of electricity because they contain metal ions that are not held rigidly in place, and because the sea of valence electrons is mobile enough to carry a current.

_____ **3.** If you hit a metal with a hammer, the metal ions slide past one another in the sea of electrons and assume new positions in the now dented sample.

_____ **4.** The metal ions in a metal sample are held just as rigidly as the ions in ionic compounds.

_____ **5.** Most metals have very high melting points but only moderately high boiling points.

_____ **6.** Metals are good conductors of heat because the delocalized electrons are mobile enough to carry heat away from whatever the metal comes in contact with.

_____ **7.** Most metals have very high boiling points because vaporizing a metal means that the attractions between the metal ions and the valence electrons have to be severed.

_____ **8.** Metals are malleable and ductile because they have polar covalent bonds.

## UNIT 3 REVIEW

Circle the letter of the correct answer.

**1.** The balanced form of the equation $FeO + O_2 \longrightarrow Fe_2O_3$ is _____.

**a.** $2\ FeO + O_2 \longrightarrow Fe_2O_3$

**b.** $4\ FeO + O_2 \longrightarrow 2\ Fe_2O_3$

**c.** $2\ FeO + 2\ O_2 \longrightarrow Fe_2O_3$

**2.** The substances formed in a chemical reaction are called the _____.

**a.** reactants

**b.** products

**c.** stoichiometric coefficients

**3.** The study of the quantitative relationships between the amounts of reactants and products in a chemical reaction is called _____.

**a.** the limiting reactant

**b.** stoichiometry

**c.** the molar ratio

**4.** 73.1073 g of $C_8H_{18}$ (MM = 114.2302 g/mol) is the same as _____.

**a.** 0.6400 mol of $C_8H_{18}$

**b.** $3.854 \times 10^{23}$ molecules of $C_8H_{18}$

**c.** both *a* and *b*

**5.** Stoichiometry can be used to calculate _____.

**a.** how much of one substance reacts with another substance

**b.** how much of a product can form from a known amount of a reactant

**c.** both *a* and *b*

**6.** According to the balanced equation $UF_4 + 2\ Mg \longrightarrow U + 2\ MgF_2$, for every 1 mol of $UF_4$ consumed, you _____.

**a.** need 2 mol Mg

**b.** get 1 mol U

**c.** both *a* and *b*

**7.** The forces that hold atoms together in compounds are called _____.

**a.** chemical bonds

**b.** limiting reactants

**c.** molar ratios

8. A bond that forms when two atoms share a pair of electrons is called ______.
   a. a metallic bond
   b. an ionic bond
   c. a covalent bond

9. A bond that forms when oppositely charged ions attract each other is called ______.
   a. a metallic bond
   b. an ionic bond
   c. a covalent bond

10. Electronegativity values ______.
    a. tend to decrease down a column and to increase across a row of the periodic table
    b. are the same for all elements except F, Cl, Br, and I
    c. neither *a* nor *b*

## UNIT 3 APPLICATION ACTIVITY 1

### Hopping Raisins

Create a chemical reaction that simulates carbonation, such as that in soda, that will make raisins hop!

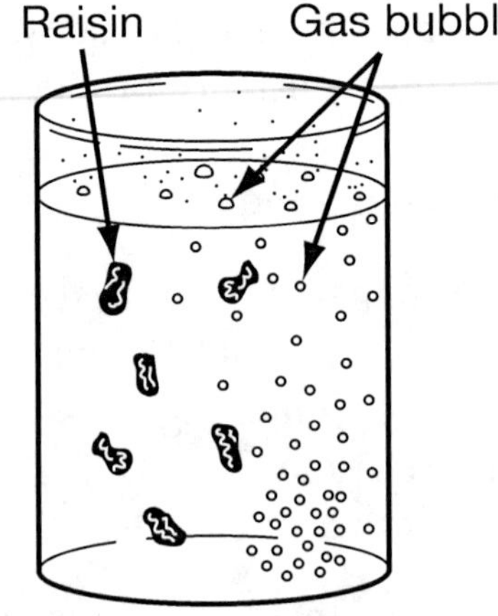


Fill a large (10- or 12-ounce), clear drinking glass with water. Add 15 ml (1 tablespoon) of baking soda and a drop or two of food coloring. Stir well.

Drop in a handful of raisins (popcorn kernels or mothballs can also be used), and stir in 45 ml (3 tablespoons) of vinegar. Observe the raisins for several minutes.

What do you observe happening?

What chemical reaction is taking place here?

## UNIT 3 APPLICATION ACTIVITY 2

### A Toast to Toast

Often you are told to eat toast when you are ill with an upset stomach. This demonstration will show you why.

Get one piece each of untoasted white bread and of toasted white bread. Fill a drinking glass half full of water. Mix in 5 ml (1 teaspoon) of household iodine. Pour the water-iodine solution into a pie dish. Tear off a strip of untoasted bread and a strip of toasted bread, each about 2 cm (1 inch) wide. Dip them both into the solution of iodine-water.

What do you observe?

Starch and iodine combine chemically to form starch iodide, which is blue-black. Therefore, iodine is used to test for starch. What does this tell you about your observations?

Is toasting an endothermic (heat-requiring) or exothermic (heat-releasing) reaction?

___

___

The process of starch digestion begins in your mouth. This process chemically changes starch to other, simpler substances. Can you now explain why toast is recommended when you have an upset stomach?

___

___

___

___

## UNIT 3 APPLICATION ACTIVITY 3

### Nature's Chemical Color

The colors of wildflowers depend on combinations of chemicals produced by nature. Just as these colors are formed, they can also be destroyed. In this activity, you will create a chemical reaction that affects flower colors.

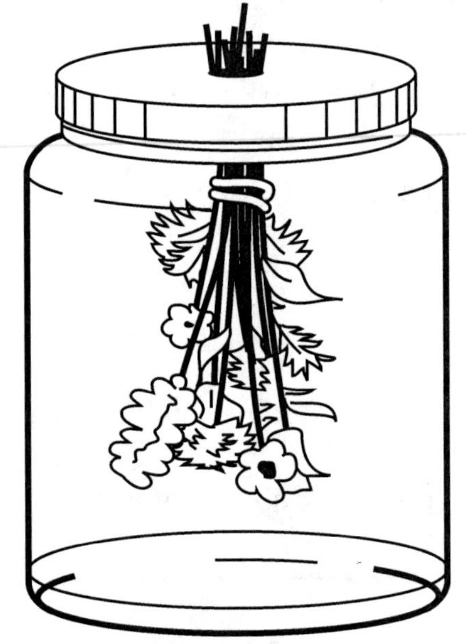

Gather a variety of wildflowers (ten different types of various colors will do). Gather the flowers so that all the stems are in a bunch. Use a rubber band to hold the stems together. Using a clean mayonnaise jar or a juice bottle with a plastic lid, cut a hole in the jar lid with scissors, so that the stems of the flowers will fit snugly through the hole. Push the stems into the hole so when the lid is put back on the jar, the flowers will be suspended upside down in the jar. Pour just enough ammonia into the jar to cover the bottom.

**Caution:** Do not breathe in ammonia vapors. Ammonia vapors could make you feel dizzy or sick.

Carefully place the lid on the jar. Let the flowers stay in the jar, suspended over the ammonia, for about 30 minutes.

What do you observe happening?

___

___

___

___

___

Why do you think this happened?

___

___

___

___

___

Why did the flowers turn green?

___

___

___

___

___

# UNIT 4

## Topics in Chemistry

# LESSON 12: Intermolecular Forces

GOAL: To learn about the forces that determine whether a substance is a solid, a liquid, or a gas

## WORDS TO KNOW

**adhesive forces**
**amorphous solids**
**cohesive forces**
**crystalline solids**
**dipolar forces**
**dipole moment**
**dispersion forces**
**hydrogen bonding**
**ideal gas equation**
**intermolecular forces**
**intramolecular forces**
**ionic solids**
**kinetic energy**
**London forces**
**metallic solids**
**molecular solids**
**network covalent solids**
**surface tension**
**universal gas constant**
**viscosity**

## Intermolecular Forces Versus Intramolecular Forces

In Unit 3, page 128, you learned that chemical bonds are the forces that hold atoms or ions together in compounds. Chemical bonds are called **intramolecular forces** because they are forces within the molecule (or ion). **Intermolecular forces** are the forces that exist between individual molecules. The forces between individual molecules may be attractions or repulsions or both.

TIP

The discussion of intermolecular forces versus intramolecular forces can be confusing if you get hung up on the words alone. The difference between *intermolecular* and *intramolecular* is the difference between *inter* and *intra. Inter* means between two of the same kind of things. *Intra* means within one of those things. For example, a farmer in Idaho sells potatoes to a potato chip maker in Portland, Oregon. This is called interstate commerce. Then the potato chip maker sells her chips to a consumer in Eugene, Oregon. This is called intrastate commerce.

Intermolecular forces are much weaker than intramolecular forces (chemical bonds). In Unit 3, on pages 133–134, for example, you learned that the covalent bonds between the atoms of covalent compounds are very strong. But the forces that hold individual molecules near one another in the bulk sample are very weak. So, it takes very little energy to separate molecules of $Cl_2$, $Br_2$, or $I_2$ from other molecules of $Cl_2$, $Br_2$, or $I_2$. It does take considerable energy, however, to separate the two chlorine atoms in $Cl_2$, the two bromine atoms in $Br_2$, or the two iodine atoms in $I_2$. This is why covalent compounds can be gases ($Cl_2$), liquids ($Br_2$), or low-melting-point solids ($I_2$) at 25°C.

Intramolecular forces tend to influence the chemical properties of a substance. Chemical properties have to do with chemical reactions (chemical changes), in which one substance is transformed into another. The only way for one substance to be transformed into another is for chemical bonds to be broken and formed.

Intermolecular forces, on the other hand, tend to influence the physical properties of a substance. Physical properties are characteristics of the substance itself. They include things like melting point and boiling point.

## PRACTICE 56: Intermolecular Forces Versus Intramolecular Forces

Decide if each statement that follows is true (**T**) or false (**F**). Write the correct letter on each line.

__T__ **1.** Chemical bonds are called intramolecular forces because they are forces within the molecule.

__T__ **2.** Intermolecular forces tend to influence the physical properties of a substance.

__F__ **3.** Physical properties have to do with chemical reactions (chemical changes), in which one substance is transformed into another.

__F__ **4.** The forces between individual molecules are attractions only.

__T__ **5.** Intermolecular forces are the forces that exist between individual molecules.

T 6. Intramolecular forces tend to influence the chemical properties of a substance.

F 7. Chemical properties include things like melting points and boiling points.

T 8. Intermolecular forces are much weaker than intramolecular forces (chemical bonds).

## How Intermolecular Forces Affect Physical State

**Kinetic energy** is the energy an object has due to its motion. The object may be anything. It may be a car speeding down a freeway, a surfer riding a wave, or a molecule in a beaker. If the speed of the molecule increases, then so does its kinetic energy. Similarly, raising the temperature of the molecule increases its kinetic energy. This is because raising the molecule's temperature increases its speed.

The physical state of a substance (whether it is a gas, a liquid, or a solid) depends on the balance between the intermolecular forces in the substance and the kinetic energy of the substance. For example, chlorine ($Cl_2$) is a gas at 25°C. This is because the kinetic energy of $Cl_2$ is much greater than the intermolecular forces between $Cl_2$ molecules. As a result, $Cl_2$ molecules are free to move about their container. Compared to a liquid or a solid, the molecules of a gas are very far apart.

Bromine ($Br_2$) is a liquid at 25°C. This is because the attractions between bromine molecules (the intermolecular forces) are much more in balance with the kinetic energy of the $Br_2$ molecules. As a result, the $Br_2$ molecules have enough kinetic energy to flow past one another. But the intermolecular forces are strong enough to hold the individual molecules close to one another.

Iodine ($I_2$) is a solid at 25°C. This is because the intermolecular forces are much greater than the kinetic energy of the $I_2$ molecules. Therefore, the intermolecular forces are strong enough to hold the $I_2$ molecules very close to one another in fixed positions.

A solid can be melted into a liquid. However, in order to melt a solid, the kinetic energy of the molecules in the solid must be raised sufficiently to overcome the intermolecular forces holding the solid together. Usually, the easiest way to raise the kinetic energy of the molecules in the solid is to raise their temperature by heating the solid. Similarly, a liquid freezes to a solid when the temperature of the liquid is lowered so that its kinetic energy can no longer compete with the intermolecular forces.

Once the solid has been melted into a liquid, the liquid can be vaporized into a gas. In order to vaporize a liquid, the temperature of the liquid must be raised so that the molecules have sufficient kinetic energy to escape the intermolecular forces holding the liquid together. Similarly, a gas condenses to a liquid when the temperature of the gas is lowered so that its kinetic energy no longer exceeds the intermolecular forces.

Finally, a solid can be sublimed to a gas if the kinetic energy of the solid molecules can be raised enough to greatly exceed the intermolecular forces. Similarly, deposition occurs when the kinetic energy of the gas molecules is lowered so that the intermolecular forces once again greatly exceed the kinetic energy. Remember that sublimation is when a substance changes from a solid to a gas without going through a liquid phase. Remember also that deposition is when a substance changes from a gas to a solid without going through a liquid phase.

## PRACTICE 57: How Intermolecular Forces Affect Physical State

Decide if each statement that follows is true (**T**) or false (**F**). Write the correct letter on each line.

_____ **1.** Kinetic energy is the energy an object has due to its motion.

_____ **2.** Decreasing the speed of a molecule raises its kinetic energy.

_____ **3.** Raising the temperature of the molecule increases its kinetic energy, because raising its temperature increases its speed.

_____ **4.** The physical state of a substance (whether it is a gas, a liquid, or a solid) depends on the balance between the intermolecular forces in the substance and the kinetic energy of the substance.

_____ **5.** Chlorine ($Cl_2$) is a solid at 25°C because the kinetic energy of $Cl_2$ is much greater than the intermolecular forces between $Cl_2$ molecules.

T 6. Bromine ($Br_2$) is a liquid at 25°C because the attractions between bromine molecules (the intermolecular forces) are in balance with the kinetic energy of the $Br_2$ molecules.

T 7. Iodine ($I_2$) is a solid at 25°C because the intermolecular forces are much greater than the kinetic energy of the $I_2$ molecules.

F 8. Compared to a liquid or a solid, the molecules of a gas are very close together.

## Dipole Moments

In Unit 3, pages 133–134, you learned that chemical bonds, in which one atom has a partial negative charge and the other atom has a partial positive charge, are called polar bonds. The H–Cl bond in HCl is a polar bond. So are the C–Cl bonds in $CCl_4$ (carbon tetrachloride), the O–H bonds in $H_2O$ (water), and the C–O bonds in $CO_2$ (carbon dioxide).

Polar bonds in a molecule tend to give the entire molecule a negative end and a positive end. Molecules that have a region of partial negative charge and a region of partial positive charge are called polar molecules. HCl and $H_2O$ are polar molecules. In the following drawing, the regions of partial negative charge are indicated by the symbol "$\delta^-$" and the regions of partial positive charge are indicated by the symbol "$\delta^+$." The arrows indicate the polar bonds and point from the positive end of the bond to the negative end of the bond.

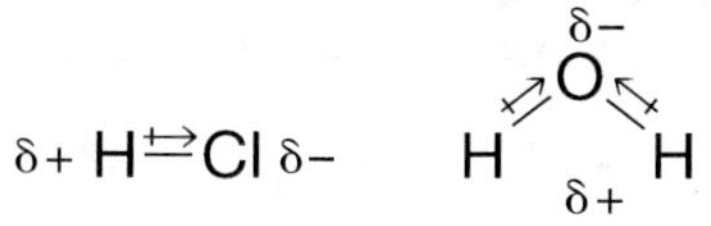

δ+ H⇸Cl δ−

HCl

δ−
O
H H
δ+

$H_2O$

Not all molecules are polar to the same extent. Some are more polar than others. For example, HF is more polar than HI because F is more electronegative than I. Electronegativity is a measure of the ability of an atom in a molecule to attract electrons to itself. The **dipole moment** of a molecule is a measure of the polarity of the molecule. The dipole moment of a molecule depends on the polarity of the individual bonds in the molecule and the shape of the molecule (that is, the structure of the molecule).

Molecules with no dipole moment are called nonpolar molecules. Examples of nonpolar molecules include $H_2$, $O_3$ (ozone), and $S_8$ (sulfur). These molecules are nonpolar because bonds between identical atoms are nonpolar.

Because the dipole moment of a molecule depends on the shape of the molecule, not all molecules with polar bonds are polar molecules. That is, not all molecules with polar bonds have a dipole moment. Examples of nonpolar molecules that have polar bonds include $CCl_4$ and $CO_2$. $CCl_4$ and $CO_2$ are nonpolar, despite their polar bonds, because their structures are such that the polar bonds cancel each other out. The drawing on the right may help you visualize how the bonds in $CCl_4$ and $CO_2$ cancel each other out.

## ■ PRACTICE 58: Dipole Moments

Decide if each statement that follows is true (**T**) or false (**F**). Write the correct letter on each line.

__F__ **1.** Molecules that have a region of partial negative charge and a region of partial positive charge are called nonpolar molecules.

__T__ **2.** HCl and $H_2O$ are polar molecules.

__F__ **3.** HF is more polar than HI because F is less electronegative than I.

__T__ **4.** The dipole moment of a molecule depends on the polarity of the individual bonds in the molecule and the shape of the molecule (that is, the structure of the molecule).

__T__ **5.** Molecules with no dipole moment are called nonpolar molecules.

__F__ **6.** All molecules are polar to the same extent.

__T__ **7.** Chemists determine the polarity of a molecule by measuring its dipole moment.

__T__ **8.** $CCl_4$ and $CO_2$ are nonpolar, despite their polar bonds, because their structures are such that the polar bonds cancel each other out.

THINK ABOUT IT

$BeF_2$ has the following linear structure: F–Be–F. The electronegativity of F is 4.0. The electronegativity of Be is 1.5. Given this information, are the two Be–F bonds in $BeF_2$ polar or nonpolar? Is $BeF_2$ a polar or nonpolar molecule? Write your answer on a separate sheet of paper.

## Dipolar Intermolecular Forces

There are two general types of intermolecular forces. The two types are called **dispersion forces** and **dipolar forces.** All substances experience dispersion forces. But only substances with permanent dipole moments experience dipolar forces. That is, nonpolar and polar molecules experience dispersion intermolecular forces. But only polar molecules experience dipolar intermolecular forces. Dispersion forces will be discussed in this lesson on page 165.

There are three types of dipolar intermolecular forces. The three types are called ion–dipole interactions, dipole–dipole interactions, and hydrogen bonds. Ion–dipole interactions are stronger than dipole–dipole interactions or hydrogen bonds. In most cases, hydrogen bonds are stronger than dipole–dipole interactions.

Ion–dipole interactions occur when a cation or an anion is attracted or repelled by the dipole moment of a polar molecule. For example, a cation is attracted to the negative end of a polar molecule. It is repelled by the positive end of the polar molecule. Similarly, an anion is repelled by the negative end of a polar molecule and is attracted to the positive end of a polar molecule. The following drawing illustrates ion–dipole interactions.

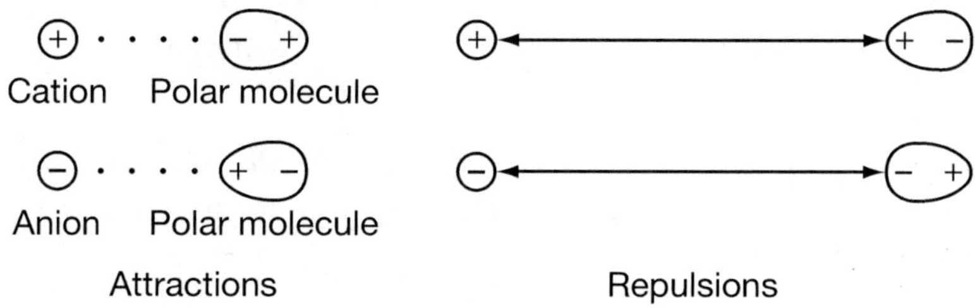


**Ion–Dipole Interactions**

**IN REAL LIFE**

Table salt (NaCl) dissolves in water because the ion–dipole interactions between $Na^+$ and the oxygen end of $H_2O$ and between $Cl^-$ and the hydrogen end of $H_2O$ are strong enough to overcome the attractions between $Na^+$ and $Cl^-$ in solid NaCl. Other salts, such as LiCl, KBr, and NaBr, dissolve in water for the same reason. This is also why ionic compounds conduct electricity so well when dissolved in water. The charges are separated from each other and are free to move about in a sea of water molecules instead of being locked rigidly into their positions in the solid.

Dipole–dipole interactions are similar to ion–dipole interactions. The difference is that they occur between two polar molecules instead of between an ion and a polar molecule. For example, dipole–dipole interactions occur when the positive end of one polar molecule attracts the negative end or repels the positive end of another polar molecule. Dipole–dipole interactions also occur when the negative end of one polar molecule repels the negative end or attracts the positive end of another polar molecule. This drawing illustrates dipole–dipole interactions.

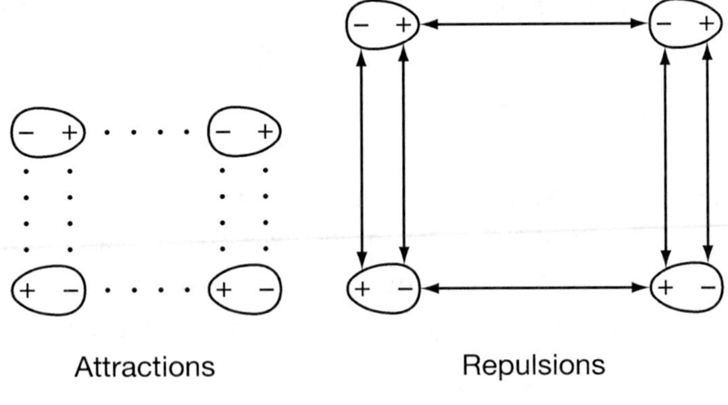


**Dipole–Dipole Interactions**

Hydrogen bonds are not bonds at all. They are particularly strong dipolar intermolecular interactions. Hydrogen bonding will be discussed on page 161.

## PRACTICE 59: Dipolar Intermolecular Forces

Decide if each statement that follows is true (**T**) or false (**F**). Write the correct letter on each line.

____ **1.** The two types of intermolecular forces are called dispersion forces and dipolar forces.

____ **2.** Only substances with permanent dipole moments experience dipolar forces.

____ **3.** The three types of dipolar intermolecular forces are called ion–dipole interactions, dipole–dipole interactions, and metallic bonds.

____ **4.** If a sodium cation, $Na^+$, is attracted to the negative end of a polar molecule such as $H_2O$, it is a dipole–dipole interaction.

____ **5.** Ion–dipole interactions occur when a cation or an anion is attracted or repelled by the dipole moment of a polar molecule.

____ **6.** If the negative end of a polar molecule such as HCl is attracted to the positive end of another HCl molecule, then that is a dipole–dipole interaction.

____ **7.** Hydrogen bonds are bonds just like covalent bonds.

____ **8.** Dipole–dipole interactions occur between two polar molecules.

## Hydrogen Bonding

Each of the halogens (F, Cl, Br, and I) has seven valence electrons. Each uses only one valence electron to form a bond. So, each has six valence electrons not involved in chemical bonding. Valence electrons not involved in chemical bonding are called nonbonding electrons. Each pair of nonbonding electrons is called a lone pair of electrons. Thus, each of the halogens has three lone pairs of electrons.

Other atoms have nonbonding electrons, too. For example, oxygen has six valence electrons, but uses only two of them to form bonds. Thus, oxygen has two lone pairs of electrons. Nitrogen has five valence electrons, but uses only three of them to form bonds. Thus, nitrogen has one lone pair of electrons.

**Hydrogen bonding** occurs when a highly electronegative atom with at least one lone pair of electrons partially shares its nonbonding electrons with a hydrogen atom in a polar bond. The resulting interaction is stronger than a dipole–dipole interaction. But it is not quite as strong as most ion–dipole interactions.

Hydrogen bonding cannot occur unless the following two criteria are satisfied:

- There must be a hydrogen atom that is electron deficient (missing an electron). A hydrogen atom that carries a partial positive charge from being in a polar bond with a more electronegative atom is electron deficient. Examples include the hydrogen atoms in N–H, O–H, and F–H bonds.
- There must be a highly electronegative atom with at least one lone pair of electrons. The pair of nonbonding electrons is needed to attract the electron-deficient hydrogen atom. The elements that have the highest electronegativities and at least one lone pair of electrons are N, O, and F.

As a result, hydrogen bonding is restricted to molecules with N–H, O–H, and F–H bonds. The bottom drawing to the right shows how hydrogen bonds can form between two of the same molecules (HF or water), between two different molecules (water–ammonia), and within the same molecule (salicylic acid). The hydrogen bonds are indicated by dotted lines, and the lone pairs of electrons are indicated by pairs of dots.

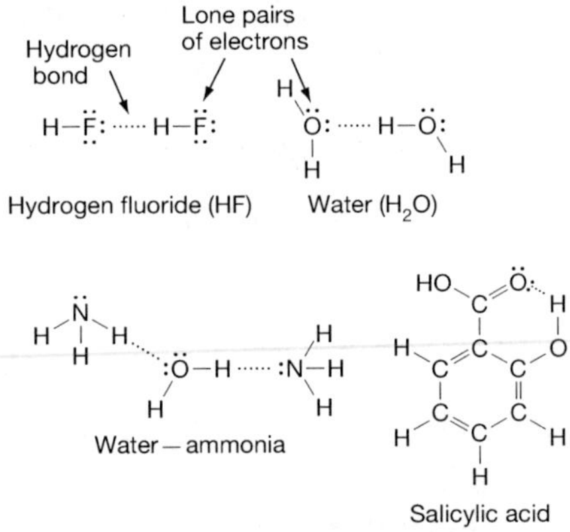

Hydrogen bond

Lone pairs of electrons

Hydrogen fluoride (HF)

Water ($H_2O$)

Water—ammonia

Salicylic acid

Molar mass and the ability to form hydrogen bonds affect the boiling points of some compounds. Molecules with similar molar masses are usually expected to have similar boiling points. $CH_4$ (methane), $NH_3$ (ammonia), $H_2O$ (water), and HF (hydrofluoric acid) have approximately the same molar mass, but their boiling points vary widely. The table on the next page lists molar masses and boiling points for $CH_4$, $NH_3$, $H_2O$, and HF.

| | $CH_4$ | $NH_3$ | $H_2O$ | HF |
|---|---|---|---|---|
| Molar mass (g/mol) | 16.04 | 17.03 | 18.02 | 20.01 |
| Boiling point (°C) | –164 | –33 | 100 | 19 |

The differences in the boiling points of $CH_4$, $NH_3$, $H_2O$, and HF are due almost entirely to their abilities to form hydrogen bonds. For example, $CH_4$ cannot form hydrogen bonds. So, its boiling point is the lowest of the group. This means that it is easier to vaporize $CH_4$ than it is to vaporize the other three molecules.

On the other hand, $NH_3$, $H_2O$, and HF can form hydrogen bonds. Of these three, N–H hydrogen bonds should be the weakest because the electronegativity difference (ΔEN) between N and H is the smallest of the three. (Remember, ΔEN is the difference in electronegativity.) Similarly, F–H hydrogen bonds should be the strongest because ΔEN between F and H is the largest of the three. Thus, the boiling point of $NH_3$ should be the lowest of the three. And, the boiling point of HF should be the highest. It turns out that the boiling point of $NH_3$ is lower than the boiling points of $H_2O$ and HF, as expected.

It also turns out, however, that the boiling point of $H_2O$ is higher (not lower) than the boiling point of HF. The boiling point of $H_2O$ is higher than the boiling point of HF because $H_2O$ can form more hydrogen bonds than HF. Each $H_2O$ molecule can form four hydrogen bonds to other $H_2O$ molecules. Each HF molecule can form only two hydrogen bonds to other HF molecules.

TIP

Both of the symbols Δ and δ are used when referring to electronegativity. The Δ is used in ΔEN when referring to electronegativity difference. δ is used with a + or – to refer to which end of a covalent bond is partially positive (+) or partially negative (–).

## THINK ABOUT IT

Chemists have predicted that the boiling point of water would be –100°C instead of 100°C if it were not for hydrogen bonding. This means that water would be a gas at normal room temperature (25°C) instead of a liquid. It also means that liquid and solid water would appear only in the very coldest places on Earth. Can you think of two ways that life on Earth would be different under these conditions? Write your answer on a separate sheet of paper.

## PRACTICE 60: Hydrogen Bonding

Decide if each statement that follows is true (**T**) or false (**F**). Write the correct letter on each line.

T **1.** Valence electrons not involved in chemical bonding are called nonbonding electrons.

F **2.** The differences in the boiling points of $CH_4$, $NH_3$, $H_2O$, and HF have nothing to do with their abilities to form hydrogen bonds.

T **3.** Each pair of nonbonding electrons is called a lone pair of electrons.

F **4.** One of the criteria for hydrogen bonding is that there must be an atom that has low electronegativity.

T **5.** Hydrogen bonding occurs when a highly electronegative atom with at least one lone pair of electrons partially shares its nonbonding electrons with a hydrogen atom in a polar bond.

F **6.** Hydrogen bonds are weaker than dipole–dipole interactions.

T **7.** One of the criteria for hydrogen bonding is that there must be a highly electronegative atom with at least one lone pair of electrons.

T **8.** Hydrogen bonding is restricted to molecules with N–H, O–H, and F–H bonds.

## Dispersion Intermolecular Forces

Remember from the earlier discussion of dipolar intermolecular forces on page 159 that all substances experience dispersion forces. But only substances with permanent dipole moments experience dipolar forces. That is, nonpolar and polar molecules experience dispersion intermolecular forces. But only polar molecules experience dipolar intermolecular forces. Dispersion forces are also called **London forces.** London forces are named for Fritz London, the German physicist who first explained them mathematically.

Although dispersion forces occur in all substances, it is easiest to understand them by considering nonpolar molecules, such as $F_2$, $Cl_2$, $Br_2$, and $I_2$. With nonpolar molecules, you do not have to separate the effects of dispersion forces from the effects of dipolar forces. That is because nonpolar molecules do not experience dipolar forces. They experience only dispersion forces.

Use $F_2$ as an example. When two molecules of $F_2$ approach each other closely or collide, the nuclei of one molecule attract the electron cloud of the other molecule. The electron clouds of the two molecules repel each other. The electron clouds change their shapes in order to minimize the repulsion. When this happens, the two molecules each end up with a region of partial negative charge and a region of partial positive charge. That is, instantaneous and short-lived dipoles are produced in the two molecules. These instantaneous and short-lived dipoles, in turn, produce instantaneous and short-lived dipoles in molecules next to them.

Dispersion forces are the forces of attraction and repulsion between molecules with these instantaneous and temporary dipoles. Dispersion forces are the weakest of all of the intermolecular forces. They are strong enough at very low temperatures, however, to condense and solidify even the noble gases (He, Ne, Ar, Kr, Xe, and Rn). You will recall from Unit 2, pages 73–74, that noble gases are very stable and rarely react with other elements or compounds.

The strength of dispersion forces depends on the polarizability of the molecules involved. Polarizability is the ease with which an electron cloud can be distorted. Greater polarizability means larger partial charges (larger induced dipoles) and stronger dispersion forces. For example, the dispersion forces between $I_2$ molecules are stronger than the dispersion forces between $F_2$ molecules. This is because the electron clouds around $I_2$ molecules are easier to distort than the electron clouds around $F_2$ molecules. That is, $I_2$ molecules are more polarizable than $F_2$ molecules.

The polarizability of a molecule depends on the size and shape of the molecule. Polarizability depends on size because large molecules have more electrons (larger electron clouds). And, larger electron clouds are easier to distort. This is why $I_2$ is a solid at 25°C, but $F_2$ is a gas at 25°C. This is also why hexane ($C_6H_{14}$) is a liquid at 25°C, but methane ($CH_4$) is a gas at 25°C.

Polarizability depends on shape because large extended molecules have more area over which their electron clouds can be distorted than small, compact molecules do. For example, pentane and neopentane both have the molecular formula $C_5H_{12}$. The structure of pentane, however, is an extended chain of the five carbon atoms. Neopentane, on the other hand, has a much more compact structure. As a result, the dispersion forces between pentane molecules are larger than the dispersion forces between neopentane molecules. The boiling point of pentane (36°C) is higher than the boiling point of neopentane (9.5°C).

TIP

Both bonding forces (intramolecular forces) and intermolecular forces are the result of attractions between oppositely charged particles. The differences between bonding and intermolecular forces are due to the magnitude of the charges on the particles and the distance between them. In chemical bonds, the charges are larger and closer together. In intermolecular forces, the charges are smaller and farther apart. Thus, the relative strengths of chemical bonds and intermolecular forces are as follows: dispersion forces < dipole–dipole < hydrogen bonding < ion–dipole < chemical bonds.

## PRACTICE 61: Dispersion Intermolecular Forces

Decide if each statement that follows is true (**T**) or false (**F**). Write the correct letter on each line.

__F__ **1.** Dispersion forces are the strongest of all the intermolecular forces.

__T__ **2.** Dispersion forces are also called London forces.

__F__ **3.** The dispersion forces between $I_2$ molecules are stronger than the dispersion forces between $F_2$ molecules because the electron clouds around $I_2$ molecules are harder to distort than the electron clouds around $F_2$ molecules.

__T__ **4.** Polarizability is the ease with which an electron cloud can be distorted.

__T__ **5.** Dispersion forces are the forces of attraction and repulsion between molecules with instantaneous and temporary dipoles.

__F__ **6.** The polarizability of a molecule depends on the size but not the shape of the molecule.

__T__ **7.** Polarizability depends on shape because large extended molecules have more area over which their electron clouds can be distorted than small, compact molecules do.

__T__ **8.** Polarizability depends on size because large molecules have more electrons (larger electron clouds), and larger electron clouds are easier to distort.

## Types of Solids

Solids can be classified as either crystalline solids or as amorphous solids. **Crystalline solids** have an orderly arrangement of atoms, molecules, or ions. The atoms, molecules, or ions in a crystalline solid are not immobile. Instead, they vibrate constantly around fixed positions in the crystal. Examples of crystalline solids include table salt (NaCl), quartz, diamond, and ice.

**Amorphous solids** have an irregular arrangement of molecules or ions. There is no observable or repeating pattern to the way in which the molecules or ions are organized. Examples of amorphous solids include rubber, plastic, wax, and glass.

**THINK ABOUT IT**

Some substances exist in both crystalline forms and amorphous forms. It all depends on how the substance is prepared. For example, silicon dioxide ($SiO_2$) exists in both forms. If molten $SiO_2$ is cooled slowly, you get crystalline quartz. If it is cooled quickly, you get amorphous glass. The cane sugar you buy at the grocery store is crystalline. If you heat it until it melts, then cool it quickly, you will get amorphous sugar. Do you think cotton candy is crystalline sugar or amorphous sugar? Write your answer on a separate sheet of paper.

Crystalline solids can be classified as atomic solids, molecular solids, ionic solids, metallic solids, or network covalent solids. Atomic solids are individual atoms held together by dispersion forces. They have very low melting points and boiling points. Only the noble gases (Group 18 in the periodic table) form atomic solids.

**Molecular solids** are individual molecules held together by combinations of dispersion forces, dipole–dipole interactions, and hydrogen bonds. The atoms in the individual molecules are held together by covalent bonds. But the molecules are held together in the solid by intermolecular forces. When the molecules are nonpolar, dispersion forces hold them together. When the molecules are polar, all three kinds of intermolecular forces hold them together. Molecular solids tend to be soft and have melting points that are usually below 200°C. This is because the intermolecular forces holding molecular solids together are relatively weak. There are many molecular solids. Examples include sucrose ($C_{12}H_{22}O_{11}$), dry ice (solid $CO_2$), ice (solid $H_2O$), and $I_2$.

**Ionic solids** are cations and anions held together by ionic bonds. That is, ionic solids are ionic compounds in the solid phase. The bonding and properties of ionic compounds were discussed in detail in Unit 3, pages 130–132. The forces holding ionic solids together are the attractions between oppositely charged ions. These forces are much stronger than the intermolecular forces holding atomic and molecular solids together. As a result, ionic solids are hard, brittle, and have high melting points. Examples of ionic solids include sodium chloride, or salt ($NaCl$); cesium chloride ($CsCl$); and calcium fluoride ($CaF_2$).

**Metallic solids** are metals such as copper, gold, tungsten, uranium, and tin. Remember from Unit 3, page 140, that the metal atoms in a sample of a metal can be viewed as cations immersed in a sea of valence electrons. Similarly, the metallic bonds can be viewed as the result of the mutual attraction of the metal cations for the mobile, delocalized electrons. Compared to intermolecular forces, metallic bonds are strong. They do exhibit a range of strengths, however. Metals vary from soft to hard, and they have melting points that vary from low to high.

**Network covalent solids** consist of atoms covalently bonded to one another in extensive arrays or networks. You learned that there are covalent bonds in molecular solids, too. In molecular solids, however, the covalent bonds are between the individual atoms in the individual molecules. The forces between the individual molecules are intermolecular forces. In network covalent solids, on the other hand, there are no individual or discrete molecules. All of the atoms are covalently bonded to other atoms throughout the network.

Covalent bonds are strong—much stronger than intermolecular forces. So, network solids tend to be very hard with very high melting points. Examples of network solids include diamond (empirical formula C), graphite (empirical formula C), quartz (empirical formula $SiO_2$), silicon carbide (empirical formula SiC), and boron nitride (empirical formula BN). There are only empirical formulas for these compounds because there are no individual or discrete molecules in network solids. You learned in Unit 3, page 139, that graphite is soft (unlike other network solids) because it consists of layers of covalently bonded carbon atoms that can slide past one another.

## PRACTICE 62: Types of Solids

Decide if each statement that follows is true (**T**) or false (**F**). Write the correct letter on each line.

__T__ **1.** Solids can be classified as either crystalline solids or amorphous solids.

__F__ **2.** Amorphous solids have an orderly arrangement of atoms, molecules, or ions.

__T__ **3.** Crystalline solids can be classified as atomic solids, molecular solids, ionic solids, metallic solids, or network covalent solids.

__F__ **4.** Only the alkali metals (Group 1 in the periodic table) form atomic solids.

__F__ **5.** Molecular solids are no different from network covalent solids because both contain covalent bonds.

__T__ **6.** Ionic solids are cations and anions held together by ionic bonds.

__T__ **7.** There are no individual or discrete molecules in network solids.

__T__ **8.** Metallic bonds exhibit a range of strengths, so metals vary from soft to hard and have melting points that vary from low to high.

## Properties of Liquids

The intermolecular forces in solids are strong enough to hold atoms and molecules in fixed positions. On page 174, you will learn that the intermolecular forces in gases are so weak that gaseous atoms and molecules can move freely about their containers. The intermolecular forces in liquids, on the other hand, are strong enough to confine liquid molecules to specific volumes, but they are not strong enough to prevent the molecules from moving about within those volumes. Thus, the intermolecular forces in liquids are stronger than the ones in gases, but not as strong as the ones in solids.

The strength of the intermolecular forces in liquids leads to two important properties of liquids. Those properties are surface tension and viscosity. **Surface tension** is the resistance a liquid has to an increase in its surface area. A liquid resists an increase in its surface area because any increase means that its intermolecular forces must be overcome.

The greater the intermolecular forces, the greater the surface tension. For example, hexane ($C_6H_{14}$) has a relatively low surface tension because the only intermolecular forces between hexane molecules are weak dispersion forces. Water, on the other hand, has a relatively high surface tension because each water molecule can form as many as four hydrogen bonds. Hydrogen bonds are very strong intermolecular forces. Mercury, the only metal that is a liquid at 25°C, has a surface tension that is almost seven times greater than that of water. This is because the metallic bonds in mercury are much stronger than the hydrogen bonds in water.

The following drawing illustrates surface tension. Note that the molecules in the interior of the liquid are completely surrounded by other liquid molecules. As a result, molecules in the interior experience intermolecular forces in all directions. These forces are indicated by arrows in the illustration below. There is no net pull in any particular direction on the molecules in the interior. Note, however, that the molecules at the surface of the liquid have only other liquid molecules below them and beside them. There are no liquid molecules above them. As a result, the intermolecular forces on the molecules at the surface tend to pull the molecules into the interior.

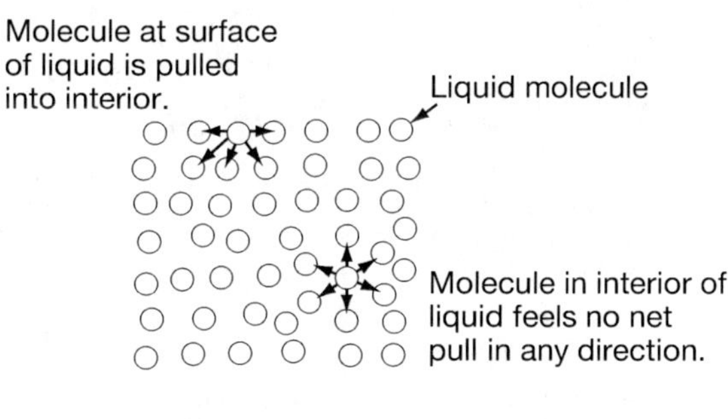

**Surface Tension**

Because molecules at the surface have fewer intermolecular interactions, they are less stable than molecules in the interior. Thus, liquids try to minimize the number of molecules at the surface. Minimizing the surface area of the liquid leads to surface tension.

You may have noticed how water beads up on a freshly waxed car but forms a film on a clean windshield. The formation of beads or a film of liquid is due to the balance between cohesive forces and adhesive forces. **Cohesive forces** are the intermolecular forces between molecules of the liquid (water, in this case). **Adhesive forces** are the intermolecular forces between molecules of the liquid and a solid surface (a waxed car body and a windshield, in this case).

Water forms spherical drops (beads) when adhesive forces are low compared to cohesive forces. Adhesive forces between water and a waxed car surface are low. There is little or no attraction between polar water molecules and nonpolar wax molecules. As a result, the water minimizes its surface area against the wax by forming beads.

Water forms a film when adhesive forces are high compared to cohesive forces. Adhesive forces between water and a clean windshield are high. The intermolecular attractions between polar water molecules and the polar glass surface are strong. In fact, they are as strong or stronger than the intermolecular hydrogen bonds between water molecules. As a result, the water maximizes its surface area against the windshield by forming a film.

**THINK ABOUT IT**

Unless you buy organically grown apples, the apples you get at the grocery store probably have been coated with a thin layer of wax to make them look shiny and more appealing. Will water bead up on the waxy surface of an apple or will it form a film? Why? For the water, are adhesive forces high or low compared to cohesive forces? Write your answer on a separate sheet of paper.

**Viscosity** is a liquid's resistance to flow. The greater the viscosity, the slower the liquid will flow. Honey, for example, flows much more slowly than water. The viscosity of honey is much greater than the viscosity of water.

At the molecular level, viscosity reflects how easily molecules flow past one another. Viscosity, therefore, depends on the shapes of the molecules and their intermolecular forces. Small, compact molecules, such as water, methanol ($CH_4O$), and benzene ($C_6H_6$), have low viscosities because their molecules can flow past one another relatively easily. Large, extended molecules, such as the ones found in cooking oils or motor oils, have high viscosities because the long, extended molecules get tangled. Tangling slows the flow of the molecules past one another, which raises the viscosity.

Viscosity depends on intermolecular forces because large intermolecular forces inhibit the flow of molecules past one another. For example, a benzene molecule ($C_6H_6$) is larger than a water molecule, but the viscosity of water is higher because water can form strong hydrogen bonds. The intermolecular forces between benzene molecules are mainly weak dispersion forces.

Viscosity decreases as temperature increases. The next time you pour cooking oil in a pan, notice how much more easily the oil flows after it has been heated. The viscosity of the oil has decreased because molecules in the oil move faster at higher temperatures. They are able to slide past one another more easily. In other words, at the higher temperature, the kinetic energy of the molecules has increased enough to overcome some of the intermolecular forces.

**IN REAL LIFE**

The viscosity of motor oil decreases as temperature increases, too. During a long car drive, the oil in the engine could become so thin that it no longer protects the moving parts of the engine. Instead, additives in the oil help compensate for the decreased viscosity. As the engine and the motor oil heat up, the additive molecules change shape from compact spheres to extended strands. The strands tangle with the molecules in the oil. This raises the viscosity of the oil to safe limits again.

## PRACTICE 63: Properties of Liquids

Decide if each statement that follows is true (**T**) or false (**F**). Write the correct letter on each line.

____ **1.** Surface tension is the resistance a liquid has to an increase in its surface area.

____ **2.** A liquid resists an increase in its surface area because any increase means that its intermolecular forces must be overcome.

____ **3.** Viscosity is a liquid's resistance to flow.

F 4. The greater the viscosity, the faster the liquid will flow.

F 5. Viscosity depends on the shapes of the molecules but not on their intermolecular forces.

T 6. Cohesive forces are the intermolecular forces between the molecules of a liquid.

T 7. Adhesive forces are the intermolecular forces between the molecules of a liquid and a solid surface.

F 8. The surface tension of water is greater than the surface tension of mercury because hydrogen bonds are stronger than metallic bonds.

## Behavior of Gases

The strengths of intermolecular forces decrease rapidly as the distance between molecules increases. Except at very high pressures, gas atoms and molecules are far apart. Intermolecular forces, therefore, are very weak in most cases. At high pressures, the gas atoms and molecules are pushed close enough to one another that intermolecular forces can become important again. Also, at very low temperatures, the kinetic energies of gas atoms and molecules are low enough that intermolecular forces can become important again, too.

Under most of the conditions found in laboratories or homes, the intermolecular forces between gas atoms and molecules are so weak that they can be ignored. Under most conditions, the volume of gas molecules is negligible compared to the volume of the container the gas is in, too. When chemists make these two assumptions, the pressure, volume, temperature, and number of moles (amount) of a gas can be described by the **ideal gas equation:**

$$PV = nRT$$

In the ideal gas equation, *P* stands for pressure, *V* stands for volume, n stands for the number of moles of the gas, and *R* stands for a proportionality constant. This constant is also known as the **universal gas constant**, the value of which changes depending on the units of the other variables. *T* stands for temperature. An ideal gas is a hypothetical gas that behaves according to the ideal gas law. There is no such thing in nature as an ideal gas. But the ideal gas equation can be applied to real gases (such as $H_2$, $O_3$, CO, and $NO_2$). This equation can be used to solve quantitative (having to do with amounts or numbers) problems involving gases.

For your purposes, the ideal gas equation makes it possible to understand how gases behave as variables such as pressure, volume, temperature, and number of moles are changed. Like all equations, the ideal gas equation can be rearranged to isolate individual variables. The possible rearranged equations are as follows:

$$\frac{P = nRT}{V} \qquad \frac{V = nRT}{P} \qquad \frac{T = PV}{nR}$$

The first of these rearranged equations, $\frac{P = nRT}{V}$, isolates pressure, *P*. This equation shows that pressure increases if the number of moles of gas, *n*, increases, but temperature, *T*, and volume, *V*, remain the same. Pressure also increases if *T* increases, but *n* and *V* remain the same. Finally, pressure decreases if *V* increases, but *n* and *T* remain the same.

The second of these equations, $\frac{V = nRT}{P}$, isolates volume, *V*. This equation shows that volume increases if *n* increases, but *T* and *P* remain the same. Volume also increases if *T* increases, but *n* and *P* remain the same. Finally, volume decreases if *P* increases, but *n* and *T* remain the same.

The third equation, $\frac{T = PV}{nR}$, isolates temperature, *T*. This equation shows that temperature increases if *P* increases, but *V* and *n* remain the same. Temperature also increases if *V* increases, but *P* and *n* remain the same. Finally, temperature decreases if *n* increases, but *P* and *V* remain the same.

**TIP**

It can get pretty confusing if you try to memorize what happens to the pressure, volume, or temperature of a gas as *P*, *V*, *T*, or *n* is changed. Instead, memorize the ideal gas equation, $PV = nRT$. Once you have done that, you can isolate the variable you are looking for (*P*, *V*, or *T*). Then you can reason out what will happen as one of the other variables is changed while the rest remain the same. For example, does the temperature increase or decrease when the pressure decreases and the volume and number of moles remain the same? $PV = nRT$, so $T = PV/nR$. Thus, *T* decreases if *P* decreases, but *V* and *n* remain the same.

## PRACTICE 64: Behavior of Gases

Decide if each statement that follows is true (**T**) or false (**F**). Write the correct letter on each line.

_____ **1.** The ideal gas equation is $PR = nVT^2$.

_____ **2.** Under most of the conditions found in laboratories or homes, the intermolecular forces between gas atoms and molecules are so weak that they can be ignored.

_____ **3.** An ideal gas is a hypothetical gas that behaves according to the ideal gas law.

_____ **4.** The strengths of intermolecular forces increase rapidly as the distance between molecules increases.

_____ **5.** In the ideal gas equation, *P* stands for pressure, *V* stands for volume, *n* stands for the number of moles of the gas, *R* stands for a proportionality constant, and *T* stands for temperature.

_____ **6.** There is no such thing in nature as an ideal gas, but the ideal gas equation can be applied to real gases (such as $H_2$, $O_3$, CO, and $NO_2$).

_____ **7.** According to the ideal gas equation, volume decreases if *n* increases, but *T* and *P* remain the same.

_____ **8.** The ideal gas equation is $PV = nRT$.

# LESSON 13: Solutions

GOAL: To learn about solutions and some of their properties

## WORDS TO KNOW

**alloys**
**amalgam**
**boiling point elevation**
**colligative properties**
**freezing point depression**
**miscible**
**saturated solution**
**solute**
**solvent**
**supersaturated solution**
**unsaturated solution**

## What Is a Solution?

You learned in Unit 1, page 9, that a homogeneous mixture has a uniform composition throughout. A solution is a homogeneous mixture of two or more chemical substances. A **solvent** is the substance in the solution that determines whether the solution is a solid, a liquid, or a gas. The solvent is usually present in the greatest amount. The substance or substances that dissolve in the solvent are called the **solute** or solutes. When water is the solvent, the solution is called an aqueous solution.

Although you may think of solutions as solids or liquids dissolved in liquids, a solution can be any combination of solids, liquids, and gases, as shown in the following table.

| Solute | Solvent | Example |
|---|---|---|
| Gas | Gas | Air |
| Gas | Liquid | Oxygen in water |
| Gas | Solid | Hydrogen in palladium |
| Liquid | Liquid | Acetone in water |
| Solid | Liquid | NaCl in water |
| Solid | Solid | Brass |

The concentration of a solution is the amount of solute dissolved in a known volume of the solution. Concentration is usually expressed as a molarity. The molarity of a solution is the number of moles of solute divided by the total volume of the solution. The volume is expressed in liters. Molarity has the units of moles per liter (or mol/L). The symbol for molarity is M. Thus, if 1.72 moles of NaCl are dissolved in water and the total volume of the solution is 1.0 L, then the concentration of the solution is 1.72 mol/L or 1.72 M.

In most cases, there is a maximum amount of solute that will dissolve in a known amount of solvent. A **saturated solution** contains the maximum amount of solute that will dissolve in a particular solvent at a particular temperature. An **unsaturated solution** is a solution that contains less than the maximum amount of solute that it can dissolve. A **supersaturated solution** is a solution that contains more than the maximum amount of solute that it can dissolve. Supersaturated solutions are unstable. Eventually, some of the solute will come out of the solution as crystals.

Some substances, such as water and acetone ($C_3H_6O$), can form solutions in all proportions. Substances that are completely soluble in each other in all proportions are called **miscible.** When substances are miscible, it is neither necessary nor meaningful to distinguish one as the solute and the other as the solvent.

## PRACTICE 65: What Is a Solution?

Decide if each statement that follows is true (**T**) or false (**F**). Write the correct letter on each line.

_____ **1.** A homogeneous mixture of two or more chemical substances that has a uniform composition throughout is called a solution.

_____ **2.** A solution can be a solid or a liquid dissolved in a liquid, but it cannot be a gas dissolved in a liquid.

_____ **3.** When water is the solvent, the solution is called a supersaturated solution.

T 4. The molarity of a solution is the number of moles of solute divided by the total volume of the solution expressed in liters.

F 5. A solution that contains LESS than the maximum amount of solute that it can dissolve is called a saturated solution.

T 6. Supersaturated solutions are unstable, so eventually some of the solute will come out of the solution as crystals.

T 7. Substances that are completely soluble in each other in all proportions are called miscible.

F 8. The substance in the solution that determines whether the solution is a solid, a liquid, or a gas is called the solute.

## Solubility of Liquids

Three things occur when one substance dissolves in another.

- Solute atoms, ions, or molecules separate from one another.
- Solvent atoms, ions, or molecules separate from one another to make space for the solute.
- Solute atoms, ions, or molecules mix with solvent atoms, ions, or molecules.

Whether or not these three things occur depends on the relative strengths of the intermolecular forces between solute molecules, between solvent molecules, and between solute and solvent molecules.

In general, one substance dissolves in another when the solute–solvent intermolecular forces are similar to, or the same as, the solute–solute and solvent–solvent intermolecular forces. Chemists summarize this observation by saying that like dissolves like.

Consider substances such as water, methanol, pentane, and octane, all of which are liquids at 25°C. The structures of these four compounds are shown in the drawing on the next page. Once again, lone pairs of electrons are shown as pairs of dots.

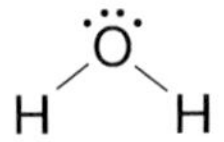

Water ($H_2O$)

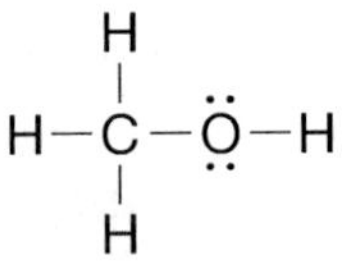

Methanol ($H_4CO$)

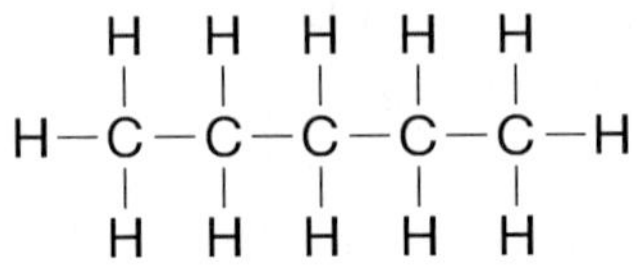

Pentane ($H_{12}C_5$)

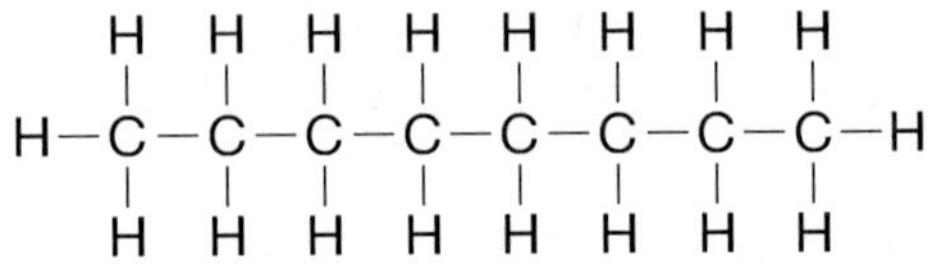

Octane ($H_{18}C_8$)

Water forms hydrogen bonds, dipole–dipole interactions, and dispersion forces. The same is true of methanol. So, water and methanol dissolve in each other. In Lesson 12, you learned that hydrogen bonds are stronger than dipole–dipole interactions or dispersion forces. Therefore, the formation of water–methanol hydrogen bonds is the most important reason water and methanol are miscible.

Pentane is nonpolar, so the only intermolecular forces it experiences are dispersion forces. The same is true of octane. So, pentane and octane dissolve in each other. In fact, there is very little difference between the pentane–octane dispersion forces and the pentane–pentane or octane–octane dispersion forces.

Neither water nor methanol dissolves in or can dissolve pentane or octane. When water is mixed with pentane, for example, the two liquids separate into two distinct layers. Dispersion forces are the only intermolecular forces between water and pentane. Water–water hydrogen bonds are much stronger than water–pentane dispersion forces, however. The formation of water–pentane dispersion forces would actually destabilize water. So, water and pentane are insoluble in each other. Water is insoluble in octane, and methanol is insoluble both in pentane and octane for the same reasons.

## IN REAL LIFE

Acetone ($C_3H_6O$) is a versatile solvent. It used to be the main ingredient in nail polish remover. Most nail polish removers now use ethyl acetate ($C_4H_8O_2$), though. This is because ethyl acetate is less harmful to your skin. The structures of acetone and ethyl acetate are shown below. On page 178, you learned that acetone and water are miscible. Acetone and water are miscible because acetone is a polar molecule thanks to its polar C–O bond. Also, the oxygen atom has two lone pairs of electrons that can form hydrogen bonds to the hydrogen atoms in water. Acetone can also dissolve nonpolar compounds, such as pentane. Acetone can dissolve pentane because acetone has a three-carbon chain that is nonpolar. The nonpolar region of acetone can form dispersion interactions with pentane molecules that are like the dispersion interactions in pentane alone. Ethyl acetate works in the same way.

Acetone

Ethyl acetate

## PRACTICE 66: Solubility of Liquids

Decide if each statement that follows is true (**T**) or false (**F**). Write the correct letter on each line.

____ **1.** In general, one substance dissolves in another when the solute–solvent intermolecular forces are similar to or the same as the solute–solute and solvent–solvent intermolecular forces.

____ **2.** Water is soluble in octane.

____ **3.** Methanol is insoluble in pentane and octane.

_____ **4.** Solute atoms, ions, or molecules must separate from one another in order for one substance to dissolve in another.

_____ **5.** Pentane is nonpolar, so the intermolecular forces it experiences are hydrogen bonding and dispersion forces.

_____ **6.** Water–water hydrogen bonds are weaker than water–pentane dispersion forces, so water should be able to dissolve pentane.

_____ **7.** Whether or not one substance dissolves in another depends on the relative strengths of the intermolecular forces between solute molecules, between solvent molecules, and between solute and solvent molecules.

_____ **8.** Acetone can dissolve polar molecules, such as water, and nonpolar molecules, such as pentane.

## Solubility of Solids

You learned in Lesson 12, page 168, that the five kinds of solids are atomic, molecular, ionic, metallic, and network covalent. "Like dissolves like" applies to these solids, too. You can ignore the solubility of atomic solids, however. This is because they are only solids at very low temperatures. At 25°C, they are all gases.

Network covalent solids are insoluble in all solvents. Network covalent solids are insoluble because covalent bonds must be broken in order for them to dissolve. Covalent bonds are much stronger than any intermolecular force. So, there is no solute–solvent interaction that can overcome the strength of the covalent bonds holding the network solid together.

Metallic solids (metals) are insoluble in most solvents for similar reasons. That is, metallic bonds are much stronger than any intermolecular force. Metals can dissolve in other metals, however. Solid mixtures of two or more metals are called **alloys.** Alloys may be either homogeneous mixtures (solutions) or heterogeneous mixtures. Brass is a homogeneous alloy of copper and zinc. Plumber's solder is a heterogeneous alloy of lead and tin. If you look at solder under a microscope, you will see distinct regions of lead and distinct regions of tin. If you look at brass under a microscope, you will see no such regions. This is because the copper atoms and the zinc atoms in brass are uniformly mixed.

Mercury, which is a liquid at 25°C, can dissolve metals, such as silver, gold, zinc, and tin, to form liquid solutions. A solution of another metal dissolved in mercury is called an **amalgam.**

**IN REAL LIFE**

The material that dentists used to fill tooth cavities is an amalgam. A compound containing silver and tin, $Ag_3Sn$, was ground with mercury to form a semisolid amalgam that could be fitted into the cavity. Upon standing, a chemical reaction occurred to form a solid mixture of $Ag_5Hg_8$ and $Sn_7Hg_8$. This mixture was hard enough to withstand the pressures of years and years of chewing.

Some ionic solids, such as NaCl, are very soluble in solvents like water. Others, such as $BaSO_4$, are not. Ionic solids dissolve if the intermolecular forces between the ions and the solvent are strong enough to compensate for, or overcome, the attractions of the cations and anions in the ionic solid. For NaCl, the ion–dipole intermolecular forces between $Na^+$ and $H_2O$ and between $Cl^-$ and $H_2O$ do compensate for the $Na^+$–$Cl^-$ attractions in solid NaCl. For $BaSO_4$, they do not.

Molecular solids are the easiest solids to dissolve. In Lesson 12, page 168, you learned that molecular solids are individual molecules held together by combinations of dispersion forces, dipole–dipole interactions, and hydrogen bonds. Molecular solids tend to dissolve in solvents with similar kinds of intermolecular forces. Thus, $I_2$ (which is nonpolar) is insoluble in water (which is polar), but is soluble in $CCl_4$ (which is nonpolar). On the other hand, sucrose (which is polar and forms hydrogen bonds), is very soluble in water but is insoluble in solvents such as $CCl_4$.

## PRACTICE 67: Solubility of Solids

Decide if each statement that follows is true (**T**) or false (**F**). Write the correct letter on each line.

_____ **1.** Network covalent solids are soluble in all solvents.

_____ **2.** Solid mixtures of two or more metals are called alloys.

_____ **3.** A solution of another metal dissolved in mercury is called an amalgam.

_____ **4.** Ionic solids dissolve if the intermolecular forces between the ions and the solvent are strong enough to compensate for, or overcome, the attractions of the cations and anions in the ionic solid.

_____ **5.** Alloys may be homogeneous mixtures (solutions) but not heterogeneous mixtures.

_____ **6.** Molecular solids are the easiest solids to dissolve.

_____ **7.** Network covalent solids are insoluble because ionic bonds must be broken in order for them to dissolve.

_____ **8.** $I_2$ (which is nonpolar) is insoluble in water (which is polar), but is soluble in $CCl_4$ (which is nonpolar).

## Solubility of Gases

You have already learned that one substance generally dissolves in another when the solute–solvent intermolecular forces are similar to or the same as the solute–solute and solvent–solvent intermolecular forces. The intermolecular forces in gases are very weak, however. Thus, solute–solute intermolecular interactions are not much of a factor when gases dissolve in liquids. But solute–solvent and solvent–solvent interactions are.

Gases tend to be relatively insoluble in water. For example, at 25°C and the pressure at sea level, only 0.64 mL of oxygen ($O_2$) dissolves in 100 mL of water. Remarkably, that is enough oxygen to sustain the lives of all aquatic animals.

In some cases, gases appear to be very soluble in a liquid. This is because they are reacting with the liquid in addition to dissolving in it. For example, at 25°C and the pressure at sea level, 81 mL of $CO_2$ appears to dissolve in 100 mL of water. However, $CO_2$ is also reacting with $H_2O$ to form $H_2CO_3$ (carbonic acid).

Gases can dissolve in solids, too. When they do, they occupy the spaces between the atoms, ions, or molecules of the solid. For example, huge amounts of hydrogen ($H_2$) can be dissolved in metals, such as palladium and niobium. Oxygen ($O_2$) dissolves in copper. Unfortunately, the oxygen dissolved in copper ends up reacting with the copper to produce $Cu_2O$ (copper oxide). This compound does not conduct electricity as well as pure copper metal. So, the electrical conductivity of copper wires is diminished by the dissolved gas.

Gases are infinitely soluble in other gases. That is, gases are miscible in other gases. The air you breathe, for example, contains mostly nitrogen ($N_2$) and oxygen ($O_2$). But more than a dozen other gases are present in varying proportions in the air you breathe.

## Practice 68: Solubility of Gases

Decide if each statement that follows is true (**T**) or false (**F**). Write the correct letter on each line.

__F__ **1.** Gases dissolve in liquids, but not in solids.

__T__ **2.** Gases are infinitely soluble in other gases.

__T__ **3.** When gases dissolve in solids, the gases occupy the spaces between the atoms, ions, or molecules of the solid.

__F__ **4.** Gases tend to be highly soluble in water.

__T__ **5.** Huge amounts of hydrogen ($H_2$) can be dissolved in metals, such as palladium and niobium.

__T__ **6.** In some cases, gases appear to be very soluble in a liquid because they are reacting with the liquid in addition to dissolving in it.

## The Effect of Temperature and Pressure on Solubility

You have already learned that three things must occur in order for one substance to dissolve in another.

- Solute particles (atoms, ions, or molecules) must separate from one another.
- Solvent particles must separate from one another to make space for the solute.
- Solute particles must mix with solvent particles.

In order to separate from one another, solute particles and solvent particles must have sufficient kinetic energy to overcome their intermolecular forces. The kinetic energies of solutes and solvents increase as their temperatures increase. As a result, liquid and solid solutes tend to become more soluble in liquid solvents as the temperature of the solution rises. For example, sugar dissolves more quickly in hot tea or coffee than in iced tea or coffee.

There are exceptions to this generalization. For example, potassium hydroxide (KOH) and sodium sulfate ($Na_2SO_4$) become less soluble in water as the temperature increases. Many compounds containing calcium do, too. As a result, the last rinse cycle in most washing machines is with cold water, in order to rinse out undissolved calcium compounds.

Gases are less soluble in liquids as the temperature increases. For example, you may have noticed that the number of gas bubbles escaping from your carbonated beverage increases as it warms up to room temperature. Gases become less soluble because they have such weak intermolecular forces to begin with. The interactions they form with the liquid solvent molecules are weak, too. So, even a slight increase in their kinetic energies shakes them loose from the solvent.

Pressure has very little effect on the solubilities of liquids and solids. This is because liquids and solids are so difficult to compress more than they are already. On the other hand, pressure has a huge effect on the solubilities of gases. In fact, the solubility of a gas in a liquid is directly proportional to the pressure exerted on the solution. Thus, more gas dissolves as the pressure increases.

IN REAL LIFE

Scuba divers can injure or kill themselves if they do not understand that pressure increases the solubility of gases in liquids such as blood. Pressure increases the farther down in the ocean they dive. This is because divers have the weight of all of the water above them pressing down on them. If they are breathing compressed air, which contains about 78% $N_2$ and 21% $O_2$, then the amount of $N_2$ that dissolves in their blood also increases the farther down in the ocean they go. If divers dive below 50 meters, they must rise to the surface again slowly to allow the excess $N_2$ in their blood to safely eliminate. If they rise too quickly, the $N_2$ bubbles out of their blood and causes the extremely painful condition called "the bends." The bends are painful because the bubbles of $N_2$ are blocking the capillaries—the fine blood vessels throughout their bodies. In extreme cases, the blockage is complete enough to cause death. As a result, divers who descend to tremendous depths, such as 90 meters, breathe mixtures of $O_2$ and helium from their tanks. Helium is a good alternative to $N_2$. This is because helium is much less soluble in blood than $N_2$, even when the pressure increases.

## PRACTICE 69: The Effect of Temperature and Pressure on Solubility

Decide if each statement that follows is true (**T**) or false (**F**). Write the correct letter on each line.

T **1.** Liquid and solid solutes tend to become more soluble in liquid solvents as the temperature of the solution rises.

F **2.** Gases are more soluble in liquids as the temperature increases.

T **3.** Pressure has very little effect on the solubilities of liquids and solids, because liquids and solids are so difficult to compress more than they are already.

__T__ **4.** The solubility of a gas in a liquid is directly proportional to the pressure exerted on the solution.

__F__ **5.** Gases become less soluble in liquids as the temperature increases, because gases have such strong intermolecular forces to begin with.

__T__ **6.** If scuba divers ascend too quickly, the excess $N_2$ bubbles out of their blood and causes the extremely painful condition called "the bends."

__F__ **7.** Less gas dissolves in a liquid as the pressure increases.

__T__ **8.** Some liquids and solids become less soluble in liquid solvents as their temperatures increase.

## Colligative Properties

The presence of a solute makes the physical properties of the solution different from the physical properties of the pure solvent. In the case of some physical properties, however, the identity of the solute does not matter, but the number of solute particles (atoms, ions, or molecules) does. Physical properties of solutions that depend on the quantity of solute particles but not on the kind of solute particles are called **colligative properties.** The two colligative properties that you will learn about are freezing point depression and boiling point elevation. **Freezing point depression** is the lowering of the freezing point of a solvent that occurs when a solute is dissolved in it. **Boiling point elevation** is the raising of the boiling point of a solvent that occurs when a solute is dissolved in it.

At the atomic/molecular level, freezing occurs for a pure liquid when molecules of the liquid collide with molecules of the solid and the liquid molecules are captured by the solid molecules. By "captured," it is meant that the intermolecular forces between the solid and liquid molecules are strong enough to compensate for or overcome the kinetic energy of the liquid molecules. At the freezing point, some solid molecules also have enough kinetic energy to escape to the liquid phase. When the rates of escape and capture are equal, a dynamic equilibrium has been established. The left portion of the drawing on the next page illustrates the dynamic equilibrium at the freezing point of a pure liquid. The number of solid molecules escaping to the pure liquid (3) equals the number of pure liquid molecules captured by the solid (3).

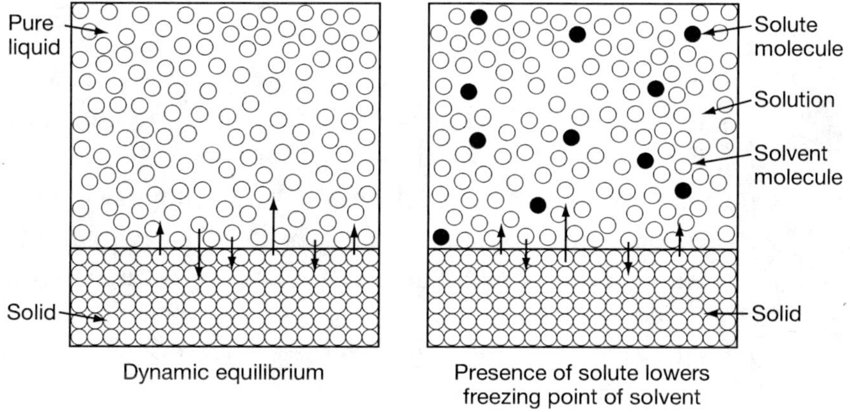


In a solution, some of the solvent molecules have been replaced by solute molecules. Thus, liquid solvent molecules collide less frequently with solid solvent molecules than they do in the pure solvent. This means that fewer liquid molecules freeze.

As the right portion of the drawing above shows, however, the rate at which solid solvent molecules escape to the liquid phase is not affected by the presence of solute molecules. The presence of the solute lowers the freezing point of the solvent because the number of solvent molecules captured by the solid (2) is less than the number of solid molecules escaping to the solution (3). Thus, the temperature of the solution must be lowered in order to freeze the solvent.

Lowering the temperature of the solution restores the dynamic equilibrium for two reasons. First, it reduces the kinetic energy of the liquid solvent molecules to the point at which more can be captured by the solid solvent molecules. Second, it reduces the kinetic energy of the solid solvent molecules to the point at which fewer can escape to the liquid phase. The end result is that a solute decreases the freezing point of a solvent.

At the atomic/molecular level, boiling occurs for a pure liquid when molecules at the surface of the liquid have sufficient kinetic energy to escape the intermolecular forces of the liquid. At the boiling point, however, some gaseous molecules are also captured by the liquid phase.

That is, there is a dynamic equilibrium in which the rate of escape from the liquid equals the rate of capture by the liquid. The left portion of the drawing below illustrates the dynamic equilibrium.

**THINK ABOUT IT**

Ethylene glycol ($C_2H_6O_2$) is the compound in antifreeze that keeps the cooling water in your car's radiator from freezing solid in the winter. It is miscible with water because it can form extensive hydrogen bonds with water. Its presence as a solute decreases the freezing point of water. What effect, if any, does ethylene glycol have on the boiling point of the water in your radiator during the summer? Write your answer on a separate sheet of paper.

In a solution, some of the solvent molecules have been replaced by solute molecules. There are fewer solvent molecules at the surface of the solvent that have sufficient kinetic energy to escape. This means that fewer liquid molecules boil.

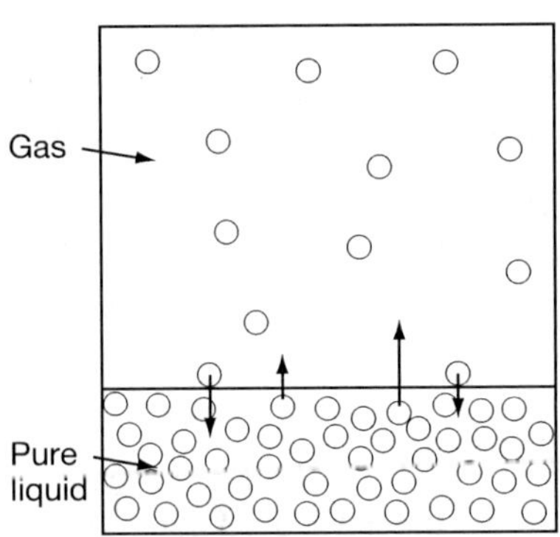


Dynamic equilibrium

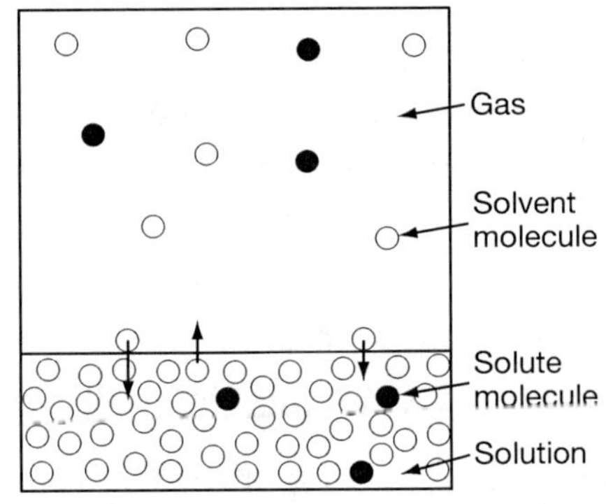


Presence of solute raises boiling point of solvent

The left portion of the drawing above illustrates dynamic equilibrium. The number of liquid molecules escaping to the gas equals the number of gas molecules captured by the liquid. As the right portion of the drawing shows, however, the rate at which gaseous solvent molecules are captured by the liquid phase is not affected by the presence of solute molecules. The presence of the solute raises the boiling point of the solvent because the number of solvent molecules escaping to the gas is less than the number of gas molecules captured by the solution. Thus, the temperature of the solution must be raised in order to boil the solvent.

Raising the temperature of the solution restores the dynamic equilibrium for two reasons. First, it increases the kinetic energy of the liquid solvent molecules to the point at which more can escape to the gas phase. Second, it increases the kinetic energy of the gaseous solvent molecules to the point at which fewer can be captured by the liquid phase. The end result is that a solute increases the boiling point of a solvent.

## Practice 70: Colligative Properties

Decide if each statement that follows is true (**T**) or false (**F**). Write the correct letter on each line.

__T__ **1.** Physical properties of solutions that depend on the quantity of solute particles but not on the kind of solute particles are called colligative properties.

__T__ **2.** A dynamic equilibrium has been established when the rate of escape from one phase equals the rate of capture from another phase.

__F__ **3.** The presence of a solute increases the freezing point of the solvent.

__T__ **4.** The presence of a solute increases the boiling point of the solvent.

__F__ **5.** Colligative properties depend on the number of solute particles in the solution and on the identity of the solute particles.

__T__ **6.** The presence of a solute decreases the freezing point of the solvent because liquid solvent molecules collide less frequently with solid solvent molecules than they do in the pure solvent.

__F__ **7.** A dynamic equilibrium occurs at the freezing point of a pure liquid but not at the boiling point.

__T__ **8.** At the atomic/molecular level, boiling occurs for a pure liquid when molecules at the surface of the liquid have sufficient kinetic energy to escape the intermolecular forces of the liquid.

# LESSON 14: Acids and Bases

GOAL: To learn the differences between acids and bases

## WORDS TO KNOW

**acid** **base** **pH scale**

## What Are Acids and Bases?

Acids and bases have many uses in everyday life. Acetic acid is the substance in vinegar that gives vinegar its bite. Citric acid gives lemons their sour taste and is used as a flavoring in many processed foods. Boric acid can be used as an antiseptic and an insecticide (especially for roaches). Hydrochloric acid is the acid in your stomach that helps digest your food. Sodium hydroxide is a base that is the active ingredient in many oven cleaners and drain cleaners. Ammonia is a base that can be used as a general purpose household cleaner. Sodium bicarbonate is the base you may know as baking soda. It can be used to help your cake rise, to deodorize your refrigerator, and to put out a kitchen fire.

An **acid** is a substance that can donate one or more protons. You learned in Unit 2, page 53, that a proton is one of the fundamental building blocks of atoms. Protons reside in the nuclei of atoms and are responsible for most of the mass of an atom. A hydrogen atom consists of one proton and one electron. Thus, removing the electron from a hydrogen atom leaves only a proton. This can be symbolized as $H^+$. When an acid donates a proton, it means that it donates an $H^+$ ion. A **base** is a substance that can accept one or more protons. That is, a base accepts an $H^+$ ion.

In order to donate a proton, an acid must have at least one polar H–X bond. X is any element that has an electronegativity greater than that of hydrogen. Water ($H_2O$) has two polar H–O bonds. HCl, HBr, $H_2S$, $H_2SO_4$, $HNO_3$, acetic acid ($C_2H_4O_2$), and many more compounds have at least one polar H–X bond.

In order to accept a proton, a base must have at least one lone pair of electrons that can bond with the proton. Water ($H_2O$) and the hydroxide ion ($HO^-$) contain oxygen atoms with lone pairs of electrons that can accept $H^+$. Ammonia ($NH_3$) has a nitrogen atom with a lone pair of electrons that can accept $H^+$. Amines, which are derivatives of ammonia, also have nitrogen atoms with lone pairs of electrons that can accept $H^+$. An example of an amine is trimethylamine, $C_3H_9N$.

Note that water can act as an acid and a base. A compound that can act as an acid and a base is said to be amphiprotic.

Acids and bases do not donate or accept protons in separate, isolated reactions. An acid can donate a proton only if there is a base ready to accept one. Similarly, a base can accept a proton only if there is an acid ready to give one up. Thus, an acid donates a proton simultaneously with a base accepting that same proton. A chemical reaction in which $H^+$ is simultaneously donated by an acid and accepted by a base is called a proton transfer reaction.

## PRACTICE 71: What Are Acids and Bases?

Decide if each statement that follows is true (**T**) or false (**F**). Write the correct letter on each line.

T **1.** An acid is a substance that can donate one or more protons.

F **2.** In order to accept a proton, a base must have at least one polar H–X bond.

T **3.** In order to accept a proton, a base must have at least one lone pair of electrons that can bond with the proton.

F **4.** An acid can donate a proton whether or not there is a base ready to accept one.

T **5.** A base is a substance that can accept one or more protons.

T **6.** Hydrochloric acid (HCl) and acetic acid ($C_2H_4O_2$) are acids because they have at least one polar H–X bond.

F **7.** Ammonia ($NH_3$) has a nitrogen atom with a lone pair of electrons that can accept $H^+$, so ammonia must be an acid.

T 8. A chemical reaction in which $H^+$ is simultaneously donated by an acid and accepted by a base is called a proton transfer reaction.

## Strengths of Acids and Bases

Acids and bases can be grouped according to how extensively they ionize when dissolved in water. To ionize means to break up into cations and anions or to react to form ions. For example, the following reaction occurs when HCl is dissolved in water.

$$HCl + H_2O \longrightarrow H_3O^+ + Cl^-$$

HCl ionizes (breaks up) into $H^+$ and $Cl^-$. But the $H^+$ is simultaneously picked up by a water molecule to form $H_3O^+$. $H_3O^+$ is called the hydronium ion. The hydronium ion is the way $H^+$ exists in water. There are no free protons floating around in the solution.

HCl dissociates completely into ions in water. Acids that ionize completely in water are called strong acids. HCl is a strong acid. Other strong acids include HBr, HI, $HNO_3$ (nitric acid), and $H_2SO_4$ (sulfuric acid).

HF, on the other hand, ionizes only slightly when dissolved in water. In fact, if you could count molecules of HF, you would find that only about 26 out of every 1000 molecules of HF are dissociated at any one time. "Dissociated at any one time" means that HF molecules dissociate into ions and then reassociate into HF molecules. So, it is not always the same 26 molecules that are dissociated. For this reason, the dissociation reaction is written with reaction arrows in both directions.

$$HF + H_2O \longleftrightarrow H_3O^+ + F^-$$

Acids that ionize incompletely, or only slightly, in water are called weak acids. HF is a weak acid. Other weak acids are $H_3PO_4$ (phosphoric acid), $H_2CO_3$ (carbonic acid), $C_2H_4O_2$ (acetic acid), and $H_2O$ (water).

The extent to which weak acids dissociate or ionize differs from weak acid to weak acid. For example, about 84 out of every 1000 molecules of phosphoric acid dissociate at any one time. Additionally, only about 4 out of every 1000 molecules of acetic acid, only about 66 out of every

100,000 molecules of carbonic acid, and only 1 out of every 10 million molecules of water dissociate at any one time. Water is a very weak acid.

$$H_2O + H_2O \longleftrightarrow H_3O^+ + OH^-$$

Bases that dissociate or ionize completely into ions in water to give hydroxide ions ($OH^-$) and metal ions are called strong bases. Examples of strong bases include NaOH (sodium hydroxide), $Ca(OH)_2$ (calcium hydroxide), $NaNH_2$ (sodium amide), and $LiCH_3$ (methyl lithium). These equations show the reactions of these strong bases with water.

$$NaOH + H_2O \longrightarrow Na^+ + OH^-$$

$$Ca(OH)_2 + H_2O \longrightarrow Ca_2^+ + 2\ OH^-$$

$$NaNH_2 + H_2O \longrightarrow Na^+ + OH^- + NH_3$$

$$LiCH_3 + H_2O \longrightarrow Li^+ + OH^- + CH_4$$

Bases that ionize incompletely or only slightly in water are called weak bases. Examples of weak bases include $NH_3$ (ammonia), $C_3H_9N$ (trimethylamine), $C_5H_5N$ (pyridine), and $NH_3O$ (hydroxylamine). The following equation shows the reaction of $NH_3$ with water.

$$NH_3 + H_2O \longleftrightarrow NH_4^+ + OH^-$$

Like the reaction of HF with water, the reaction of $NH_3$ with water is written with reaction arrows in both directions. These two reactions are examples of reversible reactions. These reactions are said to be reversible because they can go in both the forward (left-to-right) direction and the reverse (right-to-left) direction. The reversibility of these reactions explains why not all of the HF molecules are dissociated at the same time. As some HF molecules continue to dissociate, others are reassociating into HF molecules.

The reaction has reached dynamic equilibrium when there is no further net change in the number of dissociated HF molecules. The dynamic equilibrium of a chemical reaction is similar in concept to the dynamic equilibrium reached at the freezing and boiling points of liquids.

## PRACTICE 72: Strengths of Acids and Bases

Decide if each statement that follows is true (**T**) or false (**F**). Write the correct letter on each line.

__T__ **1.** Acids that dissociate completely in water are called strong acids.

__T__ **2.** Bases that dissociate or ionize completely into ions in water to give hydroxide ions ($OH^-$) and metal ions are called strong bases.

__F__ **3.** HF is a strong acid.

__F__ **4.** Reactions are reversible when they can go in the forward direction but not the reverse direction.

__T__ **5.** NaOH (sodium hydroxide) is a strong base.

__F__ **6.** $NH_3$ (ammonia) is a strong acid.

__T__ **7.** Acids that dissociate incompletely or only slightly in water are called weak acids.

__T__ **8.** Bases that ionize incompletely or only slightly in water are called weak bases.

## Measuring Acidity: pH and Indicators

You have already learned that water can be both an acid and a base. Water can act as an acid and a base because it dissociates into ions very slightly.

$$H_2O + H_2O \longrightarrow H_3O^+ + OH^-$$

This process is called self-ionization or autoionization. Chemists say that a solution is neutral when the concentration of $H_3O^+$ equals the concentration of $OH^-$. Pure water is a neutral solution. When the concentration of $H_3O^+$ exceeds (is greater than) the concentration of $OH^-$, the solution is acidic. When the concentration of $OH^-$ exceeds the concentration of $H_3O^+$, the solution is basic or alkaline.

The concentration of $H_3O^+$ can vary widely from greater than 1.0 M (that is, 1.0 mol/L) in solutions of strong acids to less than $1 \times 10^{-14}$ M in solutions of strong bases. In order to conveniently express such a wide range of concentrations, chemists have devised the pH scale.

The **pH scale** is a logarithmic scale that expresses the concentration of $H_3O^+$ in simple numbers instead of exponents. Because the pH scale is logarithmic, each unit is 10 times different from the one before and the one after it. For example, if the concentration of $H_3O^+$ is 0.1 M, then the solution has a pH of 1.0. If the concentration of $H_3O^+$ is 0.01 M, then the solution has a pH of 2.0. If the concentration of $H_3O^+$ is $1 \times 10^{-7}$ M, then the solution has a pH of 7.0. If the concentration of $H_3O^+$ is $1 \times 10^{-14}$ M, then the solution has a pH of 14.0.

Note that the higher the pH, the lower the concentration of $H_3O^+$. An acidic solution has a lower pH (a higher concentration of $H_3O^+$) than a basic solution. Note, also, that a 0.1 M solution is 10 times more concentrated than a 0.01 M solution, but their pH units differ by only one unit.

At 25°C, pure water has a pH of 7.0. That is, the concentration of $H_3O^+$ is $1 \times 10^{-7}$ M in pure water. Pure water is neutral, so the pH of a neutral solution is 7.0. The pH of an acidic solution is anything less than 7.0. The pH of a basic solution is anything greater than 7.0.

**IN REAL LIFE**

You may not realize it, but you may be familiar with other logarithmic scales. The decibel scale, which measures the power of an acoustic signal, is a logarithmic scale. So is the Richter scale, which measures the energy of ground movement and is used to indicate the strength of earthquakes.

Acid–base indicators are molecules whose color depends on the acidity or basicity of a solution. For example, an acid–base indicator called methyl orange is red in the presence of acids but orange in the presence of bases. Another indicator, called phenolphthalein, is colorless in the presence of acids but red in the presence of bases. Indicators make it possible to tell when the concentrations of $H_3O^+$ and $OH^-$ are equal in a solution. Indicators also tell when the concentration of either the acid or the base in a solution exceeds the other.

## PRACTICE 73: Measuring Acidity: pH and Indicators

Decide if each statement that follows is true (**T**) or false (**F**). Write the correct letter on each line.

_____ **1.** Chemists say that a solution is neutral when the concentration of $H_3O^+$ equals the concentration of $OH^-$.

_____ **2.** The pH scale is a logarithmic scale that expresses the concentration of $H_3O^+$ in simple numbers instead of exponents.

_____ **3.** The higher the pH, the lower the concentration of $H_3O^+$.

_____ **4.** If the concentration of $H_3O^+$ is $1 \times 10^{-14}$ M, then the solution has a pH of 1.0.

_____ **5.** Pure water has a pH of 7.0.

_____ **6.** An acid-base indicator called methyl orange is orange in the presence of acids but red in the presence of bases.

_____ **7.** If the concentration of $H_3O^+$ is 0.01 M, then the solution has a pH of 2.0.

_____ **8.** Acid–base indicators are molecules whose color depends on the intermolecular forces in a solution.

## UNIT 4 REVIEW

Circle the letter of the correct answer.

**1.** The forces of attraction and/or repulsion that exist between individual molecules are called ______.

**a.** intermolecular forces
**b.** intramolecular forces
**c.** reactant forces

**2.** A gas condenses when the temperature of the gas is lowered enough that its kinetic energy ______.

**a.** no longer exceeds the intermolecular forces
**b.** no longer exceeds the intramolecular forces
**c.** is entirely changed to potential energy

3. The substance in a solution that determines whether the solution is a solid, a liquid, or a gas is called the ______.
   a. solvent
   b. solute
   c. colligative solid

4. In general, one substance dissolves in another when ______.
   a. the solute–solvent intermolecular forces are similar to or the same as the solute–solute and solvent–solvent intermolecular forces
   b. one of the substances is a network covalent solid
   c. both *a* and *b*

5. The substance that dissolves in a solvent to form a solution is called the ______.
   a. solvent
   b. solute
   c. solid

6. Solid mixtures of two or more metals are called ______.
   a. tinctures
   b. alloys
   c. dual solids

7. A substance that can donate one or more protons is ______.
   a. an acid
   b. a base
   c. a metalloid

8. A reversible reaction ______.
   a. can go in the forward (left-to-right) direction
   b. can go in the reverse (right-to-left) direction
   c. both *a* and *b*

9. A substance that can accept one or more protons is ______.
   a. an acid
   b. a base
   c. a network covalent solid

10. When the concentration of $H_3O^+$ is greater than the concentration of $OH^-$, the solution is ______.
   a. acidic
   b. basic
   c. neutral

## UNIT 4 APPLICATION ACTIVITY 1

### The Effect of Acid Rain on "Sculptures"

If you have ever visited an old cemetery, you may have noticed the effect of acid rain. Try making your own "sculpture" and observing the effects of "acid rain" on it.

Using a piece of chalk and a nail, carve a figure from the chalk. Include some detail on the surface of your carving (a face or a design, for example).

Place your carving in a petri dish. Fill a medicine dropper with vinegar, and place three to four drops of the vinegar on your sculpture. (Vinegar is acetic acid mixed with water and is similar to the solution called "acid rain.") Repeat, placing drops of vinegar on your sculpture five more times. Observe what occurs each time.

Now pour enough vinegar into the petri dish to cover your sculpture. Cover the dish with plastic wrap, and let it soak where it will not be disturbed overnight. Observe your sculpture the next day.

What happened to the sculpture when vinegar was dropped on it?

______________________________________________________________

______________________________________________________________

How did soaking the sculpture in vinegar overnight affect it?

______________________________________________________________

______________________________________________________________

______________________________________________________________

Marble and limestone both contain calcium carbonate, the same material that makes up chalk. How might buildings and sculptures in a city be affected by acid rain?

______________________________

______________________________

______________________________

How might the effects of acid rain be slowed or stopped?

______________________________

______________________________

______________________________

## UNIT 4 APPLICATION ACTIVITY 2

### Household Acid–Base Indicators

It is easy to determine whether everyday household products are acids or bases.

Fill an 8-ounce glass half full of warm tap water. Stir one heaping teaspoon of blackberry jam in the water until it dissolves. The mixture should be a reddish color. Use a medicine dropper to add three to four drops of ammonia to the solution. Stir lightly. What happens?

______________________________

______________________________

______________________________

Use a clean medicine dropper, and add three to four drops of lemon juice (or vinegar) to the same solution to which you added the ammonia. Stir lightly. What happens?

______________________________

______________________________

______________________________

The jam solution turns green-purple when a base is added and red when an acid is added. Determine whether ammonia and lemon juice (or vinegar) are acids or bases, and record your data in the chart.

| Solution | Acid or Base? |
|---|---|
| ammonia | |
| lemon juice | |
| | |
| | |
| | |
| | |

Repeat the procedure, using a new jam solution, to try out other substances, such as milk, orange juice, soda, and baking soda. Is each of these common household substances an acid or a base?

______________________________________________________________

______________________________________________________________

______________________________________________________________

## UNIT 4 APPLICATION ACTIVITY 3

### A Crystal Garden

You can observe crystals up close in your own crystal garden. First, place a cup of water in a saucepan, and place the pan on a hot plate. Add 1 teaspoon of salt to the water. Heat the water slowly. Do not let it boil.

Continue to stir the solution while you add salt 1 teaspoon at a time. Do this until it takes a long time for the salt to dissolve. At that point, add one more teaspoon of salt, and remove the pan from the hot plate.

While the water cools, tie one end of a piece of string 30 centimeters long to a washer. Find a jar. Wind the end of the string without the washer around an ice-cream stick. Adjust the length of the string so that, when you place the ice-cream stick across the top of the jar and drop the string with the washer in the jar, the washer hangs about 1 centimeter from the bottom of the jar. After the pan has cooled enough to handle safely, pour the saltwater solution into the jar. Place the jar where it will remain undisturbed for several days.

What do you see after four to five days?

Identify the solute and solvent in the solution you prepared.

What type(s) of intermolecular forces allow these crystals to form?

# APPENDIXES

## A. Periodic Table of the Elements

### Periodic Table of the Elements

Key

| 6 ← Atomic Number |
|---|
| **C** ← Element's Symbol |
| Carbon ← Name |
| 12.011 ← Atomic Weight |

Nonmetals: groups 13–18. Transition Metals: groups 3–12. Metals: groups 1–16, periods 1–7.

| | 1<br>IA | 2<br>IIA | 3<br>IIIB | 4<br>IVB | 5<br>VB | 6<br>VIB | 7<br>VIIB | 8<br>VIIIB | 9<br>VIIIB | 10<br>VIIIB | 11<br>IB | 12<br>IIB | 13<br>IIIA | 14<br>IVA | 15<br>VA | 16<br>VIA | 17<br>VIIA | 18<br>VIIIA |
|---|---|---|---|---|---|---|---|---|---|---|---|---|---|---|---|---|---|---|
| 1 | 1<br>**H**<br>Hydrogen<br>1.0079 | | | | | | | | | | | | | | | | | 2<br>**He**<br>Helium<br>4.003 |
| 2 | 3<br>**Li**<br>Lithium<br>6.941 | 4<br>**Be**<br>Beryllium<br>9.01218 | | | | | | | | | | | 5<br>**B**<br>Boron<br>10.811 | 6<br>**C**<br>Carbon<br>12.011 | 7<br>**N**<br>Nitrogen<br>14.0067 | 8<br>**O**<br>Oxygen<br>15.9994 | 9<br>**F**<br>Fluorine<br>18.998 | 10<br>**Ne**<br>Neon<br>20.180 |
| 3 | 11<br>**Na**<br>Sodium<br>22.98977 | 12<br>**Mg**<br>Magnesium<br>24.305 | | | | | | | | | | | 13<br>**Al**<br>Aluminum<br>26.982 | 14<br>**Si**<br>Silicon<br>28.086 | 15<br>**P**<br>Phosphorus<br>30.974 | 16<br>**S**<br>Sulfur<br>32.066 | 17<br>**Cl**<br>Chlorine<br>35.453 | 18<br>**Ar**<br>Argon<br>39.948 |
| 4 | 19<br>**K**<br>Potassium<br>39.0983 | 20<br>**Ca**<br>Calcium<br>40.078 | 21<br>**Sc**<br>Scandium<br>44.956 | 22<br>**Ti**<br>Titanium<br>47.88 | 23<br>**V**<br>Vanadium<br>50.942 | 24<br>**Cr**<br>Chromium<br>51.996 | 25<br>**Mn**<br>Manganese<br>54.938 | 26<br>**Fe**<br>Iron<br>55.847 | 27<br>**Co**<br>Cobalt<br>58.933 | 28<br>**Ni**<br>Nickel<br>58.69 | 29<br>**Cu**<br>Copper<br>63.546 | 30<br>**Zn**<br>Zinc<br>65.39 | 31<br>**Ga**<br>Gallium<br>69.723 | 32<br>**Ge**<br>Germanium<br>72.61 | 33<br>**As**<br>Arsenic<br>74.922 | 34<br>**Se**<br>Selenium<br>78.96 | 35<br>**Br**<br>Bromine<br>79.904 | 36<br>**Kr**<br>Krypton<br>83.80 |
| 5 | 37<br>**Rb**<br>Rubidium<br>85.4678 | 38<br>**Sr**<br>Strontium<br>87.62 | 39<br>**Y**<br>Yttrium<br>88.906 | 40<br>**Zr**<br>Zirconium<br>91.224 | 41<br>**Nb**<br>Niobium<br>92.906 | 42<br>**Mo**<br>Molybdenum<br>95.94 | 43<br>**Tc**<br>Technetium<br>(98) | 44<br>**Ru**<br>Ruthenium<br>101.07 | 45<br>**Rh**<br>Rhodium<br>102.906 | 46<br>**Pd**<br>Palladium<br>106.42 | 47<br>**Ag**<br>Silver<br>107.868 | 48<br>**Cd**<br>Cadmium<br>112.411 | 49<br>**In**<br>Indium<br>114.82 | 50<br>**Sn**<br>Tin<br>118.71 | 51<br>**Sb**<br>Antimony<br>121.75 | 52<br>**Te**<br>Tellurium<br>127.60 | 53<br>**I**<br>Iodine<br>126.906 | 54<br>**Xe**<br>Xenon<br>131.29 |
| 6 | 55<br>**Cs**<br>Cesium<br>132.905 | 56<br>**Ba**<br>Barium<br>137.327 | 71<br>**Lu**<br>Lutetium<br>174.967 | 72<br>**Hf**<br>Hafnium<br>178.49 | 73<br>**Ta**<br>Tantalum<br>180.948 | 74<br>**W**<br>Tungsten (Wolfram)<br>183.85 | 75<br>**Re**<br>Rhenium<br>186.207 | 76<br>**Os**<br>Osmium<br>190.2 | 77<br>**Ir**<br>Iridium<br>192.22 | 78<br>**Pt**<br>Platinum<br>195.08 | 79<br>**Au**<br>Gold<br>196.967 | 80<br>**Hg**<br>Mercury<br>200.59 | 81<br>**Tl**<br>Thallium<br>204.383 | 82<br>**Pb**<br>Lead<br>207.2 | 83<br>**Bi**<br>Bismuth<br>208.980 | 84<br>**Po**<br>Polonium<br>(209) | 85<br>**At**<br>Astatine<br>(210) | 86<br>**Rn**<br>Radon<br>(220) |
| 7 | 87<br>**Fr**<br>Francium<br>(223) | 88<br>**Ra**<br>Radium<br>226.025 | 103<br>**Lr**<br>Lawrencium<br>(260) | 104<br>**Rf**<br>Rutherfordium<br>(261) | 105<br>**Db**<br>Dubnium<br>(262) | 106<br>**Sg**<br>Seaborgium<br>(263) | 107<br>**Bh**<br>Bohrium<br>(264) | 108<br>**Hs**<br>Hassium<br>(265) | 109<br>**Mt**<br>Meitnerium<br>(266) | | | | | | | | | |

| | | | | | | | | | | | | | | |
|---|---|---|---|---|---|---|---|---|---|---|---|---|---|---|
| * Lanthanide series: | 57<br>***La**<br>Lanthanum<br>138.906 | 58<br>**Ce**<br>Cerium<br>140.115 | 59<br>**Pr**<br>Praseodymium<br>140.908 | 60<br>**Nd**<br>Neodymium<br>144.24 | 61<br>**Pm**<br>Promethium<br>(145) | 62<br>**Sm**<br>Samarium<br>150.36 | 63<br>**Eu**<br>Europium<br>151.965 | 64<br>**Gd**<br>Gadolinium<br>157.25 | 65<br>**Tb**<br>Terbium<br>158.925 | 66<br>**Dy**<br>Dysprosium<br>162.50 | 67<br>**Ho**<br>Holmium<br>164.93 | 68<br>**Er**<br>Erbium<br>167.26 | 69<br>**Tm**<br>Thulium<br>168.934 | 70<br>**Yb**<br>Ytterbium<br>173.04 |
| † Actinide series: | 89<br>**†Ac**<br>Actinium<br>227.028 | 90<br>**Th**<br>Thorium<br>232.038 | 91<br>**Pa**<br>Protactinium<br>231.036 | 92<br>**U**<br>Uranium<br>238.029 | 93<br>**Np**<br>Neptunium<br>237.048 | 94<br>**Pu**<br>Plutonium<br>(244) | 95<br>**Am**<br>Americium<br>(243) | 96<br>**Cm**<br>Curium<br>(247) | 97<br>**Bk**<br>Berkelium<br>(247) | 98<br>**Cf**<br>Californium<br>(251) | 99<br>**Es**<br>Einsteinium<br>(252) | 100<br>**Fm**<br>Fermium<br>(257) | 101<br>**Md**<br>Mendelevium<br>(258) | 102<br>**No**<br>Nobelium<br>(259) |

## B. Chart of Elements

| Atomic Number | Name | Symbol | Atomic Mass | Atomic Number | Name | Symbol | Atomic Mass |
|---|---|---|---|---|---|---|---|
| 1 | Hydrogen | H | 1.0079 | 56 | Barium | Ba | 137.34 |
| 2 | Helium | He | 4.00260 | 57 | Lanthanum | La | 138.9055 |
| 3 | Lithium | Li | 6.941 | 58 | Cerium | Ce | 140.12 |
| 4 | Beryllium | Be | 9.01218 | 59 | Praseodymium | Pr | 140.9077 |
| 5 | Boron | B | 10.81 | 60 | Neodymium | Nd | 144.24 |
| 6 | Carbon | C | 12.011 | 61 | Promethium | Pm | (145) |
| 7 | Nitrogen | N | 14.0067 | 62 | Samarium | Sm | 150.4 |
| 8 | Oxygen | O | 15.9994 | 63 | Europium | Eu | 151.96 |
| 9 | Fluorine | F | 18.99840 | 64 | Gadolinium | Gd | 157.25 |
| 10 | Neon | Ne | 20.179 | 65 | Terbium | Tb | 158.9254 |
| 11 | Sodium | Na | 22.98977 | 66 | Dysprosium | Dy | 162.50 |
| 12 | Magnesium | Mg | 24.305 | 67 | Holmium | Ho | 164.9304 |
| 13 | Aluminum | Al | 26.98154 | 68 | Erbium | Er | 167.26 |
| 14 | Silicon | Si | 28.086 | 69 | Thulium | Tm | 168.9342 |
| 15 | Phosphorus | P | 30.97376 | 70 | Ytterbium | Yb | 173.04 |
| 16 | Sulfur | S | 32.06 | 71 | Lutetium | Lu | 174.97 |
| 17 | Chlorine | Cl | 35.453 | 72 | Hafnium | Hf | 178.49 |
| 18 | Argon | Ar | 39.948 | 73 | Tantalum | Ta | 180.9479 |
| 19 | Potassium | K | 39.098 | 74 | Tungsten | W | 183.85 |
| 20 | Calcium | Ca | 40.08 | 75 | Rhenium | Re | 186.207 |
| 21 | Scandium | Sc | 44.9559 | 76 | Osmium | Os | 190.2 |
| 22 | Titanium | Ti | 47.90 | 77 | Iridium | Ir | 192.22 |
| 23 | Vanadium | V | 50.9414 | 78 | Platinum | Pt | 195.09 |
| 24 | Chromium | Cr | 51.996 | 79 | Gold | Au | 196.9665 |
| 25 | Manganese | Mn | 54.9380 | 80 | Mercury | Hg | 200.59 |
| 26 | Iron | Fe | 55.847 | 81 | Thallium | Tl | 204.37 |
| 27 | Cobalt | Co | 58.9332 | 82 | Lead | Pb | 207.2 |
| 28 | Nickel | Ni | 58.70 | 83 | Bismuth | Bi | 208.9804 |
| 29 | Copper | Cu | 63.546 | 84 | Polonium | Po | (209) |
| 30 | Zinc | Zn | 65.37 | 85 | Astatine | At | (210) |
| 31 | Gallium | Ga | 69.72 | 86 | Radon | Rn | (222) |
| 32 | Germanium | Ge | 72.59 | 87 | Francium | Fr | (223) |
| 33 | Arsenic | As | 74.9216 | 88 | Radium | Ra | 226.0254 |
| 34 | Selenium | Se | 78.96 | 89 | Actinium | Ac | (227) |
| 35 | Bromine | Br | 79.904 | 90 | Thorium | Th | 232.0381 |
| 36 | Krypton | Kr | 83.80 | 91 | Protactinium | Pa | 231.0359 |
| 37 | Rubidium | Rb | 85.4678 | 92 | Uranium | U | 238.029 |
| 38 | Strontium | Sr | 87.63 | 93 | Neptunium | Np | 237.0482 |
| 39 | Yttrium | Y | 88.92 | 94 | Plutonium | Pu | (244) |
| 40 | Zirconium | Zr | 91.22 | 95 | Americium | Am | (243) |
| 41 | Niobium | Nb | 92.91 | 96 | Curium | Cm | (247) |
| 42 | Molybdenum | Mo | 95.95 | 97 | Berkelium | Bk | (247) |
| 43 | Technetium | Tc | (99) | 98 | Californium | Cf | (251) |
| 44 | Ruthenium | Ru | 101.7 | 99 | Einsteinium | Es | (254) |
| 45 | Rhodium | Rh | 102.9055 | 100 | Fermium | Fm | (257) |
| 46 | Palladium | Pd | 106.4 | 101 | Mendelevium | Md | (258) |
| 47 | Silver | Ag | 107.868 | 102 | Nobelium | No | (255) |
| 48 | Cadmium | Cd | 112.40 | 103 | Lawrencium | Lr | (260) |
| 49 | Indium | In | 114.82 | 104 | Rutherfordium | Rf | (261) |
| 50 | Tin | Sn | 118.69 | 105 | Dubnium | Db | (262) |
| 51 | Antimony | Sb | 121.75 | 106 | Seaborgium | Sg | (263) |
| 52 | Tellurium | Te | 127.60 | 107 | Bohrium | Bh | (262) |
| 53 | Iodine | I | 126.9045 | 108 | Hassium | Hs | (265) |
| 54 | Xenon | Xe | 131.30 | 109 | Meitnerium | Mt | (265) |
| 55 | Cesium | Cs | 132.9054 | | | | |

## C. Types of Chemical Reactions

| **Reaction Type** | **Process of Reaction** | **Example of Reaction** | **Example of Product(s)** |
|---|---|---|---|
| Synthesis Reaction | Two substances are joined to make a single, more complex substance. | $2H_2 + O_2 \rightarrow 2H_2O$<br>In this case, water is formed from hydrogen and oxygen. | Water |
| Decomposition Reaction | A single, complex substance is broken down into two or more simpler substances. | $2H_2O \rightarrow 2H_2 + O_2$<br>In this case, water breaks down into its component elements. | Hydrogen, oxygen |
| Single Replacement Reaction | A single, uncombined element replaces another element in a compound. Two reactants produce two products. | $2Zn + 2HCl \rightarrow$ $2ZnCl + H_2$<br>In this case, zinc replaces the hydrogen in hydrochloric acid, producing two new products—zinc chloride and a hydrogen molecule. | Zinc chloride, hydrogen |
| Double Replacement Reaction | Parts of two different compounds switch places, making two new products. | $AgNO_3 + NaCl \rightarrow$ $AgCl + NaNO_3$<br>In this case, silver nitrate joins with sodium chloride to form silver chloride and sodium nitrate. The silver and sodium switch places. | Silver chloride, sodium nitrate |

## D. pH Continuum

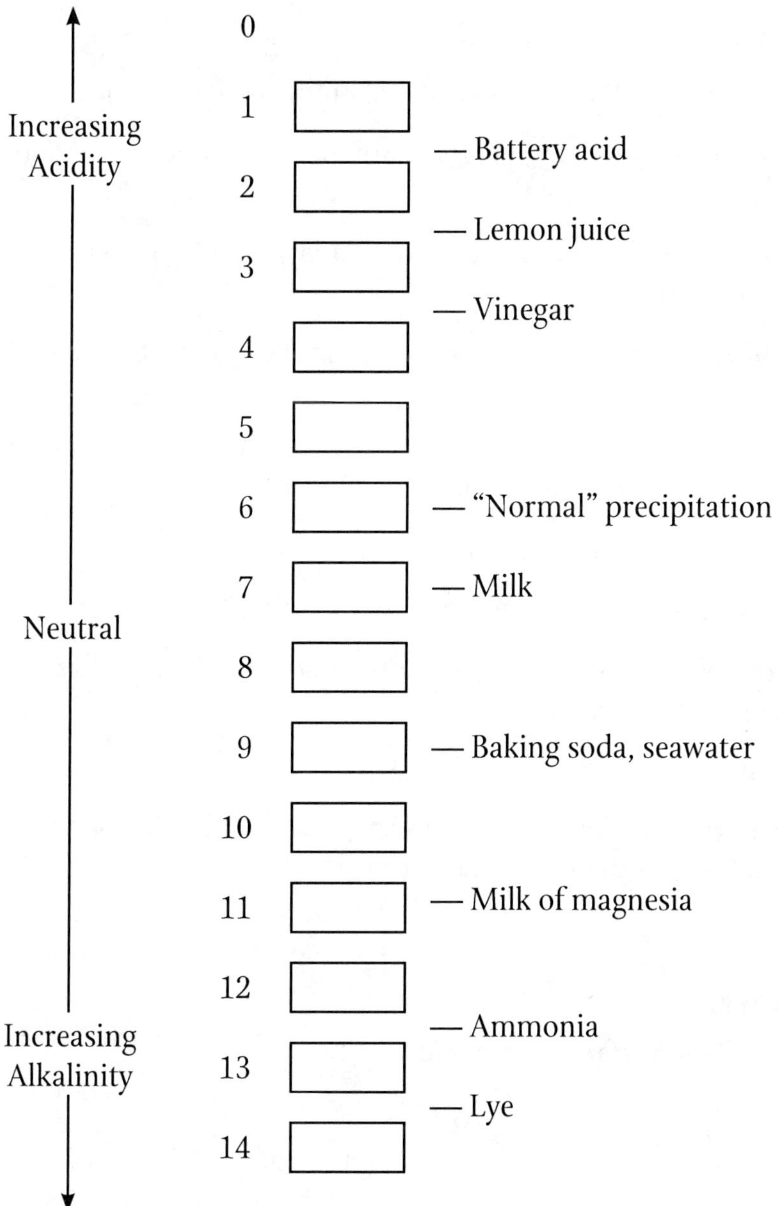

## GLOSSARY

**absolute zero** (AB-suh-loot ZEE-roh) the temperature at which all particle motion stops; this temperature is –273.15°C or –459.67°F.

**acid** (A-sud) a substance that can donate one or more protons

**actinides** (AK-tuh-nydz) elements 89–102 on the periodic table

**actual yield** (AK-chuh-wul YEELD) the amount of product that is actually obtained from a chemical reaction

**adhesive forces** (ad-HEE-siv FOR-sez) the intermolecular forces between a liquid and a solid surface

**alkali metals** (AL-kuh-ly ME-tulz) elements in the first column of the periodic table

**alkaline earth metals** (AL-kuh-lyn URTH ME-tulz) elements in the second column of the periodic table

**alloys** (A-loyz) a solid mixture of two or more metals

**amalgam** (uh-MAL-gum) a solution of a metal dissolved in mercury

**amorphous solids** (uh-MOR-fus SO-ludz) solids with an irregular arrangement of molecules or ions

**anions** (A-ny-unz) negative ions

**atomic mass** (uh-TO-mik MAS) the average mass of the naturally occurring isotopes in the sample of an element

---

**PRONUNCIATION KEY**

CAPITAL LETTERS show the stressed syllables.

| | | | |
|---|---|---|---|
| a | as in m**a**t | f | as in **f**it |
| ay | as in d**ay**, s**ay** | g | as in **g**o |
| ch | as in **ch**ew | i | as in s**i**t |
| e | as in b**e**d | j | as in **j**ob, **g**em |
| ee | as in **e**ven, **ea**sy, n**ee**d | k | as in **c**ool, **k**ey |

**atomic mass unit** (uh-TO-mik MAS YOO-nut) a unit equal to $\frac{1}{12}$ the mass of a carbon-12 atom

**atomic number** (uh-TO-mik NUM-bur) the number of protons in the nucleus of an atom

**atomic radius** (uh-TO-mik RAY-dee-us) one half the distance between the nuclei of adjacent atoms in the crystal of an element

**atoms** (A-tumz) the smallest possible particles that a substance can be and still be recognizable as that substance

**Avogadro's number** (a-vuh-GO-drohz NUM-bur) $6.022137 \times 10^{23}$

**base** (BAYS) a substance that can accept one or more protons

**boiling** (BOY-ling) the process in which a liquid turns to a gas, at a constant temperature, and can happen at any location within the liquid

**boiling point** (BOY-ling POYNT) the temperature at which a liquid turns to a gas at any location throughout the liquid

**boiling point elevation** (BOY-ling POYNT e-luh-VAY-shun) the raising of the boiling point of a solvent that occurs when a solute is dissolved in it

**bond distance** (BOND DIS-tuns) the distance at which the attractive forces between atoms exceed the repulsive forces

**bonds** (BONDZ) a pair of electrons shared between two atoms

**PRONUNCIATION KEY**

CAPITAL LETTERS show the stressed syllables.

ng as in runni**ng**

o as in c**o**t, f**a**ther

oh as in g**o**, n**o**te

sh as in **sh**y

th as in **th**in

oo as in t**oo**

u as in b**u**t, s**o**me

uh as in **a**bout, tak**e**n, lem**o**n, penc**i**l

ur as in t**er**m

y as in l**i**ne, fl**y**

zh as in vi**s**ion, mea**s**ure

**cathode-ray tube** (KA-thohd-RAY TOOB) two metal electrodes in an evacuated glass tube

**cations** (KAT-y-unz) positive ions

**Celsius scale** (SEL-see-us SKAYL) a temperature scale that sets the freezing point of water at 0°C and the boiling point of water at 100°C

**chemical bonds** (KE-mi-kul BONDZ) forces that hold atoms or ions together in compounds

**chemical change** (KE-mi-kul CHAYNJ) a change in the nature of a material in which new substances are formed

**chemical equation** (KE-mi-kul i-KWAY-zhun) uses formulas to identify the substances involved in a chemical reaction and numbers to identify the amounts of those substances

**chemical formula** (KE-mi-kul FOR-myuh-luh) uses numbers and symbols for the elements to indicate which elements are present in a substance and how many atoms of each element are present in that substance

**chemical properties** (KE-mi-kul PRO-pur-teez) those properties of a substance that can be determined only by the formation of new materials

**chemistry** (KE-muh-stree) the study of the composition, structure, and properties of matter and the changes that matter undergoes

**cohesive forces** (koh-HEE-siv FOR-sez) intermolecular forces between molecules in a liquid

**PRONUNCIATION KEY**

CAPITAL LETTERS show the stressed syllables.

| | | | |
|---|---|---|---|
| a | as in m**a**t | f | as in **f**it |
| ay | as in d**ay**, s**ay** | g | as in **g**o |
| ch | as in **ch**ew | i | as in s**i**t |
| e | as in b**e**d | j | as in **j**ob, **g**em |
| ee | as in **e**ven, **ea**sy, n**ee**d | k | as in **c**ool, **k**ey |

**colligative properties** (kuh-LI-guh-tiv PRO-pur-teez) physical properties of solutions that depend on the quantity of solute particles, but not the kind of solute particles

**compound** (kom-POWND) a substance made up of two or more elements that are chemically combined

**condensation** (kon-den-SAY-shun) the process in which a gas turns into a liquid

**conversion factor** (kun-VUR-zhun FAK-tur) a number that tells how many of one unit equals the same amount in another unit

**coulombs** (KOO-lomz) the unit for measuring electric charge

**covalent bond** (koh-VAY-lunt BOND) formed when two atoms share a pair of electrons

**crystalline solids** (KRIS-tuh-lun SO-ludz) solids that have an orderly arrangement of atoms, molecules, or ions

**density** (DEN-suh-tee) the amount of mass in a given volume

**deposition** (de-puh-ZI-shun) the process by which a gas becomes a solid without becoming a liquid in between

**dipolar forces** (DY-poh-lur FOR-sez) intermolecular forces experienced only by polar molecules

**PRONUNCIATION KEY**

CAPITAL LETTERS show the stressed syllables.

| | | | |
|---|---|---|---|
| ng | as in runni**ng** | u | as in b**u**t, s**o**me |
| o | as in c**o**t, f**a**ther | uh | as in **a**bout, tak**e**n, lem**o**n, penc**i**l |
| oh | as in g**o**, n**o**te | ur | as in t**er**m |
| sh | as in **sh**y | y | as in l**i**ne, fl**y** |
| th | as in **th**in | zh | as in vi**s**ion, mea**s**ure |
| oo | as in t**oo** | | |

**dipole moment** (DY-pohl MOH-munt) a measure of the polarity of a molecule

**dispersion forces** (di-SPUR-zhun FOR-sez) See London forces.

**double bond** (DUH-bul BOND) a bond containing two pairs of shared electrons

**ductile** (DUK-tyl) the property of metal that allows it to be drawn into wires

**effective nuclear charge ($Z_{eff}$)** (i-FEK-tiv NOO-klee-ur CHARJ) the nuclear charge that an electron actually experiences

**electronegativity** (i-lek-troh-ne-guh-TI-vuh-tee) the ability of an atom to attract bonding electrons to itself in a chemical compound

**electrons** (i-LEK-tronz) negatively charged particles that have very little mass but take up most of the space in an atom

**element** (E-luh-munt) a substance made of only one kind of atom

**empirical formula** (im-PIR-i-kul FOR-myuh-luh) shows the relative number of atoms of each element in a compound

**evaporation** (i-va-puh-RAY-shun) the process in which a liquid turns to a gas, but only at the surface of the liquid

**experiment** (ik-SPER-uh-munt) a series of steps used to test the validity of a hypothesis

---

**PRONUNCIATION KEY**

CAPITAL LETTERS show the stressed syllables.

| | | | |
|---|---|---|---|
| a | as in m**a**t | f | as in **f**it |
| ay | as in d**ay**, s**ay** | g | as in **g**o |
| ch | as in **ch**ew | i | as in s**i**t |
| e | as in b**e**d | j | as in **j**ob, **g**em |
| ee | as in **e**ven, **ea**sy, n**ee**d | k | as in **c**ool, **k**ey |

**Fahrenheit scale** (FAR-un-hyt SKAYL) a temperature scale that sets the freezing point of water at 32°F and the boiling point of water at 212°F

**families** (FAM-leez) vertical columns on the periodic table

**freezing** (FREE-zing) the process in which a liquid turns into a solid

**freezing point** (FREE-zing POYNT) the temperature at which a liquid turns into a solid

**freezing point depression** (FREE-zing POYNT di-PRE-shun) the lowering of the freezing point of a solvent when a solute is dissolved in it

**gas** (GAS) a material without a fixed volume and without a fixed shape

**graphite** (gra-FYT) a form of pure carbon

**groups** (GROOPS) vertical columns on the periodic table

**halogens** (HA-luh-junz) elements in column 17 of the periodic table

**heat** (HEET) the energy that flows between objects that are of different temperatures

**heterogeneous mixture** (he-tuh-ruh-JEE-nee-us MIKS-chur) a mixture that has visible boundaries between the substances of which it is composed

**heteronuclear diatomic molecule** (he-tuh-roh-NOO-klee-ur dy-uh-TO-mik MO-li-kyool) a molecule with two atoms, each of which is a different element

---

**PRONUNCIATION KEY**

CAPITAL LETTERS show the stressed syllables.

| | | | |
|---|---|---|---|
| ng | as in runni**ng** | u | as in b**u**t, s**o**me |
| o | as in c**o**t, f**a**ther | uh | as in **a**bout, tak**e**n, lem**o**n, penc**i**l |
| oh | as in g**o**, n**o**te | ur | as in t**er**m |
| sh | as in **sh**y | y | as in l**i**ne, fl**y** |
| th | as in **th**in | zh | as in vi**s**ion, mea**s**ure |
| oo | as in t**oo** | | |

**homogeneous mixture** (hoh-moh-JEE-nee-us MIKS-chur) a mixture that has a uniform and changeless composition throughout

**homonuclear diatomic molecule** (hoh-moh-NOO-klee-ur dy-uh-TO-mik MO-li-kyool) a molecule with two atoms that are both the same element

**hydrogen bonding** (HY-druh-jun BON-ding) when a highly electronegative atom with at least one lone pair of electrons partially shares its nonbonding electrons with a hydrogen atom in a polar bond

**hypothesis** (hy-PO-thuh-sus) a proposed explanation for gathered information

**ideal gas equation** (y-DEE-ul GAS i-KWAY-zhun) $PV = nRT$

**inner transition elements** (I-nur tran-SI-shun E-luh-munts) lanthanides and actinides

**intermolecular forces** (in-tur-muh-LE-kyuh-lur FOR-sez) forces that exist between individual molecules

**intramolecular forces** (in-truh-muh-LE-kyuh-lur FOR-sez) forces within a molecule

**ionic bond** (y-O-nik BOND) formed when oppositely charged ions attract each other

**ionic compound** (y-O-nik kom-POWND) a substance formed when anions and cations combine to form an electrically neutral compound

**PRONUNCIATION KEY**

CAPITAL LETTERS show the stressed syllables.

| | | | |
|---|---|---|---|
| a | as in m**a**t | f | as in **f**it |
| ay | as in d**ay**, s**ay** | g | as in **g**o |
| ch | as in **ch**ew | i | as in s**i**t |
| e | as in b**e**d | j | as in **j**ob, **g**em |
| ee | as in **e**ven, **ea**sy, n**ee**d | k | as in **c**ool, **k**ey |

**ionic radius** (y-O-nik RAY-dee-us) the radius of a cation or an anion

**ionic solids** (y-O-nik SO-ludz) cations and anions held together by ionic bonds

**ions** (Y-onz) atoms that have a net charge caused by gaining or losing one or more electrons

**isotopes** (Y-suh-tohps) atoms of the same element that have different numbers of neutrons

**Kelvin scale** (KEL-vun SKAYL) temperature scale in which the lowest possible temperature is zero

**kinetic energy** (kuh-NE-tik E-nur-jee) the energy an object has due to its motion

**lanthanides** (LAN-thuh-nydz) elements 57–70 on the periodic table

**law of mass conservation** (LO UV MAS kon-sur-VAY-shun) The total mass of matter does not change during a chemical reaction.

**limiting reactant** (LI-muh-ting ree-AK-tunt) the reactant that is used up first in a chemical reaction

**liquid** (LI-kwud) a material with a fixed volume but without a fixed shape

**London forces** (LUN-dun FOR-sez) the forces of attraction and repulsion between molecules with instantaneous and temporary dipoles

**luster** (LUS-tur) the shininess of a metal

**PRONUNCIATION KEY**

CAPITAL LETTERS show the stressed syllables.

| | | | |
|---|---|---|---|
| ng | as in runni**ng** | u | as in b**u**t, s**o**me |
| o | as in c**o**t, f**a**ther | uh | as in **a**bout, tak**e**n, lem**o**n, penc**i**l |
| oh | as in g**o**, n**o**te | ur | as in t**er**m |
| sh | as in **sh**y | y | as in l**i**ne, fl**y** |
| th | as in **th**in | zh | as in vi**s**ion, mea**s**ure |
| oo | as in t**oo** | | |

**malleable** (MA-lee-uh-bul) able to be hammered into thin sheets

**mass** (MAS) the amount of matter that an object possesses

**mass number** (MAS NUM-bur) the total number of protons and neutrons in the nucleus of an atom

**matter** (MA-tur) anything that occupies space and has mass

**melting** (MEL-ting) the process by which a solid turns into a liquid

**melting point** (MEL-ting POYNT) the temperature at which a solid turns into a liquid

**metallic bonds** (muh-TA-lik BONDZ) bonds that hold metal atoms together; they are the result of the mutual attraction of the metal cations for mobile, delocalized electrons.

**metallic solids** (muh-TA-lik SO-ludz) solids held together by the attraction of metal cations for mobile, delocalized electrons

**metalloids** (ME-tul-oydz) elements between the metals and nonmetals on the periodic table; these elements generally have some properties of the metals and some properties of the nonmetals.

**metals** (ME-tulz) elements located toward the left side of the periodic table, known for having fairly loosely held valence electrons

**miscible** (MI-suh-bul) property of substances that are completely soluble in each other in all proportions

**PRONUNCIATION KEY**

CAPITAL LETTERS show the stressed syllables.

| | | | |
|---|---|---|---|
| a | as in m**a**t | f | as in **f**it |
| ay | as in d**ay**, s**ay** | g | as in **g**o |
| ch | as in **ch**ew | i | as in s**i**t |
| e | as in b**e**d | j | as in **j**ob, **g**em |
| ee | as in **e**ven, **ea**sy, n**ee**d | k | as in **c**ool, **k**ey |

**mixture** (MIKS-chur) a combination of two or more substances, each of which maintains its individual identities

**molar mass** (MOH-lur MAS) the mass of one mole of a substance

**molar ratio** (MOH-lur RAY-shoh) proportion that shows the relationship between the number of moles of one reactant or product and the number of moles of a different reactant or product

**mole** (MOHL) a constant ($6.022137 \times 10^{23}$) for counting large numbers of atoms, molecules, or other particles

**molecular formula** (muh-LE-kyuh-lur FOR-myuh-luh) shows the actual number of atoms of each element in a compound

**molecular mass** (muh-LE-kyuh-lur MAS) the sum of the atomic masses of the atoms in a molecule

**molecular solids** (muh-LE-kyuh-lur SO-ludz) individual molecules held together by combinations of dispersion forces, dipole–dipole interactions, and hydrogen bonds

**molecule** (MO-li-kyool) a combination of two or more atoms that are chemically bound together in a specific shape

**network covalent solids** (NET-wurk koh-VAY-lunt SO-ludz) atoms covalently bonded to one another in extensive arrays or networks

**PRONUNCIATION KEY**

CAPITAL LETTERS show the stressed syllables.

| | | | |
|---|---|---|---|
| ng | as in runni**ng** | u | as in b**u**t, s**o**me |
| o | as in c**o**t, f**a**ther | uh | as in **a**bout, tak**e**n, lem**o**n, penc**il** |
| oh | as in g**o**, n**o**te | ur | as in t**er**m |
| sh | as in **sh**y | y | as in l**i**ne, fl**y** |
| th | as in **th**in | zh | as in vi**s**ion, mea**s**ure |
| oo | as in t**oo** | | |

**neutrons** (NOO-tronz) particles that have no charge and have a slightly greater mass than a proton

**noble gases** (NOH-bul GAS-ez) elements in column 18 of the periodic table; these elements generally do not form bonds.

**nonmetals** (non-ME-tulz) elements toward the right of the periodic table; they generally have very tightly held valence electrons.

**percent yield** (pur-SENT YEELD) the actual yield of a chemical reaction expressed as a percentage of the theoretical yield

**periodic table** (pir-ee-O-dik TAY-bul) a chart that organizes the elements by their atomic numbers and groups them according to their properties

**periods** (PIR-ee-udz) horizontal rows on the periodic table

**pH scale** (PEE AYCH SKAYL) a logarithmic scale that expresses the concentration of $H_30^+$ in simple numbers instead of exponents

**physical change** (FI-zi-kul CHAYNJ) when a material is changed in a manner such that no new substances are formed

**physical properties** (FI-zi-kul PRO-pur-teez) those properties of a substance that can be determined without the formation of new materials

**polar covalent bonds** (POH-lur koh-VAY-lunt BONDZ) covalent bonds that form between different atoms

**PRONUNCIATION KEY**

CAPITAL LETTERS show the stressed syllables.

| | | | |
|---|---|---|---|
| a | as in m**a**t | f | as in **f**it |
| ay | as in d**ay**, s**ay** | g | as in **g**o |
| ch | as in **ch**ew | i | as in s**i**t |
| e | as in b**e**d | j | as in **j**ob, **g**em |
| ee | as in **e**ven, **ea**sy, n**ee**d | k | as in **c**ool, **k**ey |

**problem** (PRO-blum) a specific question under investigation by the scientific method

**products** (PRO-dukts) the substances formed during a chemical reaction

**protons** (PROH-tonz) positively charged particles that have more than 1800 times the mass of an electron, but take up very little of the volume of an atom

**reactants** (re-AK-tunts) the substances that react during a chemical reaction

**reversible reaction** (ri-VUR-suh-bul ree-AK-shun) a reaction in which reactants react to form products, and then the products react with other products to re-form the reactants

**saturated solution** (SA-chuh-ray-tud suh-LOO-shun) a solution that contains the maximum amount of solute that will dissolve in a particular solvent at a particular temperature

**scientific method** (sy-un-TI-fik ME-thud) a process for proposing and testing to find a suitable explanation for observed events

**scientific notation** (sy-un-TI-fik noh-TAY-shun) a method of rewriting very large or very small numbers in a manner that makes them easier to use

**shielding** (SHEEL-ding) a process by which inner shell electrons reduce the force of attraction for outer shell electrons

---

**PRONUNCIATION KEY**

CAPITAL LETTERS show the stressed syllables.

| | | | |
|---|---|---|---|
| ng | as in runni**ng** | u | as in b**u**t, s**o**me |
| o | as in c**o**t, f**a**ther | uh | as in **a**bout, tak**e**n, lem**o**n, penc**i**l |
| oh | as in g**o**, n**o**te | ur | as in t**er**m |
| sh | as in **sh**y | y | as in l**i**ne, fl**y** |
| th | as in **th**in | zh | as in vi**s**ion, mea**s**ure |
| oo | as in t**oo** | | |

**side reactions** (SYD ree-AK-shunz) when small amounts of products react with one another or with some of the reactants to form different or unwanted products

**single bonds** (SIN-gul BONDZ) bonds containing one pair of shared electrons

**solid** (SO-lud) a material with a fixed shape and volume

**solute** (SOL-yoot) the substance or substances that dissolve in the solvent

**solvent** (SOL-vunt) the substance in a solution that determines whether the solution is a solid, a liquid, or a gas

**stoichiometric coefficients** (stoy-kee-oh-ME-trik koh-uh-FI-shunts) numbers to the left of the chemical formulas of the reactants and products in a chemical equation

**stoichiometry** (stoy-kee-O-muh-tree) the study of the quantitative relationships between the amounts of reactants and products in a chemical reaction

**structural formula** (STRUK-chuh-rul FOR-myuh-luh) shows the number and kind of atoms present in a compound, as well as the way the atoms are connected to one another

**sublimation** (suh-bluh-MAY-shun) the process by which a solid changes to a gas without becoming a liquid in between

**PRONUNCIATION KEY**

CAPITAL LETTERS show the stressed syllables.

| | |
|---|---|
| a as in m**a**t | f as in **f**it |
| ay as in d**ay**, s**ay** | g as in **g**o |
| ch as in **ch**ew | i as in s**i**t |
| e as in b**e**d | j as in **j**ob, **g**em |
| ee as in **e**ven, **ea**sy, n**ee**d | k as in **c**ool, **k**ey |

**subscript** (SUB-skript) a number that is written below the symbol of an element in a chemical formula, such as the 2 in $H_2O$

**substance** (SUB-stuns) a material that has unchanging composition and distinct properties

**supersaturated solution** (SOO-pur-SA-chuh-ray-tud suh-LOO-shun) a solution that contains more solute than the amount the solvent can contain

**surface tension** (SUR-fus TEN-shun) the resistance a liquid has to an increase in its surface area

**temperature** (TEM-puh-chur) a measure of the average kinetic energy of the particles in a substance, also, the measure of the hotness or coldness of an object relative to another object

**theoretical yield** (thee-uh-RE-ti-kul YEELD) the amount of product predicted by stoichiometry

**theory** (THEE-uh-ree) an explanation of a phenomenon based on experimental results

**transition metals** (tran-SI-shun ME-tulz) elements in columns 3–12 on the periodic table

**triple bond** (TRI-pul BOND) a bond containing three pairs of shared electrons

**PRONUNCIATION KEY**

CAPITAL LETTERS show the stressed syllables.

| | | | |
|---|---|---|---|
| ng | as in runni**ng** | u | as in b**u**t, s**o**me |
| o | as in c**o**t, f**a**ther | uh | as in **a**bout, tak**e**n, lem**o**n, penc**i**l |
| oh | as in g**o**, n**o**te | ur | as in t**er**m |
| sh | as in **sh**y | y | as in l**i**ne, fl**y** |
| th | as in **th**in | zh | as in vi**s**ion, mea**s**ure |
| oo | as in t**oo** | | |

**universal gas constant** (yoo-nuh-VUR-sul GAS KON-stunt) R in the ideal gas equation

**unsaturated solution** (un-SA-chuh-ray-tud suh-LOO-shun) a solution that contains less solute than the maximum amount the solvent can dissolve

**valence electrons** (VAY-luns i-LEK-tronz) the electrons in the outermost shell (energy level) of an atom

**viscosity** (vis-KO-suh-tee) a liquid's resistance to flow

**volume** (VOL-yum) the amount of space an object occupies

**weight** (WAYT) the force that gravity exerts on an object

**yield** (YEELD) the amount of product obtained from a chemical reaction

# INDEX